"This exploratory work proposes a multimodal method—a fusion of prior approaches informed by linguistics, visual communication, and other disciplines—for descriptive online content analysis. Simultaneously capturing visual and textual elements (and the relationships between them) is a promising development."

—Patrick Meirick, *University of Oklahoma*

"Provides an interesting and comprehensive exploration of political communication as it evolves in concert with advances in communication technologies. This is an excellent volume for scholars interested in keeping apace of the current state and possible future of global political communication."

—Brian Houston, *University of Missouri*

Political Communication Online

The impact of the Internet on political communication has been significant and multifaceted: it has expanded the reach of political messages, opened the floodgates of decontextualization and intercultural misunderstanding, made room for new genres and forms, and allowed for the incorporation of every previously existing communication mode into complex, multilayered documents.

Political Communication Online places these developments in their social and media contexts, covers various disciplinary backgrounds and how they can contribute to a common understanding of the evolving online media landscape, and proposes a novel methodological tool for the analysis of political communication online. Ognyan Seizov offers an approach that places context at the core of the theoretical and methodological discussion, by discussing the traits of online communication that make it a unique communication environment. The book then brings together different disciplines that have important contributions for the study of political communication online, but which have not been integrated for this purpose so far, such as visual communication, multimodal research, and cognitive psychology. Seizov introduces the book's main theoretical and methodological contribution to multimodal document analysis, the annotation scheme "Imagery and Communication in Online Narratives" (ICON), and explores how the ICON approach works in practice. Taking four distinct genres of online political communication—news, election campaigns, NGOs, and social movements—the book presents the analyses of convenience samples from each genre in detail.

This text features a comprehensive theoretical discussion of vital current developments in online political communication, places these developments in context, and couples that with a practical demonstration of the novel methodology it proposes.

Ognyan Seizov is currently a Visiting Postdoctoral Fellow at the Research Center "Visual Communication & Expertise" at Jacobs University Bremen, Germany. His research interests include multimodal and online communication, new media, political and social campaigning, document analysis, and mixed-method media research.

Routledge Research in Political Communication

1 **Political Campaigning in Referendums**
Framing the Referendum Issue
Claes H. de Vreese and Holli A. Semetko

2 **The Internet and National Elections**
A Comparative Study of Web Campaigning
Edited by Nicholas W. Jankowski, Randolph Kluver, Kirsten A. Foot, and Steven M. Schneider

3 **Global Political Marketing**
Edited by Jennifer Lees-Marshment, Jesper Strömbäck, and Chris Rudd

4 **Political Campaigning, Elections and the Internet**
Comparing the US, UK, Germany and France
Darren G. Lilleker and Nigel A. Jackson

5 **Public Broadcasting and Political Interference**
Chris Hanretty

6 **Social Media and Democracy**
Innovations in Participatory Politics
Brian Loader and Daniel Mercea

7 **Political Leadership, Nations and Charisma**
Vivian Ibrahim and Margit Wunsch

8 **The Media, Political Participation and Empowerment**
Edited by Richard Scullion, Roman Gerodimos, Daniel Jackson, and Darren Lilleker

9 **Digital World: Connectivity, Creativity and Rights**
Edited by Gillian Youngs

10 **Political Marketing**
Strategic 'Campaign Culture'
Edited by Kostas Gouliamos, Antonis Theocharous, Bruce Newman, Stephan Henneberg

11 **Politics and the Internet in Comparative Context**
Views From the Cloud
Edited by Paul G. Nixon, Rajash Rawal, and Dan Mercea

12 **Political Communication Online**
Structures, Functions, and Challenges
Ognyan Seizov

Political Communication Online
Structures, Functions, and Challenges

Ognyan Seizov

LONDON AND NEW YORK

First published 2014 by Routledge

2 Park Square, Milton Park, Abingdon, Oxon OX14 4RN
711 Third Avenue, New York, NY 10017, USA

Routledge is an imprint of the Taylor & Francis Group, an informa business

First issued in paperback 2016

Copyright © 2014 Taylor & Francis

The right of Ognyan Seizov to be identified as author of this work has been asserted by him in accordance with sections 77 and 78 of the Copyright, Designs and Patents Act 1988.

All rights reserved. No part of this book may be reprinted or reproduced or utilised in any form or by any electronic, mechanical, or other means, now known or hereafter invented, including photocopying and recording, or in any information storage or retrieval system, without permission in writing from the publishers.

Notice:
Product or corporate names may be trademarks or registered trademarks, and are used only for identification and explanation without intent to infringe.

Library of Congress Cataloging-in-Publication Data

Seizov, Ognyan.
 Political communication online : structures, functions, and challenges / Ognyan Seizov.
    pages cm. — (Routledge research in political communication ; 12)
 1. Communication in politics—Computer network resources.
2. Communication in politics—Technological innovations. 3. Internet in public administration. I. Title.
   JA85.S46 2014
   320.01'4—dc23
   2013046244

ISBN 978-0-415-73738-8 (hbk)
ISBN 978-1-138-69685-3 (pbk)

Typeset in Sabon
by Apex CoVantage, LLC

Contents

List of Tables and Figures		ix
Preface		xi
Acknowledgements		xiii
1	Political Communication Online: A Field in Flux	1
2	ICON: A Visual Approach to Multimodality in Political Communication	19
3	Investigating Political Communication Online: Analytical Levels and Procedures	36
4	Political Communication Online at a Multimodal Glance: General Trends and Characteristics	58
5	News and Campaigns: Findings From Two Traditional Genres of Political Communication	78
6	NGOs and Social Movements: Political Communication With Social Origins	104
7	Moving Forward: Evolving Genres and Future Research Directions in Political Communication Online	128
	Works Cited	145
	Index	157

Tables and Figures

TABLES

1.1	An image family tree according to Mitchell	9
2.1	The main elements of the GeM annotation framework	26
2.2	A systemic functional multimodal discourse analysis framework for printed texts	32
3.1	The coding options for ICON Layer 1	39
3.2	The coding options for ICON Layer 2	41
3.3	The coding options for ICON Layer 3	43
3.4	The coding options for ICON Layer 4	45
3.5	The coding options for ICON Layer 5	48
3.6	The coding categories embedded into ICON's five layers	54
4.1	Coding results from ICON's visual layers based on the whole sample	60
4.2	Coding results from ICON's multimodal layers based on the whole sample	62

FIGURES

4.1	Fragments of the two Al Jazeera webpages that feature the only cases of dissonant image-text relations in the sample	65
4.2	A fragment of a webpage with split-attention design that still maintains a consonant image-text relationship from CNN's US edition	67
4.3	A policy page from Barack Obama's campaign website as an example of dual scripting design	70
5.1	CNN's Web article "Latino boom makes Orlando proving ground for Obama"	83
5.2	The MSNBC online article "First thoughts: Romney's immigration challenge"	85

5.3 The BBC news article "North Carolina rejects funds for sterilization victims" 87
5.4 The Al Jazeera English news story about the death of Rodney King 88
5.5 US Attorney General Eric Holder's contempt charge. Coverage from (left to right) BBC, CNN, and Al Jazeera English 90
5.6 The economic policies as seen on Mitt Romney's (left) and Barack Obama's campaign websites 96
5.7 Mitt Romney's (left) and Barack Obama's healthcare policy webpages 99
6.1 "Damaging cuts to foreign operations..."—a typical webpage from the Freedom House website 109
6.2 "US sanctions on Iranian and Syrian entities and individuals..."—RSF news story 112
6.3 "Internet advocacy coalition announces..."—RSF news story 113
6.4 "We Are the 99 Percent" 120
6.5 "June 21: National day of action against PNC"—Occupy Wall Street news story 122
6.6 "Bed-Stuy: Juneteenth Free University"—news story from Occupy Wall Street 123
7.1 The distribution of the sample across the three typical structures and their respective functions. 134

Preface

The origins of this monograph are in the eponymous doctoral dissertation I completed at Jacobs University Bremen, Germany, in early 2013. It started out as a purely visual project: a comparison of visual styles in presidential campaigning around the globe. Then I discovered the exciting world of multimodal research, and I realized analyzing images alone would not do. Always a fan of the written word, I chose to pair visuals and text. Luckily for me, there was a lot of research in linguistics that also considered visuals; in fact, it considered everything on the page as part of the "text." But I was not quite happy with that either. My heart was still stuck on the visual as being a major bearer of meaning. As a result, I decided to cross the best of both worlds and come up with a new analytical construct that would cover images and texts with equal, or at least similar, diligence. Four years down the road, the project is completed, and you are holding its latest and most thorough incarnation in your hands right now.

Synthesis often produces a precipitate; combining different theories and methods does not make a clean solution. Purists from visual studies or applied linguistics will be quick to spot some shortcuts and freedoms I have allowed myself in creating the synergetic annotation framework, which is it at the heart of this volume. Just as the precipitate is an important and useful product of many chemical reactions, these sharper theoretical corners are a welcome part of the creative scientific process. They invite comments, revisions, and reinventions—and so they take us further down the collaborative path.

Doing research across disciplines is somewhat in vogue today, at least in principle. The idea of a physicist, a psychologist, and an engineer sitting in a room and working out the problems of mediated human communication online (an arbitrary but still real-life example!) has an instant appeal. However, the notion of a single researcher being the physicist and psychologist is still frowned upon. It is much harder to do interdisciplinary research and be convincing about it if you do not have a team of mono-disciplinary experts around you. For all the praise scientific dialogue and collaboration get in press releases and mission statements, reviewers, search committees, and funding agencies like to keep disciplinary borders intact. I did not know that when I embarked on my ICON-ic journey (pardon the pun). I would do it again nevertheless. While it demands much more from both the author and the reader, transdisciplinary research opens up a world of possibility, insight, and understanding. I hope that my book does that too, and that it adds momentum to this new trend in science so more of those obstructive fences come down—in research departments, science foundations, and our minds alike.

Acknowledgements

A monograph is a solo project by definition, but in reality it always constitutes a team effort. I wish to thank the following people and institutions who played a crucial role in the development of this book:

- Marion G. Müller, Margrit Schreier, and John Bateman, for supervising the doctoral dissertation which forms the basis of the current volume; their valuable feedback and advice expanded the original scope of my work to new exciting horizons.
- The anonymous reviewers, for their sober assessment of my initial book proposal; their constructive criticism and pointers helped turn a dissertation into a research monograph.
- The Research Center "Visual Communication & Expertise" at Jacobs University Bremen, for the intellectual and financial support, especially during the final stages of preparation of the manuscript.
- The German Ministry for Education and Research, for supporting the innovative, multidisciplinary research project "Visual—Film—Discourse" (2008–2011); being part of it opened my eyes to the intrinsic value of dialogue within and between different sciences, and it inspired me to take my own research in that direction.

1 Political Communication Online
A Field in Flux

Political communication as a research field is going through major changes, both in terms of scope and method. What was once the discrete study of campaign materials or news coverage is now forced onto a fast track towards analyzing any media artifact which is even "barely political" (after the famous ObamaGirl YouTube channel from 2007–2008), as Richardson, Parry, and Corner (2012) note in their volume on political culture beyond the news. The quick expansion of the field is driven by technological innovation in the professional practice of political PR, as well as by the growing active involvement of the wider public in the creation and exchange of political messages (e.g. Coleman, 2001). These developments invite novel scholarly approaches that are in pace with the changing parameters of political communication. This also implies looking at political communication outside its traditional manifestations. Richardson et al. (2012) call for going beyond the news and explore print cartoons, politically flavored talk shows, and the blogosphere, among other less commonly scrutinized communication channels. The wider inclusion of such complex data sources, however, necessitates the development of similarly complex analytical methods.

One side of the complexity associated with political communication online is the increase in interactivity and the ample opportunities audiences have to make the jump from receivers to participants in a virtual dialogue. Nowadays, the average member of the media audience is anything but passive, producing as much content as he or she consumes. This is the main quality of the media "prosumer" (e.g. Bianco, 2009; Ritzer & Jurgenson, 2010). The term merges "producer" and "consumer," and it has been in use in the market research context since the 1980s (e.g. Toffler, 1980; Kotler, 1986). Bruns (2007, 2008) uses the term "produsage" to denote a similar phenomenon, especially in the context of Web 2.0, an environment built upon an "architecture of participation" (O'Reilly, 2007, p. 17). Nowadays, with the advent of the Internet as a major communication medium, prosumers occupy a central place in the creation and distribution of content (Comor, 2011). The literature on the subject draws a direct link between the prosumer movement and the political economy of capitalism. This puts the phenomenon firmly in a Western context and links prosumers' growing numbers to, among other environmental features, widespread online access. As individuals become more and more interconnected—as they join the "network society" (e.g. Castells, 2000, 2005)—sharing texts, visuals, and the meanings they carry has hardly been as easy, painless, and quick. Nevertheless, this ease of communication brings along a number of challenges.

Comor (2011, p. 309) notes that "both mainstream and progressive analysts conceptualize prosumption to be a liberating, empowering and, for some, a prospectively revolutionary institution." Indeed, Toffler (1980), the term's originator, believed prosumption would bring about nothing short of a new, better human civilization. However, the phenomenon is not without its pitfalls, especially in the field of mass communication, which is in focus here. In particular, Ritzer and Jurgenson (2010, p. 13) point to the trend towards amateur, unpaid, and abundant content generation within a system where scarcity used to be the norm. While "scarcity" and "abundance" are relative terms in the mass communication context, the implications of the statement are that mass media are losing their monopoly over the generation and dissemination of information, and that this happens rapidly at the hands of prosumers who produce content and make it ready for consumption, all for free (or at negligible personal expense)—something professional mass media cannot hope to match, economically speaking. In the context of the mass audience's "feeding frenzy"—the constant hunger for more news even if none exists—online media prosumption surely sounds like a blessing. However, amateur production and especially amateur dissemination can have significant and far-reaching consequences, involving topics of crucial importance such as social responsibility, fact checking, and reporting bias, to name but a few.

Toffler's vision of prosumption was always technology centered; according to Comor (2011, p. 312), the revolutionary potential of this new socioeconomic phenomenon is locked inside the technology itself (i.e. networked computers). Indeed, computer networks grow massively, and the constraints of the online canvas shrink by the minute as new platforms, new functionalities, and new tools emerge. This myriad of fresh communication opportunities begins to penetrate all spheres previously dominated by the "traditional" media. Political communication, on the battle for "hearts and minds" since its inception in the early 1800s (e.g. Müller, 1997), has also moved online and established itself firmly in this new environment in the past 15–20 years—virtually since the World Wide Web became available to the masses in 1990 (Zakon, 2010). As political persuasion and political discussion took to the Web, hopes for informed, two-way communication between campaigners and constituents grew (e.g. Coleman, 2001; Endres & Warnick, 2004). Simultaneously, there appeared fears that the status quo of sleek, "professional" campaigns, which tend to ignore interactivity and dialogue, would merely transfer into the new medium (e.g. Foot & Schneider, 2002; Gibson & Römmele, 2001; Xenos & Foot, 2005). Research is still on the fence about the benefits, costs, and pitfalls of online political communication. A range of analyses look at various aspects of political participation and information spread online: from social determinants of participation (e.g. Best & Krueger, 2005; Gibson, Lusoli, & Ward, 2005) to campaign creativity in using online tools (e.g. Druckman, Kiefer, & Parkin, 2007; Farnsworth & Owen, 2004), to purely Internet-based political systems with their own rules and values (Gueorguieva, 2008; Howard, 2005; Ward, 2005).

Prosumption is the first crucial component at the heart of this book's empirical and theoretical offering. The rapid infusion of amateur or semi-professional content into online communication channels necessitates a comprehensive media-analytical toolbox. So far, it has been possible and in fact widely accepted for scholars to focus on a single communication mode because high levels of professionalization (e.g. Hallin & Mancini, 2004) provide reasonable guarantee that the combinations of text and image at the center of a media artifact have been carefully crafted to carry an unambiguous message. With that axiomatic conviction, it was easy to draw conclusions about campaign strategy and style or about journalistic bias. When we tread into prosumer territory, however, the guarantee does not hold anymore. The nature of mass prosumption is heterogeneous, international, and heavily contextualized. Under these conditions, it is not enough to analyze the text or the visual only. While media professionals may be expected to streamline their communicative effort and to integrate their visual-verbal messages, prosumers are neither trained nor constrained to operate in this way. Rather, they let their own competences and strengths shine through their composition choices; thus, looking at the whole picture is key to yielding representative results, for both prosumer and professional political communication in the context of the World Wide Web.

Media hybridization is another source of inspiration and direction for this book. Hybridization has been present in numerous forms within the social sciences. The very first use of the term "hybrid" comes from ancient times; in Latin, it was used to denote the crossbreeding between "a tame sow and a wild boar" (Young, 1995, p.6). With time, the term has grown in scope tremendously and, indeed, has become one of the "emblematic notions of our era" (Kraidy, 2005, p.1). In its purist sense, hybridity refers to cultural exchange and sociocultural change in general, and numerous scholars have worked on the problem:

> Indeed, a coterie of thinkers have written about cultural exchange and mixture, including Argentinian-Mexican cultural theorist Nestor Garcia-Canclini (1989), Spanish-Colombian media scholar Jesus Martin-Barbero (1993), Russian literary theorist Mikhail Bakhtin (1981), French historian Serge Gruzinski (1999) and French philosopher Michel Serres (1969, 1972, 1974, 1977, 1980), French Guyanese literary critic Roger Toumson (1998), Saudi sociologist and novelist Turki al-Hamad (2001), and Iranian intellectual Jalal Al-I Ahmad (1984) (Kraidy, 2005, p. 3)

4 A Field in Flux

Hybridity in the mass-media context retains a very strong bond with culture and transculturality, to the extent that Berger (2009) claims the demarcation lines between local, foreign, and international news are fading. Much of the extant body of research on this phenomenon is bound to the theory of cultural imperialism (e.g. Boyd-Barrett, 1998; Morris, 2002; Baird-Olson, 2003). However, here we leave much of the ideological debate aside in favor of a practical approach to hybridity, one centered on the amalgamation of previously separate communication modes into monolithic media artifacts. The Internet presents the opportunity to fuse communication modes seamlessly, but this is also a challenge for both producers and researchers who must bridle this newly found media complexity.

One way to fathom the process of media hybridization is to conceptualize it through convergence. According to Appelgren (2004, p. 239), "in 1997, the European Union presented a definition of convergence suggesting two possible uses of the concept, the first one being the possibility for many types of networks to distribute principally similar services and *the second one being the merging together of different electronic appliances such as telephones, television sets and computers*" (emphasis added). The growing co-deployment and effective merging of different communication modes into single cohesive multimodal documents also comes with a slow but steady fusion of traditional and new media—print, TV, and online outlets share an increasing number of visual features nowadays (e.g. Cooke, 2005). It is also plain to see that the Internet as the medium of choice has taken over all defining features of traditional media and transformed them into its own palette of multimodal communication patterns. This development presents a formidable challenge to media scholars, and novel methodologies that can handle high levels of context complexity need to be developed.

RESEARCH QUESTIONS AND GOALS

As prosumption and media convergence grow in prominence within the field of online political communication, research is pressed for time and resources to keep up with the beat of technological innovation. Studies and theories center on the textual messages propagated by campaigners or bloggers, the tone of political news coverage, or the pictures from political events that appear on television and in the press. Each of these aspects of political communication, on- and offline, has been researched to varying extents, and a few have been studied comparatively as well. The next step, therefore, is an integrated multimodal approach for analyzing political communication, one that encompasses numerous communication modes present in a single document (visual—still and/or moving, textual, audio, layout) and takes into account each of their contributions to the meaning-making process. This development is a natural continuation of all the work that has been done in the field of online political communication research so far. An approach like that would unify and streamline previous efforts into thorough and telling analyses that command even more explanatory power.

This book offers a contribution to the above goal. It tackles the following research questions:

1. How do the different communication modes (visual and verbal) interact in the multimodal documents examined?
2. How do the different communication modes relate to meaning-construction patterns of the content?
3. How do political websites contextualize their content visually and verbally?
4. Are there clearly identifiable medium- and genre-specific patterns of multimodal interaction?

The relationship between the research questions is linear. The answers to the first two questions stem directly from the empirical component of the monograph, which proposes a novel multimodal annotation tool for politically flavored online media. Testing that tool sheds light on visual-verbal interaction and tests the boundaries of the new methodological construct. The findings generated there assist in tackling the third research question, where semantic interactions are embedded in the larger theoretical frame of context. Contextualization practices grow in both importance and complexity, and they become especially relevant in the case of new media. After generating systematic knowledge about what visual and verbal elements are present in the data, it is paramount to embed this knowledge in its proper contextual settings and further inform the interpretations and conclusions of the first two research questions. Finally, the fourth research question looks for media and genre dependencies. This endeavor is made easier by answering the previous research questions because they aim to provide a thorough, positive, and contextual overview of the data. Therefore, they set the stage for preliminary generalizations and conclusions about the structures, functions, and challenges that characterize political communication online in its manifestations considered here. This sequence of research questions also serves as one viable blueprint for multimodal media analysis, one where visual and verbal semantic elements are first categorized, then contextualized, and finally embedded into tentative typologies, which can then be tested through further investigation. Such a stepwise procedure is well suited for the challenge of constantly evolving media phenomena, due to the systematic principles that govern it and at the same time allow for all necessary amendments that play a role at each level. This means of organization keeps the system in check and makes sure that tweaks at any one analytical stage affect all further analyses as well.

For the purposes of the project, "political websites" are exemplified here by the online presence and presentation of: a) political news, b) election campaigns, c) political and media-related NGOs, and d) social movements.

6 A Field in Flux

The selection of political websites also aims to tap into the prosumption phenomenon that was already introduced at length. These and other research design decisions are explained in the following chapters. Some of these research questions have been asked, in part or in full, about offline political communication before. However, transferring answers across media is not an option, particularly with the booming development that we see in online communication technologies. While the challenge of the constantly evolving technological landscape remains a formidable one, it is not too ambitious to aim at an analytical model that offers a sound understanding of the semantics involved in online political communication. The present volume proposes one such comprehensive solution. To realize it, it borrows theoretical and methodological considerations from political communication, visual communication, iconography, systemic-functional linguistics, and multimodal document analysis. This array of disciplines and methods is thoroughly explained further on, and strong arguments are made for their interrelation and powerful combination.

RESEARCH DESIGN ACROSS DISCIPLINES AND MODES

Robert Yin (2009) defines research design "colloquially [as] *a logical plan for getting from here to there,* where *here* may be defined as the initial set of questions to be answered, and *there* is some set of conclusions" (p. 26). The research design "guides the investigator in the process of collecting, analyzing, and interpreting observations" (Nachmias & Nachmias, 1992, p. 77). The empirical component of this book takes the form of a series of exploratory case studies in the field of online political communication. Yin (2009) identifies the case study design as especially suitable for answering "how" questions, and the book's guiding research questions take this form almost entirely. Each case study involves the multimodal analysis of a particular genre of political website, which explores and then systematizes its visual-verbal meaning-making mechanisms. Therefore, the unit of analysis (e.g. Ragin & Becker, 1992) is the political communication website, since the research questions revolve around similarities and differences between these entities (Yin, 2009), either individually or united by their common genre (e.g. campaign website, online news, etc.). Finally, the findings from all case studies are discussed comparatively, genre-specific and inter-genre typologies are fleshed out, and a preliminary evaluation of the new multimodal annotation scheme ensues. The results are then set into the larger framework of the book, namely, the structures, functions, and challenges lying before political communication online in the new media environment of the 21st century. Naturally, all findings correspond to one or more of the research questions posed in the previous section and illustrate the overall methodological construct of mutual dependency, which this book singles out as most viable for research into current and constantly evolving media fields.

The design has to be of an exploratory nature due to the relative novelty of the research topic. As such, it throws a wide net, figuratively speaking, in order to get preliminary data from four major varieties of political communication outlets online and to paint a general picture of the visual-verbal relations that dominate each subgenre. This book is as much an empirical investigation as an exercise in theory building and method testing. Theory development is a central characteristic of case studies, which sets them apart from related methods, such as ethnography (e.g. Lincoln & Guba, 1985) or "grounded theory" (e.g. Corbin & Strauss, 2007). Robert Yin (2009) emphasizes the importance of "field contacts [which] depend upon an understanding—or theory—of what is being studied" (p. 35). The book follows this advice. It has a solid foundation in already existing research fields and methods, as outlined in the following chapters, but it also aims to take a step in a new direction by presenting a new theory of multimodal document analysis and testing it empirically. Therefore, a good exploratory analysis of the status quo against the proposed methods and theories is the necessary first move to solidify the ideas and approaches proposed here.

The concrete research steps involve theory development and elaboration, collection of data from the four genres of political websites, and their annotation via a novel analytical tool that combines the exploratory powers of different qualitative methods from the humanities and the social sciences. The tool in question is ICON ("Imagery and Communication in Online Narratives") and is described in greater detail in subsequent chapters. It relies on the power of political iconology to identify and trace visual motifs and compositions and to extract meanings from them. It combines this visual approach with careful attention to the textual messages that surround the images, as well as the layout and composition of the total webpage space. To achieve this combination, ICON relies heavily on knowledge generated in different branches of linguistics, most of all on Hallidayan systemic functional linguistics and the currents of multimodal research it inspired.

The rationale behind combining these research disciplines' methods and approaches is manifold. On one hand, each of these (mostly) qualitative approaches offers far-reaching insight into its focal area, i.e. text *or* visuals. However, these communication modes rarely exist in isolation from each other, and the growing freedoms of document and web design allow numerous combinations of visual and text elements. These combinations, in turn, create a constantly widening array of meaning potentials, which are realized in the modes' *interplay* and *co-deployment*—a classic situation of the whole being more than the sum of its parts. Therefore, it takes a combined visual-verbal analytical approach to make full sense of the potent multimodal combinations that pour out of computer screens nowadays. On the other hand, combining linguistics and iconology presents a formidable problem of terminological and analytical negotiation and realignment. This is where the exploratory nature of the volume comes into play and allows for careful gauging in order to produce a reusable multimodal analytical tool that pays due attention to both

8 *A Field in Flux*

visual and verbal data features. The mixed disciplinary environment allows for a good balance between reliance on existing iconographical and linguistic practice and explorations of new hybrids between the two.

The research design briefly outlined above also caters to the aim and scope of this volume, namely to shed light on the structures, functions, and challenges that characterize political communication online. By confining the research to this specific area and focusing all theory building and empirical analyses there, it maintains a high level of external validity (e.g. Kidder & Judd, 1986). It follows the replication logic of multiple case studies (e.g. Yin, 2009), namely theoretical replication (i.e. it predicts expected differences for anticipated reasons). The interdisciplinary approach reflects the complexity of the study's aims, and each discipline is meant to cater to specific aspects of the task at hand. Linguistics-based multimodality provides tools for describing and classifying structures as well as for extracting verbal semantics in a systematic fashion. Political iconography adds the necessary visual focus and expertise to the semantic landscape and also gives more reasoning grounds for interpretation of visual-verbal relationships as they appear on the computer screen. Both approaches necessitate careful attention to document design, layout, and context in their semantic explorations. This makes for a potentially exhaustive account of political communication processes online, at least as far as individual webpages are concerned, and is a clear methodological move towards a closer fit between technological developments in the field and matching research tools and methodologies.

TERMINOLOGY

The premise of this book hinges on four key terms: namely, *visuality, multimodality, political communication,* and *online communication.* Each of these terms represents an important starting point for the transdisciplinary task that is at hand here. All of the terms are directly relatable to the general field of communication science, which is also the parent discipline of this volume. Each one touches upon a crucial aspect of communication as it is tackled here. Every new term builds upon the previous ones or extends the structure to neighboring domains in order to expound on the foundation of this book, which is dedicated to both theory building and methodology testing. The sections below define each of the four main terms and elucidate their interconnectedness in the context of this book. The sequence of the subchapters also reflects the disciplinary hierarchy of the project. Visuality and visual communication take center stage, aided by multimodality—another discipline with clear focus on visually based communication norms. Their principles and insights are then embedded in the contexts of political communication, which is a field with its own long history—the most recent development in its timeline is the move to the realm of the World Wide Web, and this leads to the fourth key term for this book, namely online communication.

VISUALITY

The term *visuality* and its close relative *imagery* have deep and far-reaching roots. W. J. T. Mitchell (1984), in his widely cited academic essay *What Is an Image?*, goes on to "examine some of the ways we use the word *image* in a number of institutionalized discourses" (p. 504). He points to the vast scope of what is normally considered imagery—from pictures to statues and from paintings to optical illusions—and provides an image "family tree," broken down according to the distinct institutionalized discourses which make up the branches.

This family tree reflects the centuries of philosophical thought dedicated to the notion of "image." The images that this volume concerns itself with can find a place on any of the five branches of this tree: they are pictures projected on a computer screen, which create perceptions and appearances ingrained in the viewer's mind; they evoke ideas, memories, and associations; finally, they relate to the textually drawn-up images and function together with them to create a single semantic unit. The flexibility and inclusiveness of this project is yet another pointer towards the hybridization of modern media and the (at least partial) breakdown of the institutionalized, exclusive discourses, which led Mitchell to develop these strands in image theory about three decades ago.

Kress and van Leeuwen (1996, p. 4) are among the first scholars to prominently refer to the term *visuality*; they use it to signify the visual aspect(s) of communication artifacts and sometimes employ it interchangeably with *visual communication*. The latter term has been in use for a longer period of time and is gaining more and more prominence in present day. Müller (2007) provides a detailed overview of the field of visual communication, with particular focus on the German tradition. The authors above agree that visuals are universally perceivable yet culturally coded communication artifacts that need contextualization to be properly understood. Müller (2003), Kappas and Müller (2006), and Müller and Kappas (2011) detail the basics of visual communication, with special attention to both production and reception contexts and the variety of combinations thereof. The sound understanding of visuals' contextual baggage is of utmost importance for their proper interpretation, and, conversely, ignoring the context from which they come and

Table 1.1 An image family tree according to Mitchell (1984, p. 504).

IMAGES				
Graphic	**Optical**	**Perceptual**	**Mental**	**Verbal**
• pictures	• mirrors	• sense data	• dreams	• metaphors
• statues	• projections	• "species"	• memories	• descriptions
• designs		• appearances	• ideas	• writing
			• fantasmata	

in which they were meant to be viewed can lead to misunderstandings with sometimes grave consequences (e.g. Müller, Özcan, & Seizov, 2009).

The field of visual literacy, which found its origin in the 1970s and 1980s (e.g. Dondis, 1973; Braden & Hortin, 1982; Curtiss, 1987) and later on was helmed by Paul Messaris (1994; 1998), is closely associated with the recent prominence of visual communication as an academic area. Müller (2008b), among other mostly European scholars, discusses the similar concept of visual competence. Both are relevant to the understanding of visual messages and conceptualize the necessary skills one needs in order to make sense of the increasingly visual information around us. Visuality is, therefore, both a mode of information transfer based in images, material or immaterial (e.g. Müller, 2007), and a quality of modern media, one which requires a certain amount of skills and competences from audiences who wish to make sense of the information they perceive.

This brief overview outlines a number of challenges in front of visual communication research as such and in front of the present volume in particular. From its core definition, visuality is a somewhat elusive concept: are not *all* aspects of a document, in whatever form, essentially visual? Indeed, vision is the means of perceiving all that is on the page or the screen. The fundamental dividing line between "visual visuals" and "textual visuals," to which we refer simply as "text," has also created another, deeper division between the importance communication research traditionally ascribes to each of those cases. As a result, the methodologies available for the analysis of texts and visuals have been developing at different paces and in different directions. The emphasis habitually falls on text, as evident both in academia and society at large. Education is hinged upon learning to understand and produce texts, with visuals always being awarded the role of illustrating or summarizing the textual information in more concise form. This secondary role of visuals has hampered the development of numerous and sophisticated methodologies which adequately analyze both the visual itself and its place within the concrete document under scrutiny. It has even led to the dubious practice of applying non-visual methodologies to the task, as decried by Müller (2007). The current project takes upon itself to bridge the text-visual gap and restore the balance between the two. It does so in full awareness that such balance is warranted on the normative level, and the importance of visuals and text as meaning carriers still needs to be carefully verified and tested empirically.

MULTIMODALITY

Multimodality, in turn, builds upon the already complex concept of visuality and pertains to the interactions of different communication modes and their artifacts. Van Leeuwen (2008) even proposes abolishing visual and textual analysis proper in favor of a multimodal approach. Bateman (2008) provides a detailed overview of the booming research field and of its present and future significance. He focuses his study on the *multimodal document,* in which "a variety of visually-based modes are deployed simultaneously in order to fulfill an orchestrated collection of interwoven communicative goals" (Bateman, 2008, p. 1). It follows, therefore, that multimodality and visual communication are inseparable in their reliance on visual perception and on understanding the compositional and symbolic meaning-making conventions of the artifacts they study. The "*interaction* and *combination* of multiple modes within single artefacts [sic]" (p. 1) are of major interest, along with their potential for *multiplication of meaning* (Lemke, 1998). The simultaneous deployment of several communication modes is by far superior to the use of text alone (e.g. Thibault, 2001), and the multimodal document decidedly carries more information than merely the sum of its monomodal parts. Contemporary documents seem to be innately multimodal, due to both technological developments that allowed this change and the necessity to provide more and more information in little space. Therefore, they display much higher *modal density* (Norris, 2004) or *co-deployment* (Baldry & Thibault, 2006). These developments lead to increased talk of the necessity for "multimodal literacy"—an extension of the visual literacy debate introduced above—as well as for a "visual turn" in communication (Bateman, 2008, p. 2). It follows, therefore, that visuality and multimodality are closely intertwined as defining qualities of modern communication artifacts and especially of the mass-mediated ones, since technological innovations quickly find their way into the media and thus enable them to make full use of the meaning-making and meaning-expansion opportunities that visuality and multimodality bring. To this end, Bateman, Delin, and Henschel (2002) developed an analytic-synthetic model: GeM ("Genre and Multimodality"), which will be introduced at length in the following chapter, and which played a central role in the development of this project's own multimodal annotation tool.

Given the online focus of the present research effort, it is crucial to keep in mind the uniqueness of the World Wide Web as a communication interface for the mass medium that the Internet has become. In a series of technological breakthroughs and innovations, more and more enhanced communication opportunities became available to producers and consumers of online information. The defining feature of this wave of new media is the concept of the hypertext: a text with readily accessible and multiple connections to other texts, all one click away. This is arguably the most revolutionary development in online information relay, as it provides a semantic structure of the information available online as well as a hands-on, fluid navigation grid that individual users can tailor to their own unique information needs and interests. This is the phenomenon Lemke (2002) refers to as "hypermodality," a combination of multimodality and hypertextuality. In Lemke's (2002) words, it "is one way to name the new interactions of word-, image-, and sound-based meanings" (p. 300). The term is complex and points in the important direction of information design. A wide variety of information modes and means mix in the effort of providing a navigable collection of information nodes that offers individual users freedom of exploration. This freedom, as Djonov (2007) notes, is a double-edged sword, however. Free and fluid though it is, a webpage is still a more or less traditional page-based document (e.g. Bateman, Delin, & Henschel, 2002) and, as such, conforms to organizational rules that allow it to produce an intended meaning. In a hypermodal environment, this becomes increasingly difficult due to the freedoms granted to the user by the fluid document design and features.

Needless to say, this fluidity puts considerable pressure on Web designers and online communicators to balance the freedom of navigation with the information structures that cannot be bypassed without losing their intended meanings. On a related note, both Lemke (2002) and Bateman (2008) prominently refer to *constraints* when analyzing page-based multimodal documents. Despite the negative connotation of the term, to both scholars constraints also play the positive role of keeping the expanding design possibilities in check and providing a certain level of harmony between meaning complexity and design complexity. While this project does not analyze Web content from the designer point of view, it is expected to have a range of contributions to solving the problem of setting up meaningful and unequivocal image-text relations in hypertext documents. An admitted shortcoming in the present project is the lack of real professional input into the interpretations of certain design decisions and moves. It is the mark of the layman to overanalyze and ascribe meaning to elements that are there for purely technical reasons and carry little additional significance. This exercise in "reverse engineering," nevertheless, offers insights into the perception experience of both audiences and scholars without profound expertise in the field of multimodal document design. An avenue worth exploring as an aid to this and similar future research projects would be a series of expert interviews with professional online communicators whose expertise and insights could greatly inform the work of future online communication scholars and, thus, help bridge the expertise gap between the professional and the academic spheres.

POLITICAL COMMUNICATION

Political communication is the third academic pillar of this book. Denton and Woodward (1990, p. 14) focus their definition of this term on verbal and written political rhetoric. In his seminal book on the subject, McNair (2003) retains the intentionality embedded in Denton's and Woodward's impression of the concept and defines it simply as "purposeful communication about politics" (p. 4). He then breaks it down to three distinct forms:

1. All forms of communication undertaken by politicians and other political actors for the purpose of achieving specific objectives.

2. Communication addressed *to* these actors by non-politicians such as voters and newspaper columnists.
3. Communication about these actors and their activities, as contained in news reports, editorials, and other forms of media discussion of politics. (McNair, 2003, p. 4)

So defined, political communication is inextricably connected to visuality and multimodality through the mass media: "[P]olitical actors must use the media in order to have their messages communicated to the desired audience" (McNair, 2003, p. 12). In other words, the core features of mass media help shape or obscure, intentionally or not, political messages on their way from the political actors (senders) to the citizens (receivers). According to Kaid, Gerstle, and Sanders (1991), three political realities exist: objective (political events as they occur), subjective (political events as perceived by people), and constructed reality (political events as they are presented or spun in the media). What neither Kaid and colleagues nor McNair emphasize sufficiently, however, is the fact political events reach mass audiences in their "constructed" shape more often than not; hence, the media hold immense power in shaping political attitudes and keeping the electorate informed—a steeple of healthy democracies (e.g. Dahl, 1990; Howard, 2005, 2011). Ample research focuses on political communication's power to use visual, multimodal, and emotional constructs to mobilize the electorate (e.g. Brader, 2006; Luntz, 2006; Green & Gerber, 2008) as well as to scare, confuse, or deter it from participating in the democratic process altogether (e.g. Ansolabehere & Iyengar, 1997; Patterson, 2002; Brader, 2006). The current volume builds and expands upon that rich tradition and promises to deliver information on how online media construct political reality visually and multimodally. It also faces the major challenge of the constantly evolving world of online political communication: As social networks penetrate people's lives more deeply, political campaigners become increasingly proficient at utilizing them. In this race of expertise, academia is bound to lag behind, but it is one of the major aims of this volume to contribute to closing this gap.

The technological developments outlined in the opening chapters of this book spell out a major challenge for political communication research, namely the diversification of researchable political content. For instance, analyzing and comparing political and campaign communication in pre-Internet times used to be a fairly clear-cut process: It used to come from a limited number of well-defined sources and allowed for encompassing generalizations regarding political strategies (e.g. Müller, 1997), while the limited scope of traditional outlets provided narrow research foci on local media (e.g. Lang, 2004) or local political events (e.g. Holtz-Bacha, 2004; Kriesi, 2004). In the new media age, data come from a host of new sources and in exponentially growing forms as new political communication channels and actors emerge. While many hail the Internet as a blessing to democracy and an instrument for enhancing equality, here is the place to also remember the challenges of information overflow, non-professional communicators recycling unverified content, and also the wraith of path dependency, which postulates that the online democracy bubble will soon burst and that the status quo of insider politics will merely transfer onto the Web. The normative debate will not find resolution for quite some time, but it is already apparent that political communication has changed profoundly and rapidly, and it is no longer trivial to narrow down a research question and design onto a specific medium and draw meaningful conclusions regarding the overall phenomenon out of that limited sample alone. This is a challenge not only for research but also for the democratic process: Despite Internet optimism, variety and freedom also hamper our thorough understanding of how the landscape of political communication is changing, and this already casts a shadow on the process that many take as a panacea for struggling democracies. What is difficult to research is also hard to understand, both professionally and privately, and this is a thought to keep with us throughout future discussions of politics' move to the World Wide Web.

The following major expression of the Internet's insusceptibility to thorough research was already discussed earlier. Media convergence peaks online, and there it commands a seemingly limitless potential for means of expression. These means, in turn, come with an equally far-reaching incentive and empowerment for audiences to share, to relay the messages and, more importantly, to make them their own along the way. This empowerment can turn relayed information into a loaded gun, and each prosumer just might pull the trigger. The current book picks up on this trend and aims to gauge its reach by including typical prosumer examples of political communication and comparing them with the products of professional political communication, be it news or campaign material. Through its exploratory design, this project sheds some of the first rays of light on this new, possibly very fruitful field for comparative research and tests a novel annotation scheme with the same purpose.

ONLINE COMMUNICATION

Any discussion of online communication has to first consider the history of the Internet's development as a medium. Steven Thorne (2008) provides an excellent overview of the Internet's origins and growth: from the limited ARPANET designed for US scientists to exchange data in the 1960s, to the development of e-mail and voice communication in the 1970s and 1980s, and finally to the mass availability of Internet through Internet Service Providers (ISPs) from 1990 onwards (pp. 1–2). At this point, the World Wide Web was born and the user base began to grow exponentially, pushing the technological and communicational limits of the new medium further. As Thorne (2008) remarks, "In the current era, and especially for people born after the mid-1980s, email is no longer the primary digital conduit for everyday social, school, and work interaction" (p. 2). He points to instant-messaging software and wireless communication devices, and social networking sites such as Facebook, Twitter, and Google+ (Pinterest should be added to this list as well). While in earlier times the Internet was deemed not suited even for simple task-centered information exchanges (Daft & Lengel, 1984) and its text-only environment resulted in great reduction in non-verbal communication cues (e.g. Parks & Floyd, 1996), nowadays the Web's communicative options cover a much broader modal spectrum. The times when the Internet provided "scant social information" (Dubrovsky, Kiesler, & Sethna, 1991, p. 119) and was unfit for interpersonal communication are now long gone.

The early criticisms of the World Wide Web's communication limitations reflect a pitfall for communication research: When a prominent new medium positions itself center stage and commands as much power and influence as the Internet does nowadays, this development has an invariable effect on how we approach communication and media as a whole. In the words of Marshall McLuhan (1960), "The advent of a new medium often reveals the lineaments and assumptions, as it were, of an old medium" (p. 567). The rise of the Internet and the variety of communication modes and interactions it offers, therefore, calls for a review of previously existing theory, some of which is at the very core of communication science, such as Dennis McQuail's (1987) mass communication theory and, more importantly, the different levels of communication he identifies. As Morris and Ogan (1996) note, the Internet's initially interpersonal communication character morphed to a new level of information production and sharing. Attributes like "one-to-many," "one-to-one," or "many-to-many" cannot be applied without transferring old-media characteristics and constraints onto the new medium. The impersonal character of early Internet interaction rapidly acquired an interpersonal dimension, comparable with face-to-face interactions (e.g. Jones, 1995), and then evolved further into what Walther (1996) deems "hyperpersonal communication" (p. 3), which is also a negation of the "reduced cues" perspective. Writing a decade before the heyday of social media, the author already identifies the birth of "[computer-mediated interaction] that is more socially desirable than we tend to experience in parallel [face-to-face] interaction" (p. 17). In a review of extant research, Derks, Fischer, and Bos (2008) find "no indication that [computer-mediated communication] is a less emotional or less personally involving medium than [face-to-face]" (p. 766). This quick development of Internet communication to cover the full spectrum of impersonal to hyper- (i.e. excessively) personal also points to the necessity of analyzing it and theorizing about it in new ways.

The exponential growth in the Internet's communicative potentials, and the rapid development of more and more "personal" forms of interaction in particular, have led a number of researchers to consider the social psychological ramifications of the new medium's growing prominence. The synergies between computer science and social psychology in understanding computer-mediated communication had already raised scholarly interest in the 1980s: Newell and Card (1985) saw the integration of psychology findings into the design and development of human-computer interaction as an indispensable part of the process. Grudin (1990) was among the first computer scientists to emphasize the shift from human-computer interaction proper to human interaction *via* a networked set of computers. Wright, Fields, and Harrison (2000) outline the gradual analytical shift from linear task analysis to distributed cognition to account for the human element in computer interaction, and McFarlane and Latorella (2002) discuss the integration of human interruption into interaction designs. These are only a couple of important developments that nevertheless send a clear signal of the deepening ties between communicating individuals and their machines. As the hyper-personal character of the new communication channel solidified, the social psychological study of emotional displays in online settings (e.g. Chmiel et al., 2011; Kappas & Krämer, 2011) came along to explore the displays and effects of emotions in computer-mediated interactions. This relatively recent research focus testifies to the computer's ever-growing sophistication in capturing and transmitting essential aspects of human communication that not long ago were thought to be unique to face-to-face settings alone. A good amount of insight into this development comes from the field of human-computer interaction:

> Human–computer interaction (HCI) is a discipline concerned with the design, evaluation, and implementation of interactive computing systems for human use. The field formally emerged out of computer science, cognitive psychology, and industrial design through the 1960s, formulating guidelines for the development of interactive computer systems, highlighting usability concerns, and providing the impetus for improved interfaces. Computing devices are becoming more prevalent and integrated into both our social and work spaces, and in some cases, they are already essential elements of these environments. HCI therefore plays an increasingly important role in ensuring that computer systems are not only functional but also respect the needs and capabilities of the humans that use them. (Cooperstock, 2007, n.p.)

So defined, the HCI research field stands to make numerous valuable contributions to understanding the developments in online communication that occur nowadays; furthermore, it is very likely to actively shape and guide them. Although from the vantage point of the current project the computer plays the role of facilitator, insights from this strand of research are still important for understanding the complex communication situation in which Internet users operate. While this book does not have the breadth of scope to cover these aspects of online communication, it is still crucial to remain aware of them and to consider them in a possible follow-up study. For the time being, it suffices to acknowledge the existence of a dedicated research field which deals with the design and procedural features of human-computer interaction and, more importantly, to reaffirm its impact on current developments there.

The solid multidisciplinary foundation of human-computer interaction combines with another key feature of the Internet as a communication medium, namely its tendency to grow organically and virally. This happens at the interface of prosumption, and the more centralized conventions developed through HCI research and practice. According to Rheingold (1994), the Internet grows in small chunks developed by scholars, students, and regular people on their own time. It is very telling to pair the rapid technological development of the Internet with the requirements each stage of innovation imposed on the users who wished to remain active and up-to-date in their online communications and interactions. Additionally, the trend of the Internet to develop in small bits has trickled down to the mode of content creation in the Web 2.0 context—prosumers come up with *microcontent*, a term presented by Alexander and Levine (2008) to signify how "authors create small chunks of content, with each chunk conveying a primary idea or concept" (p. 40).

Computer-mediated communication (CMC) is an essential part of our understanding of online communication processes. Thorne (2008) defines CMC as "multimodal [and] often (but not exclusively) Internet-mediated" (p. 1). Simpson (2002) defines it simply as "human communication *via* computers" and distinguishes between synchronous/asynchronous varieties, while also emphasizing the importance of networks for the process, be it LANs or the Internet as a whole (p. 414). Walther and colleagues (2011) explore the "communication dynamics" (p. 230) that CMC offers, enumerating ranges of information outlets and community-building online spaces that are at every user's fingertips. Ramirez, Walther, Burgoon, and Sunnafrank (2002) point towards the growing body of archived information about events and persons, also readily accessible to any Internet-savvy user. These "repositories of impression-enabling information" (Walther et al., 2009, p. 231) suggest that the Internet's inclusiveness, accessibility, and interactivity mean the new medium not only mediates but also potentially modifies and directs the communication processes it hosts. Furthermore, CMC diffuses into numerous spheres of life, ranging from crisis and disaster response (Palen et al., 2009), to dating and friend finding (Ramirez et al., 2002; Walther et al., 2009), to identity formation and shifts (Walther et al., 2011), to an updated battery of ethnographic methods for online research (Garcia, Standlee, Bechkoff, & Cui, 2009) and new frontiers for public deliberation (Xenos, 2008). This inclusiveness and pervasiveness of online communication makes it all the more worthwhile for scholarly analysis, which has to match its integrated, multimodal nature outlined in this section.

CHAPTER PLAN

The book pursues its theoretical, methodological, and empirical explorations in the following fashion:

Chapter 2 introduces the multidisciplinary principles behind the development of the ICON annotation scheme. It discusses its origins in visual communication studies and political iconography and relates them to multimodal document analysis inspired by systemic functional linguistics. A review of previously existing annotation models clarifies the theoretical and methodological underpinnings and advantages of the new scheme.

Chapter 3 presents the empirical portion of this book in detail. It introduces the five annotation layers of ICON with their disciplinary origins and application rules. It also discusses the data sources, sampling, and comparability matters of the study that tests the new annotation scheme. The research design and the steps of designing and implementing a multidisciplinary media study are clarified here, and ICON's advantages in terms of reach and explanatory power shine through.

Chapter 4 presents the annotation results for the complete sample of political webpages. The general view reveals consistently high levels of multimodal integration amid varying levels of design complexity. Visuals prove to be a crucial meaning-making component, indeed, holding prominent spots in many examples. A comparison with previous mono-modal research in political communication boosts ICON's worth.

Chapter 5 focuses on political news and election campaigns as traditional forms of political communication. Both demonstrate high levels of multimodal sophistication along with idiosyncrasies such as occasional impassioned news reporting or fact—rather than emotion—based persuasion. In addition, ICON uncovers distinct communicative strategies between and within the two genres.

Chapter 6 considers webpage content from NGOs and social movements, an extension of the usual research focus of political communication. Clear communicative strategies and styles are evident there as well, also with varying degrees of complexity and modal density. Overall, the original demarcations between the four different genres of webpage content appear to blur in favor of structure-functional forms of expression.

Chapter 7 provides a summary of the findings. Three distinct patterns of visual-verbal organization emerge from the analyses, and they correspond to three clearly delineated communication goals. These structure-functional pairings transgress the four original genres' boundaries, which is a clear sign the Internet is reshaping traditional political communication patterns and styles. After providing concrete answers to the initial research questions, the chapter outlines the future development ahead of ICON and similar multimodal annotation schemes, and places the current volume in a thematic series of innovative research in political communication.

2 ICON
A Visual Approach to Multimodality in Political Communication

Approaching multimodal analytics from a visual standpoint is a relatively new idea that has not seen much practical implementation yet. While images' importance receives growing acknowledgement from a number of disciplines, it is not habitual for visuality to be an analytical anchor, especially not in media research across modes. The complexity of the tasks at hand when it comes to analyzing image-text relationships in any multimodal document is daunting, let alone in online pages, which offer design possibilities that are wider than ever before. The undertaking is additionally complicated by the practice of various communication-related disciplines to stay strictly within their own boundaries and to look at portions of content as if in a vacuum. For instance, visual communication scholars tend to look at images in isolation from their surroundings, that is from their publication context as defined by Müller (2007). Another problem, pointed out by Bateman (2008), among other scholars, is that linguistics and much of multimodality research tends to consider visuals as layout elements only. These approaches, mostly inspired by Hallidayan systemic-functional linguistics (e.g. Bateman et al., 2002; Bateman, 2008), take visuals into account as another form of "text" or as artifacts of document design. Many analytical frameworks forgo the much-needed closer look into the specifics of what is visualized and how—in terms of meaningful realization choices like color, angle, distance, and other image characteristics with a semantic load.

Such superficial treatment of visual meaning making is somewhat characteristic of psychological studies with a communication streak as well. In such studies visuals are merely stimuli; their content is pre-tested for the study's purposes without further consideration. A general example is the International Affective Picture System (IAPS, pronounced "eye-aps"), a database of standard visuals that undergo careful screening with respect to the emotions they elicit in viewers. The selection process of those visuals involves subjects' ratings of emotional response and deliberately does not center on objective image content. The only visual characteristics which play a role in picture selection are basic, technical features such as color, clarity of composition, recognizable visual focus, etc. (Lang, Bradley, & Cuthbert, 1997). Hence, the studies that use the IAPS photo battery cannot include visual semiosis in their research designs or their discussions of results.

Nevertheless, there are also positive examples in the field of psychology and emotion research which pay a good deal of attention to visuals' content and not only to what emotions they elicit. For instance, Iyer and Oldmeadow (2006) tested the emotional effects of news items about a prominent hostage situation with and without visual illustration. Naturally, the illustrated stories elicited stronger emotional responses, and the content of the images used figures prominently both in the research design and in the discussion. Also, very recently Müller, Kappas, and Olk (2012) proposed a new model for analyzing the perception of press photography, where visual meaning goes hand in hand with perception and interpretation. These positive examples, however, do not change the general condition of images as research props. Additionally, whenever more thorough insight into visuals is required, this comes about through methodologies that were transferred from other disciplines without much adaptation. This practice does not negate the findings of previous research, but it points to a potential loss of meaningful information, especially when we keep in mind the visual turn of contemporary media.

These strands of analysis involving mass-mediated visuals are not inherently suboptimal. Quite on the contrary: Different fields ask their own research questions and have their own adequate methodological toolboxes. The problem arises only when the research project at hand aims to address a wider goal that its methodology cannot cover. This is when cooperation between disciplines and methodologies that share a research focus or tackle scientific problems in similar ways can close some of the gaps in communication research and create notable synergies. In this chapter, I will introduce one such interdisciplinary cooperation, which paints a multimodal picture of political communication online. It offers an analytical look at visual meaning-making elements and enhances that look with attention to the verbal and layout features that interact with it. In other words, by combining political iconography with multimodality, this project puts the visual into an analytical focus without overlooking the other important mediators in the process of semiosis. It introduces the annotation scheme "Imagery and Communication in Online Narratives" (ICON) and provides empirical examples of how it can be applied to the specific topic of political communication online, which offers content that is rich, varied, and at the same time challenging in its diversity and social resonance. These characteristics ensure a fruitful testing ground for new methodologies that the scientific field needs. Going into the trying terrain of informational complexity and constant technological and design evolution ensures a thorough test of the new analytical hybrid's features, of its strengths and weaknesses.

Before going into the details of ICON, a word of clarification is in order. After all the advocating for transdisciplinary approaches and giving all semantic elements their due attention, the focus on images in the model's title might seem like a step back. This book is, indeed, grounded in the field of communication science with a special interest in visual political communication; nevertheless, the impression of a step back into mono-disciplinarity is a wrong one. The task of ICON is to provide image analysis and classification as well as semantic analysis of complete multimodal documents, and this cannot be achieved without eliciting other disciplines' help in order to grasp the images' contextual semantic bearings and their relationship to the surroundings on the webpage. This in itself already moves a level up from standard visual communication research, much of which tends to view and analyze visuals in isolation. An early shift towards multimodal integration in visual communication seeps through the words of one of the field's founding fathers, Roland Barthes:

> Images [. . .] can signify [. . .], but never autonomously; every semiological system has its verbal admixture. Where there is a visual substance, for example, the meaning is confirmed by being duplicated in a linguistic message [. . .] so that at least a span of the iconic message is [. . .] either redundant or taken up by the linguistic system. (Barthes, 1964, p. 10)

While the claim above has been occasionally characterized as "too logocentric" (Nöth, 2011, p. 300), it goes without saying that visual communication research needs to become multimodal and needs to consider additional semantic contexts in order to make a real impact. This is also in line with W. J. T. Mitchell's (2005) influential article titled "There Are No Visual Media": In terms of sensory-perceptual involvement, all media are mixed. Furthermore, the analytical logic behind the layers of ICON, discussed in the following chapter, reflects the topical and methodological characteristics of each major discipline that has influenced the model's development. The reasoning behind the model's design and scope cannot be confined to a single discipline, since no sharply delineated field has the tools and means of generating the necessary answers. The end result is a better understanding of visuals' roles and contributions to online political communication's *narratives,* a term which is more at home in linguistics, literature, or rhetoric studies (e.g. Aronoff & Rees-Miller, 2003). The general notion of narrative appears here in a very specific context, which provides an opportunity for thorough exploration of its linguistic functions. These narratives are then embedded in the context of political, online, and visual communication. The end result takes the form of a test for a new multimodal analytical approach geared towards online media artifacts in all their complexity. Therefore, the theoretical underpinnings of ICON embody the principles of transdisciplinarity, with the explicit goal of exploring its synergetic benefits.

PREVIOUSLY EXISTING ANALYTICAL APPROACHES

Before presenting ICON in detail and applying it to concrete empirical cases, it is important to keep in mind the various distinct forms or traditions of visual and multimodal analysis from which it stems. *Visual content analysis* (e.g. Bell, 2001; Grittmann & Ammann, 2011, 2009; Grittmann & Lobinger, 2011; van Leeuwen, 2001) is one starting point, mainly with its capability of data reduction and classification. The categories in ICON are developed inductively (e.g. Boyatzis, 1998) since the scope of the study does not allow effortless reliance on any of the pre-existing coding schemes. This is also the first important step in the analytical procedure because it provides the opportunity to summarize and systematize the types of visualizations in the sample according to fixed characteristics. In that sense, visual content analysis enforces the comparative backbone of the project. It also gives a smooth entry into the meaning-analytical mode of ICON, upon which further layers build and add extra visual, verbal, and layout information, with the goal of painting a fuller picture of the semantic canvas. As Schreier (2012) emphasizes, qualitative content analysis's flexibility and combinative affordance are also significant methodological advantages. The correct performance of this visual content analysis also provides insights into the particular visual rhetoric (e.g. Wright, 2011), which informs the ensuing discussions of intersemiosis.

Political iconography is another important visual method for ICON's development. All images undergo iconographical analysis (e.g. Müller, 2011a; 2011b; 2008a; van Leeuwen, 2001) to identify motifs and underlying symbolism. Originally an art historical method, iconology provides the in-depth qualitative visual insights that enhance the content analysis outlined previously. It employs the logic of patterns of visual representation (stemming from Aby Warburg's concept of "pathos formulae"), which create a rich visual tradition over time. With its careful attention to detail and concern for composition and visual meaning making, iconology also serves as a bridge to the notion of narratives, which in itself is further away from visual communication than from linguistics, for instance. However, by drawing parallels and comparisons with prior visualizations, iconology builds motif families and interrelations, in a similar way to how a verbal narrative weaves a storyline. Therefore, iconology is an essential method in the framework of ICON for two reasons: It allows for a deeper qualitative visual analysis of the visual material, and it also lends its narrative logics to the transdisciplinary scrutiny of the multimodal artifacts.

Eye-tracking and similar visual attention studies play an important role in the analytical scope of ICON as well. Given the vast amount of design options available in online communication, reading attention becomes a crucial topic of interest. The attention-guiding principles discovered thanks to eye-tracking research appear as an integral part of the ICON annotation framework and shed light on patterns of information design. Since only a few of those studies scrutinized webpages, the present book also offers a look at the viability of the print designs online, however limited and preliminary. Due to the exploratory and non-experimental nature of the current project, its purpose is not to test theories of visual attention; nevertheless, those theories have the power to inform the analytical process, and they hold the potential to guide further work in the field as well. As such, this instance of academic cross-pollination reflects another, less often considered aspect of interdisciplinarity: namely the validation or exploration of theories across disciplinary boundaries.

Finally, the *semantic image-text relations* angle is inspired by the work of Martinec and Salway (2005) whose very complex and systematic approach to the problem was the author's very first contact with multimodal research. The shape and form of the actual analyses here owe much to the "Genre and Multimodality" (GeM) model developed by Bateman and colleagues (2002) and systematized in Bateman's (2008) monograph. Like this precursor, ICON employs different layers of annotation, each of which refers to specific characteristics of the visual-verbal semantic construct. The difference between models such as GeM and ICON is in the goal: while the unit of analysis remains the multimodal document, the questions each model can answer differ. While in corpus-based multimodal research it is customary to "cut up" multimodal documents at various levels and to differentiate layers of elements and semantic functions, the present project focuses on an initial exploration of the roles visually based modes play in political communication online without explicitly dissecting the data. To achieve this, ICON departs from the tradition of thorough transcription and breakdown of layout elements. While the standard linguistics-based approach would seem a natural choice when the questions revolve around structures and functions, the current project's exploratory nature will benefit from a more in-depth look at the actual contents, that is, at what the discernible visual-verbal messages and narratives are in each webpage. This also reflects a point of criticism towards previous attempts for being too focused on reverse-engineering design and layout structures with a lesser focus on the content. In that sense, the present project's departure point is meaning and message, which then naturally leads into discussions of presentation and design; not the other way around.

While this book does not employ *semi-automatic multimodal content analysis* and makes use of human coders only, the structure and nature of ICON lends itself to automation in varying degrees. While complex layers such as the iconographical or the contextual one (1 and 5, respectively) still require the multimodal perceptual competence of human researchers, others, such as the coding of various visual features (angle, distance, color scheme) as well as spatial image-text relationships, may be done by a machine. The human involvement naturally raises questions of reliability— an issue that this project and any follow-up research projects must cover. There are already numerous studies which demonstrate the growing visual and multimodal literacy of computers (e.g. Costa et al., 2011; Jacobs, 2006) as well as their ability to extract visuals from complex, though not necessarily page-based, environments and to outline their basic characteristics (e.g. Nixon, Liu, Direkoglu, & Hurley, 2011; Tellaeche, Pajares, Burgos-Artizzu, & Ribeiro, 2011). In that sense, the ICON annotation scheme is ready for semi-automatic implementation and, thus, has the potential to generate quantities of data much larger than the ones presented in this book.

This would also be the most natural extension and further application of this analytical tool. Such a move towards the processing of ever-larger corpora would be a valuable contribution to standardized quantitative multimodal content analysis.

The review of disciplinary roots paints an eclectic picture for ICON as an analytical tool. In combining the ideas and approaches of different research fields whose meeting point is mediated human communication, a reproducible and accessible pathway towards tackling the semantic challenge of online communication is presented. Since this project unveils ICON in its exploratory stage, it is normal for expectations to run high and also for criticism to be abundant and usually well founded. Both sides of the coin are considered during the evaluation stage of ICON; for the time being, it is sufficient to view it as a move towards a transdisciplinary model in motion that aims to show how subject matter is capable of taking precedence over disciplinary boundaries, institutionally or methodologically founded. It also has the goal of illustrating the practical implications of combining methods in a way that allows scholars from any of the involved disciplines to take a step beyond their methodological comfort zones and tap into the potential benefits of mixed-method research without the prolonged time and intellectual investment that is normally required for mastering a new scientific realm.

SYSTEMIC FUNCTIONAL LINGUISTICS AS A BASIS FOR MULTIMODAL DOCUMENT ANALYSIS

Despite ICON's roots in visual communication and content analysis, its ambitious comprehensive outlook requires the help of other disciplines, too, most notably systemic functional linguistics, with its drive for thorough narrative descriptions and social-contextual embedding. It is one of the best approaches for total document analysis at present. The idea of taking media artifacts apart and analyzing them from beginning to end, however, is certainly not new in itself. The search for (mass-) mediated meaning has been going strong since the 1940s (e.g. Schramm, 1997; Schreier, 2012). Throughout these decades, different aspects of the texts (in the widest sense of the term) came into analytical focus, including but not limited to structure, readability, authorship traits, discourse, or propagandistic aspects. All these analyses were characterized by a very narrow focus, mostly on content, which required a methodology geared towards data reduction and standardization. While this yielded excellent results for the specific purposes of each such study, the crucial aspect of growing document complexity remained somewhat in the background. A preoccupation with identifying what is being said superseded the concern with *how* it was being said. Eventually, the increase of multimodal co-deployment (Baldry & Thibault, 2006) became too apparent to ignore, and methodologies that accounted for structural and semantic multimodal interaction started evolving. Returning to Bateman (2008), despite the conviction that multimodal meaning making relies "on the simultaneous orchestration of diverse presentational modes, analytical methods for handling this orchestration are few and far between" (p. 1).

Amid the relative scarcity of research that deals with multimodal documents comprehensively, systemic functional linguistics has spawned a number of specific approaches to the problem. The models reviewed below are examples of that. The close scrutiny of structures and systems of meaning in the realm of language provides a good start on the quest to transcending modal boundaries. At the same time, they lay bare the challenges ahead of multimodal media research. Although systemic functional linguistics has the necessary semantic gear, the models it inspires continue treating visuals as base or layout elements and do not yet give visual meaning nearly the same weight that content analysis or political iconology do. All such analyses embark on a quest for better understanding of multimodality, yet the final product does not truly leave the realms of linguistics. The sheer time and labor investment as well as the complexity of document stratification and classification presents a whole different challenge, too. The available visual methods, on the other hand, often lack the rigid structure and clear decision rules to offer reproducible results. They leave much to contexts, both communicational and personal. This is not to be taken as critiques to either approach. Quite on the contrary: each of these fields and its methods has evolved in response to the respective research goals, questions, and topics. The results they provide are adequate in their reach and complexity. Still, the premise of this book is to present and test ICON, a new tool for tackling the multimodal challenge of contemporary online communication with a combination of established methods. Its contribution is to prove that both the visual and the verbal communication modes can be scrutinized in sufficient detail, and that new synergies and interactions can be uncovered, which could not be by earlier approaches. The ensuing review of multimodal annotation schemes presents the origins of ICON in context as well as the premises and approaches that have been prevalent in recent research on complex documents, on- and off-line.

GENRE AND MULTIMODALITY (GeM)

The "Genre and Multimodality" (GeM) annotation model is presented at length in John Bateman's (2008) monograph. The model's goal is "to articulate a framework within which it is possible to frame precise questions concerning the mechanisms by which a multimodal document goes about creating the meanings that it does," while being very wary of the danger of falling into "superficial interpretations" or "applying rich interpretative schemes" which obscure whatever real meaning can be extracted from the multimodal document under scrutiny (p. 13). To avoid these pitfalls, the model concerns itself with testable hypotheses and borrows empirical methods from corpus-based linguistics. Corpus here is defined as a "large principled collection of natural text" (Biber, Conrad, & Reppen, 1998, p. 4). The focus on linguistic corpora allows a double-pronged approach: On the one hand, the rich data offer search room for patterns, and on the other hand, they present ample evidence for the verification of those patterns' existence. This "empirical anchoring" (Bateman, 2008, p. 15) is one of GeM's major assets. Another asset is the model's attention to constraints as important bearers of meaning: canvas constraints (physical), production constraints (technological), and consumption constraints (access and usability) all have crucial implications for the extent and directions of interpretation (p. 18). From here on, the model is presented in its different descriptive and analytical levels, a form of organization already seen in the work of Waller (1987) but modified to fit the current research's goals and needs. The initial stage is recognizing the building blocks of a multimodal document and coming up with segmentations that are appropriate to the semantic structures as well. Various disciplines lend a helping hand in this endeavor: design studies, systemic functional linguistics, and social semiotics. Each of these disciplines adds facets that are crucial for the analysis's reliability and reproducibility. The result is an exhaustive list of base units that, for a Louvre two-page spread brochure, exceed 100. The presence of what is on the page, as well as the absence of what is not, then undergo functional, rhetorical, and generic analyses as they go through the different layers of the GeM framework (see Table 2.1).

Table 2.1 The main elements of the GeM annotation framework (based on Bateman, 2008, p. 19).

Content structure	The content-related structure of the information to be communicated–including propositional content
Genre structure	The individual stages of phases defined for a given genre: i.e., how the delivery of the content proceeds through particular stages of activity
Rhetorical structure	The rhetorical relationships between content elements: i.e., how content is argued, divided into main material and supporting material, and structured rhetorically
Linguistic structure	The linguistic details of any verbal elements that are used to realize the layout elements of the page / document
Layout structure	The nature, appearance and position of communicative elements on the page, and their hierarchical interrelationships
Navigation structure	The ways in which the intended mode(s) of consumption of the document is / are supported: this includes all elements on a page that serve to direct or assist the reader's consumption of the document

Careful attention is then paid to layout elements, textual and graphical, and how they group together visually. The result is a thorough layout structure analysis that also lays bare visual, typographical, and spatial hierarchies, which have important implications for the ensuing rhetorical analysis. The departure point for this analytical level is that "combinations signal meaningful relationships between elements that would not be available to those elements in isolation" (Bateman, 2008, p. 143). The linguistic notion of cohesion helps shed light on such relationships, but what lies at the base of this analytical level is Rhetorical Structure Theory (Mann & Thompson, 1986; 1988) with its notion of semantic dependency structures, namely nucleus (main material) and satellites (subparts, additional support), which Bateman (2008) extends to graphical elements as well (pp. 148–151), a move that reshapes classical RST and makes it applicable to multimodal documents with a series of tweaks, such as allowing visuals to be nuclei and adopting spatiality instead of sequentiality when pairing document parts. Genre is then incorporated, in its "precise, *linguistically motivated*" (Bateman, 2008, p. 182) form, with the important distinction between two main definitions: genre as social semiotic (e.g. Halliday, 1973; Kress, 2003) and genre as social action (e.g. Miller, 1984). A definition that is exhaustive and applies equally to both of these schools of thought is the following, provided by Swales:

> A genre comprises a class of communicative events, the members of which share some set of communicative purposes. These purposes are recognized by the expert members of the parent discourse community, and thereby constitute the rationale for the genre. [. . .] In addition to purpose, exemplars of a genre exhibit various patterns of similarity in terms of structure, style, content and intended audience. (Swales, 1990, p. 58)

Bateman (2008) takes up the view of genre as defined by content, form, and functionality (p. 216), and suggests three distinct modeling approaches: typology ("genre networks"), topology ("dimensions of variation"), and facets ("genre [is] a multidimensional construction combining aspects both of the documents described and the purposes for which they are being taken up") (p. 218). He then commences with an illustration of genre by tracking changes across a series of ornithology entries (1924–1996) on one and the same bird species and running all these examples through the GeM framework. The analytical potential of genre as a predictive characteristic that can guide multimodal document analyses is confirmed, but much broader empirical analyses are necessary before we can reach such a point of distinctly defined, truly predictive genres as reliable analytical tools.

GeM is among the most systematic multimodal analytical frameworks developed in the past decade, and it is based on a very solid foundation of prominent strands in linguistics and, to a lesser extent, communication studies. Its corpus-based nature is among its major assets, as it emphasizes the empirical element in a field that is easily overwhelmed by interpretations and results whose reproducibility is often questionable. The exhaustive list of page elements and their precise classification bring subjectivity to a negligible level, and the machine-readable XML format, in which the analysis is logged, allows for quick transfer and multiple manipulations and computations involving the collected data. However, the major contribution of GeM to the multimodality challenge of modern media is the inclusion of genre into the equation. The main point of these exhaustive analyses is for genres to crystallize out of what stands in the multimodal document rather than from some predefined classification. This is, arguably, a more objective approach because it is data-driven and systematic. As Bateman (2008) himself asserts, however, it will take immense work and application of this model to large multimodal corpora before enough information is generated that can reliably define genres and circumscribe their essential characteristics. This is what makes GeM an important analytical tool in the field of multimodal research, one whose evolution and usage deserves close scrutiny.

With its systematic framework and clear classifications and stances, GeM is a major inspiration for both the theoretical and empirical components of this book and for the inclusion of genre as an analytical component in particular. However, the approach that is taken here to this contentious category differs from the inductive, data-driven choice Bateman and colleagues have made. For the purposes of this project, "genre" still encompasses the essence of Swales's definition cited previously, as well as the notions of semiotic affordances and expectations associated with particular forms of mass-mediated content. Due to the brevity of the empirical portion, however, an inductive approach to genre would be counterintuitive. Therefore, genre is operationalized with a focus on visual form (e.g. photograph, caricature, etc.) and document publication context (e.g. political campaign, news item, etc.), which are both major sources of peripheral information and also powerful framing tools, against whose backdrop semiosis takes place. This view of genre is also more appropriate to the analytical focus of the current project, since it finds its departure point in visual communication studies. From that vantage point, GeM is unfit for the level of visual analysis which is required here since it treats visuals as base elements and gives their meaning-carrying potentials limited consideration relative to other modes and design features present in the multimodal documents under scrutiny.

INTERSEMIOTIC COMPLEMENTARITY

The term "intersemiotic complementarity" was first used by functional linguist Terry Royce (1998) to reflect the conviction that the visual and the verbal modes do not merely co-exist on a page, but that they interact and create a common meaning, each in its own specific ways. To tap into this semiotic process, the author refers to Michael Halliday's postulate of three metafunctions that operate in every language:

> the Ideational metafunction, which is the resource for "the representation of experience: our experience of the world that lies about us, and also inside us, the world of our imagination. It is meaning in the sense of 'content.'"
>
> the Interpersonal metafunction, which is the resource for "meaning as a form of action: the speaker or writer doing something to the listener or reader by means of language."
>
> the Textual metafunction, which is the resource for maintaining "relevance to the context: both the preceding (and the following) text, and context of situation." (Halliday, 1985, p. 53, in Royce, 2007, p. 65)

These three metafunctions are at work simultaneously during the reading and processing of every text. Despite their origin in linguistics and subsequent focus on language, Halliday and Hasan (1985) develop a method for analyzing text cohesion, which Royce (2002; 2007) finds easily applicable *across* semiotic modes as well. In his chapter dedicated to an article in *The Economist,* Royce (2007) conducts a thorough analysis of both the visual and the verbal meanings, as well as their observable interactions, through the following sense relations, postulated by, for example, Halliday (1985): repetition, synonymy, antonymy, hyponymy, meronymy, and collocation. Both visuals and text go through these categories, and visuals are further analyzed according to Kress and van Leeuwen's (1990) criteria of visually representing social relations and actions. In the intersemiotic complementarity analysis, for instance, the co-occurrence of verbal and visual elements is thoroughly analyzed (e.g. the visual depiction of a mountain and the mention of "mountain" in the text are coded "R" for "repetition"), and meaningful conclusions about the visual-verbal relationships and the compositional elements present on the page are drawn. In sum, intersemiotic complementarity manifests itself:

> when the ideational meanings in both modes are related lexico-semantically through intersemiotic sense relations [. . .].
>
> when interpersonal meanings in both modes are related through intersemiotic *reinforcement of address,* and through intersemiotic *attitudinal congruence* and *attitudinal dissonance* (modality) relations.
>
> when the compositional meanings are integrated by the compositional relations of *information value, salience, visual framing, visual synonymy,* and *potential reading paths.* (Royce, 2007, p. 103)

The analysis is complemented by a clear sentence division inventory, which sheds further light on the process. The author also draws connections to the implications multimodal semiosis of this sort has in the context of teaching English as a foreign language—a topic on which he has worked previously (e.g. Royce, 2002) and which often appears in other studies of multimodal meaning making as well.

Terry Royce's analysis is also an excellent example of multimodal research inspired by systemic functional linguistics, which is evident in the framework and terminology at its core. Relying on established Hallidayan concepts and theories of language and meaning lends credibility to the interpretive analyses and lays a solid foundation for the further development of the analytical method. Still, the identified semantic relations remain in the realm of linguistics, and the wide definition of "text" does not escape the precedence of the verbal component despite the plentiful attention allotted to the visual and design features of the examined document. The leap to intersemiotic complementarity also appears somewhat wide. The semantic correlations, though extensive and informative, do not convincingly convey the idea of "a total effect that is greater than the sum of the individual elements or contributions" (Royce, 2007, p. 103). While it is possible to argue that repetitions and visual-verbal synonymy enhance the salience and impact of the repeated meaningful elements (and the same or opposite effects can be ascribed to antonymy, for instance), a purely analytical approach without an experimental or reception study component cannot make such far-reaching claims with absolute certainty. This is also a source of caution for the current project, where the assumption of visual-verbal synergies in multimodal documents is present but where the research design as such does not claim to offer conclusive empirical backing for it.

Royce's (2007) chapter also presents a somewhat rare example of deep research into the visual component as well. The visual analyses do not involve traditional methods (e.g. visual content analysis, iconology, semiotics), but they still succeed in making a valuable semantic contribution to the investigation of the multimodal document at hand. The instances of interpersonal and compositional meaning scrutiny are particularly useful for this book, with their attention to attitudinal congruence and dissonance as well as to visual synonymy and potential reading paths (as cited previously). These are the prime loci for intersemiotic complementarity in Royce's study of the *Economist* article, which he approaches with SFL tools in order to arrive at meaningful conclusions about visual-verbal interactions. The current project approaches the same investigative goal—visual-verbal semantic interaction—from the vantage point of visual communication, focusing on a thorough visual analysis first and then linking it with the adjacent verbal and design components. Both approaches work with the conviction that the two modes "complement each other semantically to produce a single textual phenomenon" (Royce, 2007, p. 103), and both analyses yield findings that buttress this important point.

MULTIMODAL DISCOURSE ANALYSIS

Systemic functional linguistics has given rise to another strand of research on multimodal documents, namely multimodal discourse analysis (e.g. O'Halloran, 2004; 2008). According to O'Halloran (2011), it is "an emerging paradigm in discourse studies which extends the study of language per se to the study of language in combination with other resources, such as images, scientific symbolism, gesture, action, music and sound" (p. 120). Multimodal discourse analysis is, once again, rooted in Michael Halliday's (e.g. 1973; 1985) theory of meaning generation as a context-dependent process built on semiotic choices within the realm of language, which is then extended to other realms of human communication such as art (O'Toole, 1994; 1999) or visual communication (Kress & van Leeuwen, 1996). The specific strength of SFL theory in this case is the metafunctional principle already outlined in the previous section, which provides a base for theories of multimodal semantic interaction (e.g. Baldry & Thibault, 2006; Kress & van Leeuwen, 2006). Nevertheless, challenges continue standing in the way of an integrated approach due to a lack of unified theoretical and methodological frameworks for analyzing the different modes reliably and reproducibly.

Kay O'Halloran provides a telling overview of the major caveat of doing systemic functional multimodal discourse analysis:

> [SFL] is concerned with the study of the sequence of parts (i.e. the words, word groups, clauses, clause complexes and paragraphs), which form stages in the development of the text. The progressive structures are modeled according to metafunction [, while] the perception of the whole visual image takes precedence of perception of the parts, which may consist of a series of happenings within the overall work. There are factors, such as the size of the image and the ratio and density of the whole to the parts which need to be taken into consideration, but generally the whole is perceived before the parts in visual imagery. (O'Halloran, 2008, pp. 447–8)

This major difference, also stated within the field of visual communication (e.g. Müller, 2007), poses a challenge, which O'Halloran solves by applying the same set of analytical strata to both communication modes, mainly "content" and "expression," referring to Martin (1992) and Halliday (2004) for the verbal account and to the model developed by O'Toole (1994) for the visual components. Both strata, thus, address semiosis through similar approaches based on grammar, discourse, and formal characteristics (e.g. typography, phonology, graphics). The visual analysis, however, realizes the metafunctions differently in accordance with the semiotic resource's idiosyncrasies and requires "descriptive categories and analytical approaches which do not necessarily involve SFL categorical-type system networks" (O'Halloran, 2008, p. 452). The resulting mixed-mode semiosis realizes

32 ICON: A Visual Approach to Multimodality

semantic expansion through the creation of new spaces for interpretance, where the co-deployment of different modes and their respective semantic logics result in the creation of new systems of meaning organization and perception (Lemke, 2000). The resulting analytical framework is best summarized in Table 2.2.

As it is evident from the different levels in the table, visual and verbal elements can be analyzed through similar linguistics-based frameworks. The ensuing analysis involves a similar battery of linguistic and semantic inventories as the ones cited by Royce (2007), with a particular focus on the visual and verbal creation of ideational and logical meaning. The visual analysis in particular takes the form of action and narrative interpretation, which are both open to a certain degree of subjective view. Digital technology comes to aid the analyses through image editing and superimposition of the investigative categories upon the analyzed document; digital enhancement "demonstrates how semiotic choices can be visually marked in a way which gives rise to detailed semantic and ideological interpretations of the text" (O'Halloran, 2008, p. 470). This relates nicely to Bateman's (2008) notion that multimodal analysis should also concern itself with what is *not* there, as such absences are often best highlighted through enhancing and exaggerating what *is* there.

Table 2.2 A systemic functional multimodal discourse analysis framework for printed texts (based on O'Halloran, 2008, p. 457).

	Ideology	
	Generic mix	
	Registerial mix	
Content stratum	Intersemiosis Mini-genres, Items, and Components (Linguistic, Visual, and/or Other)	
	Language	Visual Images
	Intersemiosis Discourse Semantics	
	Discourse	Intervisual Relations Work
	Intersemiosis Grammar	
	Clause complex Clause Word Group / Phrase Word	Scene Episode Figure Part
Display Stratum	Intersemiosis Materiality	
	Typography / Graphology and Graphics	

The discourse-analytical take on multimodal document analysis adds another facet to the challenge of studying intersemiosis. While still relying on the same basic theory that underpins the other approaches reviewed in this chapter, it also expands on the notion of the multimodal whole exceeding the sum of its mono-modal parts by involving Lemke's (2000) proposition of new spaces for interpretance in the debate, and backing it up through operationalizing expression and content-analytical strata specific to verbal and visual communicative elements. The particular attention paid to the material layers of both communication modes is of relevance to this book, which also considers the physical attributes or "attributes of realization" of multimodal documents. O'Halloran (2008) emphasizes the relevance of this analytical layer through the usage of digital technology for modifying the image component of a printed document and the investigative insights which result from this manipulation. At the same time, this technique once again points towards the deficiency which all SFL-inspired multimodal research tools summarized here seem to share, namely the lack of visual methodology proper to complement their undoubted linguistic prowess. In the case of multimodal discourse analysis, visuals are analyzed in the most systematic fashion of all three models, but even this scrutiny does not leave the realm of linguistics in its treatment of visuals as texts (this time in the verbal sense of the word), albeit acknowledging their fundamentally different perceptual logic. This is also the area where ICON makes a contribution by starting out with a visual analysis, which then turns multimodal, contrary to the established practice in this branch of the field.

TOWARDS AN ALTERNATIVE MULTIMODAL ANALYTICAL TOOL

The approaches outlined in this chapter each offer considerable insight into the emerging field of multimodal document analysis. Now we set out to systematize those insights, and to prepare the ground for the introduction of another analytical approach to tackle the scientific problems of increased multimodal meaning-bearing content and intersemiosis present in contemporary media documents. This analytical approach also aims to make the case for a visually based approach, namely one that does not habitually gloss over images as part of the "text" which can be treated with methodologies developed by other disciplines and for other purposes. While dismissing previous efforts in multimodal annotation is definitely not on the agenda, acknowledging the primary importance of visuals in online communication is. In the spirit of transdisciplinarity, the goal is to generate a synergetic approach that adopts some of the best practices of current analytical tools and incorporates them into the visual paradigm of this book. To do so, a review of major insights follows.

The first and most obvious conclusion stemming from this overview is the important place of systemic functional linguistics in the recent move towards sophisticated research in multimodality. This is easily attributable to Michael Halliday's crucial choices of making context a central point of semantic reference and, thus, tying language, culture, and communication to social action. Grounded in this way, the theory is much more easily applied in non-verbal and multimodal contexts, as demonstrated in all of the discussed models' reviews. By creating such a pliable, society-centered theory of language, Halliday has also made it infinitely *applicable* through its recognition of and adaptability to context. The breakdown of four metafunctions (ideational, interpersonal, logical, and textual) ensures the coverage of all major communicative aspects of language, but it allows for applications outside the realm of the written/spoken word as well, since every text, regardless of mode, fulfills each of the four metafunctions by definition within the SFL framework. The careful attention to nuances of meaning and modality complement this analytical thoroughness. In sum, flexibility combined with exhaustive exploration of semantic potentialities makes the systemic functional view of multimodality a supreme base for research into different communicative modes.

The social component of Michael Halliday's linguistic theory also resonates well with communication studies' interest in society and social developments. This interest figures prominently in this book as well, as evident from the thorough review of prosumption in the introductory chapter. In that sense, the attention to semiotic choices and the view of language (and by extension, communication) as social action both harmonize with the prosumer challenge, which has already been outlined. As the variety of semiotic resources available to media producers increases, the specific choices for content realization and presentation gain increasing importance, and the significance of what is *not* on display in a given document grows and adds to the meaningfulness of what is there. In that train of thought, SFL is an excellent theoretical framework for tackling the vast variety of online intersemiosis with an open mind and systematic effort.

While its advantages cannot be denied, SFL still does not come as a panacea in the face of the intersemiotic challenge that contemporary multimodal documents present, and this is another crucial insight that the previous review makes clear. While it is thorough in its consideration of semantic elements, and although it inspired numerous multimodal analytical frameworks, SFL cannot offer enough of a departure from its mono-disciplinary, linguistic roots. This is not meant as critique towards a prominent field but as a word of caution against its ready application to the task of explaining intersemiosis. Among the authors reviewed above, O'Halloran (e.g. 2004; 2008) sets a good example by admitting adjustments are needed to the general framework whenever visuals are the analytical focus, and she offers a set of appropriate modifications in order to take SFL principles into the visual field. Nevertheless, even adjustments to the original framework retain the structures and approaches that were prompted and guided by language and by principles of verbal communication. O'Halloran's (2008) approach to "linguistic visual analysis" presented previously goes as far as to modify the original image under scrutiny in order to support its analyses and interpretations. This is where the need for an integrated approach with proper visual methodology becomes undeniable. Although it crosses modal boundaries, SFL remains anchored in its original mono-disciplinary realm. Therefore, it propagates the suboptimal practice of applying methods and modes of scientific thought to problems they are not equipped to tackle, and this makes for incomplete findings and unrealized information potentials.

Therefore, the most important insight to be gained here is the need for a truly transdisciplinary approach to the phenomenon of increasing multimodality and its implications for mass-mediated semiosis. Along with the undeniable contribution of SFL-based approaches to the problem, the addition of proper visual methodology to shed light on the visual semantic processes is a key factor in understanding the issue to a significantly larger extent. Naturally, this runs head-on into the problems of transdisciplinary dialogue and negotiations of terminology and research focus, but this is a non-optional part of modern communication studies, thanks to burgeoning technological, economic, and social developments which make mass-mediated multimodal expression an integral part of everyday life—as already pointed out in Chapter 1 of this book. The present project is also based on the premise that SFL and visual methodologies such as political iconography and visual content analysis have a lot to learn from each other, and they do not need to change their nature and approaches in order to make valuable common contributions. Unified by their ultimate interest in explicating human communication, verbal and visual methods can and should work side by side and do their respective jobs, while it is the task of the researcher to make sense of their findings and bring them together into a unified transdisciplinary network. ICON makes a step in that direction, and the following chapter presents it in detail.

3 Investigating Political Communication Online
Analytical Levels and Procedures

ICON has five distinct layers of annotation, each of which provides insights into the features of the visual and, where applicable, the image-text relationships found in the multimodal artifact under scrutiny. Some layers stem from a single discipline, while others draw bridges across different fields in order to provide deeper insights into semantic and multimodal relations. Because of their varied disciplinary origins, some layers pertain to individual page elements (images or texts only), while others pertain to the complete webpage. The order of the layers is not strictly hierarchical despite a palpable increase of complexity and abstraction as we progress through the scheme. Still, it is more accurate to speak of interconnectedness rather than hierarchy; each layer makes a valuable contribution that supports the overarching analytical effort. The layer structure here is inspired by the work of John Bateman and colleagues (2002; 2004) on the GeM document annotation system as well as by the SFL tradition. The concept of a layered annotation effort is a good illustration of the co-dependence of different analytical approaches. It also tackles the complexity of multimodal annotation in a clear stepwise fashion. Again, communication in its most general sense is at the core, and all individual disciplines contribute to the research goal with their communicative functions and methodologies. The detailed outline of ICON's layers below also emphasizes the disciplinary origins of each layer and makes the interactions between different fields and methodologies clear.

This chapter also serves as introduction into the empirical procedure that the analyses in this book follow. The ICON layer descriptions are accompanied by illustrations from the coding scheme and discussions of procedural rules and decision guides. Before delving into these descriptions, however, it is important to introduce the material under scrutiny. The main interest of this research lies in political communication that takes place through the website medium. Since analyzing complete websites is an arduous task, the decision was made to place the focus on individual webpages that display political content multimodally. The next important question is, "How much content is enough?", or how much of each webpage should be analyzed in order to paint an accurate picture of the communication structures and functions at work there? In the literature, there are different examples of how to approach this problem. Some scholars (e.g. Fahmy, 2004; Fahmy & Kim, 2008; Griffin & Kagan, 1996; Mellese & Müller, 2012) prefer to handpick only certain portions of content—title image, headline, lead, image captions, first (few) paragraph(s), etc.—and they usually come up with sound explanations as to why some content segment is more important, fitting, or telling than others. This approach, however, goes against the book's call for inclusion; it is not broad enough to allow for a meaningful field test of the new framework.

The same goes for the recent practice of taking screenshots of webpages and analyzing everything that fits into that screenshot. This is an objective way of going about the selection of content that gets scrutinized, and it has the additional merit of taking limited attention spans into account: very often, the top of the article is what users read carefully (or at all), and especially longer articles are seldom read in full. This procedure would be appropriate for a research design with a clear audience focus, and screenshot analysis is also one recommendation that Hinduja and Patchin (2008) make when presenting their quantitative content analysis of MySpace profiles. Apart from the advantage of saving the webpage as it was in the particular sampling period, taking such limited screen views would provide good insights into what kind of information designs have the most information impact on today's impatient, quick online readers. Since, however, the goal of this project is to shed light on multimodal meaning making in online documents as they stand, the decision is to analyze complete webpages, with the notable exceptions of extra-small images (e.g. the mug shots of reporters, which sometimes appear under news headlines) and hyperlinks that are not specific to the material at hand (e.g. "About Us," "Contact," "Terms of Use"—which are standard content on any organization's website). All other visual-verbal materials have a place in the analyses. The complete webpages are saved in JPEG format using the Mozilla Firefox add-on "Abduction!", which is a free extension for the open-source browser and allows users to take partial or complete snapshots of any website and save them to their hard disks in a variety of image file formats. This feature guarantees that a high-definition, exact copy of each webpage at the time of accessing is permanently available and ready for analysis.

As the ICON layers below are conceptualized, the coding procedures and decision rules are also presented in the second half of each layer's description. The illustrations come from the software that was chosen to assist with the coding and summary of results, namely the UAM Image Tool version 2.2 (beta), which is a free annotation tool for image corpora made available by Mick O'Donnell from his personal website. The UAM tool is a good program for the purposes of this particular project because it allows for the clear, hierarchical representation of the coding layers as well as for the quick and comprehensive summary of results. Its default XML format makes the information readily exportable and transferable between different software applications, for instance for statistical and

38 *Analytical Levels and Procedures*

other analytical purposes. The program's simple interface also facilitates straightforward data entry and offers a departure from the traditional coding sheet format. The software also differentiates between categories that describe the webpage snapshot as a whole and categories that pertain to specific areas or elements of those snapshots (e.g. particular visuals and layout elements in our case). In the latter case, there are no limits to the elements to which codes can be applied, which gives the researcher the necessary freedom to select and code meaningful visual and multimodal artifacts on the page. The discussion of each layer will make it explicit whether the layer applies to the whole webpage snapshot or to individual images or areas inside it. In the latter case, all image-specific layers are applied to each such snapshot segment, according to the procedures described below.

THE FIVE LAYERS

The layer sequence of ICON is not meant to be hierarchical or to assign different degrees of semantic importance to the various document elements and communication modes it deals with. Rather, it illustrates the growing level of semiotic complexity as more elements and modes enter the communicative flow. The sequence reflects the focal points of this particular book, which is grounded in communication science and makes use of visual and multimodal analytical methods for its purposes. Therefore, the first three layers focus on the prominent visuals found on each webpage and describe them in detail in terms of content (what can be seen and how it is presented; what the presentation genre, format, and style are; what production values are evident in the visual). The third layer also investigates the ratio between visuals and text in order to determine the space and, hence, weight assigned to each communication mode. When the thorough descriptions of each prominent visual have been included, the fourth layer maps the semantic relationships between visuals, as well as the presence and kinds of attention guides, to shed more light on the semantic structures evident in the page. Finally, the fifth layer examines the visual-verbal intersemiosis and the content organization principles that each webpage displays. Each of the following subchapters presents one layer in detail and puts its contribution into the wider context of the ICON analytical tool.

MOTIF (ICONOGRAPHICAL LAYER)

The starting layer has its roots in visual communication studies. It applies the method of political iconography (e.g. Müller, 2011a; 2011b) to the visuals that play a central role in a webpage's narrative. A main visual motif

Analytical Levels and Procedures 39

and an accompanying secondary motif are identified. Every visual that is directly embedded into the multimodal narrative is characterized separately in this layer, and its meanings are taken up for further analysis. This process, inspired by linguistics, aims to map out the possible visual narratives that the multiple visuals tell through the persons, objects, and actions they depict. In another linguistic move, text-in-image is considered a plausible secondary visual motif as well, since it appears often and makes a valuable contribution to meaning formation. At this analytical level, the visual receives an amount of attention untypical for most multimodal annotation schemes, and this is a major point behind the creation of ICON: to put visuals (back) into the analytical focus and to admit their semantic contents and potentials go beyond illustrative usage.

The coding principles for the "main motif" category follow the hierarchy of actions, then persons, then objects, meaning that the main motif can be person(s) only in the absence of visible action(s), and that it can be object(s) only in the absence of person(s). The rule is in place because depicted actions contribute the most to the creation of each page's multimodal narrative. In the absence of such actions, human readers are most strongly drawn to and affected by depictions of other humans. Therefore, they receive precedence over any depicted objects, except in cases where an object covers a significant part of the view and human figures form an insignificant backdrop for it. For instance, a photograph showing US President Barack Obama shaking hands with another government official documents a political action: a handshake. Therefore, its main motif is "112-action(s)." In another example, a photograph of Barack Obama giving a press conference would be coded as "111-person(s)," regardless of the small area his head and shoulders might occupy in relation to the lectern, multiple microphones, White House insignia, and US flags around him. In the case of multiple persons present in the photograph, the most

Table 3.1 The coding options for ICON Layer 1. The main motif is always the dominant actor in the visual, performing an action. If no animate objects are found in the visual focus, the dominant object becomes the main motif. Secondary motifs are other notable persons or objects. Identifiable actions are always coded within the main motif. Text integrated into visuals is always the leading secondary motif.

1 – Motif (iconographical layer)	11 – Main motif	111 – person(s) 112 – actions(s) 113 – objects(s) 119 – n/a
	12 – Secondary motif	121 – person(s) 122 – object(s) 123 – text in image 129 – n/a

widely recognizable one in the US context is coded as the person in the main motif. Barack Obama surrounded by his bodyguards would be coded as "111-person(s)," too. Lastly, a photo of the presidential car with the driver and passengers hidden behind tinted glass would receive the code of "113-object(s)." The last code "119-n/a" applies to maps and other information visualizations which do not carry the semantic density of photographs or cartoons, as well as to unconventional images without a discernible focus or meaning, if any such should appear in the sample. This code is also applied to webpages that do not feature any visuals at all—a rare but not unseen case.

Looking at the secondary motifs, a similar hierarchy applies. The most important secondary visual motif, perhaps ironically, is text: Oftentimes verbal elements are embedded into a visual and do not merely accompany it as a caption below or on the side. These instances present important examples of visual-verbal interaction and are of great interest to the current project; therefore, the presence of text within an image automatically makes it the top secondary motif or "123-text-in-image." The next significant secondary motif is "121-person(s)"—typically the ones carrying out the action or interacting with the person coded as the image's main motif. In the absence of such persons, the "122-object(s)" involved in the action or otherwise associated to the main motif are considered. The "129-n/a" code covers the complete lack of secondary motifs or, again, examples of information visualization or purely verbal online documents. Although it is possible to have multiple secondary motifs (e.g. persons accompanying the main actor as well as text integrated into the image), a choice is made for the most prominent secondary motif according to the hierarchy above. In this way, a simple dyad of a main motif supported by a prominent secondary motif covers the foundation of visual meaning making. While actions and objects are the most powerful main motifs, verbal messages integrated into the visual are the leading secondary motif in cases of conflict, due to text's relative lack of ambiguity and, therefore, its power to direct visual meaning and interpretation. This approach is comprehensive when it comes to visual element inclusion and at the same time evades excessive information collection.

The classification of visual motifs above was applied in detail only to the visuals that appeared in the main text of the webpage or that were directly related to it in terms of content, layout, or both. This was done with the explicit purpose of covering the intended meanings embedded in the visual composition without watering them down by including the visuals from a "most read stories" sidebar, for instance. Nevertheless, while the visual analysis proper encompasses only those "visual nuclei" (see "Consociation" in this chapter), the secondary visuals ("visual satellites" such as ads, links to related stories, etc.) also find their place in the ICON annotation framework, and their meaning contribution is considered when judging the overall visual makeup of each webpage.

GENRE (MATERIAL LAYER)

Genre is a category of growing importance in media research. It often circumscribes the communicative ranges and interpretations for different media artifacts, and it is a prominent part of previous constructs for multimodal document analysis (e.g. Bateman, 2008). When we speak of "genre" here, we mean both the *material property* (e.g. photograph, caricature/drawing, information graphic), and the *type of media outlet* (e.g. tabloid news website, serious news website, and online campaign, among others). Both of these aspects play a role in how we approach the multimodal material. They also make a clear reference to target audiences as well as structural and stylistic patterns, as per Swales's (1990) definition discussed previously.

Kress and van Leeuwen (1996), among other media scholars and semioticians, empower genre as a semantic category through the notion of genre-specific semiotic affordances. This concepts describes the limited number of expression means and communicative goals that a given message format may possess. Our reading of genre as a meaning-relevant category covers both the material dimensions of the term as well as the communication context, in which multimodal artifacts appear. This lends credibility to the in-depth analyses of complex documents and also sheds light on the production and reception contexts that shape meaning making as well.

The coding options in both sub-layers are straightforward, as laid out in Table 3.2. The material property list reflects the most common types of visuals that appear in online documents. It does not pretend to be exhaustive, so there is a "miscellaneous" category for visuals that do not comply with any of the common genres, and the "n/a" category covers the option that the document does not feature any visuals at all. There are no additional options since all the material comes from one of the four publication contexts without exception.

Table 3.2 The coding options for ICON Layer 2. Both the characteristics of the visual and its publication context receive attention.

2 – Genre (material layer)	21 – Material property	211 – photograph 212 – cartoon / caricature / drawing 213 – infographic 214 – map 215 – misc 219 – n/a
	22 – Media outlet	221 – news 222 – campaign 223 – NGO 224 – social movement

COMPOSITION (PRODUCTION LAYER)

This layer scrutinizes the *visual characteristics* of the image (color scheme, camera distance and angle) and its *dimensions* (portrait, landscape, cutout, etc.). Thus, it provides continuity to the iconographical analysis, which started in the very first layer, and amends it with additional data. It also sheds light on the realizations and manifestations of genre. Color schemes are significant determinants of moods and attitudes towards the image subject (Kress & van Leeuwen, 2002). In the present analysis, they supply additional interpretative information for both the visual and the narrative functions of a webpage. The spatial relationship between the visuals and the text on the page is also considered in this layer. This is done by measuring the share of screen space each mode occupies. The webpage is then characterized as predominantly textual, predominantly visual, or evenly distributed.

In terms of coding options, the color scheme sub-layer covers all possible options and, thus, does not offer a "miscellaneous" category, forcing the coder to make a decision. It is important to note that all codes refer to the *predominant* color scheme, since it is rare that images, especially press photographs, are ideal examples of a degree of color warmth. Therefore, an image with a "warm" color scheme features colors mostly in the red gamut; a "neutral" scheme features no bright colors and emphasis on white, grey, and brown among others; and a "cold" color scheme emphasizes the blue specter and dark and/or metallic shades. There are also visuals that combine a multitude of colors from different color schemes; the "rainbow" code is for these instances. While color can bear various meanings and acts as a particularly effective framing and priming tool, it also happens that images come in gray scale—be it for artistic reasons or production constraints (e.g. archive photos or simple information visualizations). The coding scheme takes that option into account, too. The "n/a" option is reserved for online documents that do not feature visuals; otherwise, a characterization of the color scheme of the visual, regardless of its genre, is due.

The two camera-related categories only apply to photographs, since they are the only material genre that is produced via a camera. (This does not mean to completely negate the potential of drawings and maps to feature play on perspective; the current sample, however, does not include such examples.) They are also the categories that enhance our understanding of the main motif of the photograph. We now know not only *what* is being shown but also *how*. The two "n/a" categories are assigned to all other visual genres automatically. Camera distance is broken down to four categories, which include the most common camera positions in relation to its object(s). Close-up refers to a tight shot of a person's face or of an object, which takes up most of the photograph's area. A medium shot of a person features at least their shoulders and extends down to around their waist. For objects, it clearly focuses on a given object but also makes its immediate surroundings visible. A long shot of a person shows the

Analytical Levels and Procedures 43

Table 3.3 The coding options for ICON Layer 3, which cover different aspects of visual production as well as the webpage's visual or verbal emphasis.

3 – Composition (production layer)	31 – Color scheme	311 – warm 312 – neutral 313 – cold 314 – grayscale 315 – rainbow 319 – n/a
	32 – Camera distance	321 – close-up 322 – medium shot 323 – long shot 324 – panorama 329 – n/a
	33 – Camera angle	331 – high 332 – level 333 – low 339 – n/a
	34 – Visual-verbal ratio	341 – visual 342 – verbal 343 – even

person's whole body along with the immediate environment—be it other people, objects, settings, or all of the above. The same applies for visuals where objects are the main motif. Finally, panorama shots usually have a hardly discernible visual focus and instead offer a wide view of a scene, which may or may not include recognizable objects or persons. The difference between a long shot and a panorama is the minuscule presence of the main motif and the vastness of the image. For instance, a photo of US President Obama, German Chancellor Merkel, and French President Hollande standing side by side at the next G20 summit would be a long shot, while the traditional group photo of all 20 world leaders which also shows a prominent location feature as a venue marker would be classified as panorama.

Camera angle is another photographic feature. Whether the photograph's object is shown from a high, level, or low angle carries potential implications for how the object is to be perceived, as discussed previously. The meaning of a medium shot of Chancellor Merkel interacting with rally-goers on her re-election campaign trail may change dramatically depending on the camera angle. A level shot positions Merkel on an equal social plane as her voter base, which makes her more relatable; a shot from above belittles her and carries implications of weakness; a shot from below frames her visually as a leader and one above the masses, and can alienate her from the voters around her or emphasize her desire to show them the way. Ceteris paribus, the shot angle commands considerable powers to influence a photograph's message. Nevertheless, it is important to note camera angle refers to *potential* readings of power relations; it is more a tool for framing visual narratives and discourses rather than an absolute semantic agent.

The visual-verbal ratio reveals much about the narrative structure of the webpage. It is also the first coding category here that casts a global view at the webpage as a complete document. Visuals and texts have different reading logics, and the way they coexist can hint at hierarchies of meaning and intended reading paths. The "weight" of each communication mode, therefore, spells out different communicative ends and can also hold implications for the intended audiences and the nature of the messages. Webpages which feature visuals on substantially more than half their total area are coded as "visual"; webpages which rely more on text are coded as "textual"; and pages where text and visuals occupy somewhat equal space are characterized as "even." There is no "n/a" category here since all pages feature at least one of the two communication modes. As in the case of color scheme, the final classification involves a bit of fuzziness, and pages labeled "textual" or "visual" as shown above should be treated with the qualifier "mostly" unless they are extreme cases of mono-modal domination.

CONSOCIATION (COMMUNICATION LAYER)

This fourth layer considers the interaction between the different visuals and other non-textual elements across the main text of each webpage. After the thorough descriptions of each visual and the mapping of visual-verbal space distributions, we start looking for visual narratives here (nuclear consociation, nucleus-satellite consociation, and satellite-satellite consociation, depending on visuals' size and placement). In addition to standard images (photographs, information graphics, etc.), navigation elements are also considered here. They often play a central role in the steering of complex online narratives—what Lemke (2002) dubs *hypermodality*. They also act as gaze guides. While this project does not employ eye-tracking or similar methods to investigate reading paths, there is good grounding in previous research that encourages us to look at navigation in its own right and ascribe significance to it. Visually salient layout elements (arrows, bullets, hyperlinks) help check for the presence of the *signaling principle* which Holsanova, Rahm, and Holmqvist (2006) identify as an important attention guide in print newspapers. The number and kind of such layout elements is noted. Due to the hypermodal nature of online documents, however, signaling can operate within the specific page, as well as direct the reader outside the page, that is to other relevant information. Emilia Djonov (2007) also ascribes importance to hyperlink orientation in her analysis of several children's websites, and she warns that "website-external links may blur the boundaries of a website, [while] website-internal ones may obscure its structure" (p. 146). In the present analyses, the *nature* of

Analytical Levels and Procedures 45

Table 3.4 The coding options for ICON Layer 4 cover visual narratives and attention guidance.

4 – Consociation (communication layer)	41 – Visual nucleus relations	411 – nuclear consociation 412 – nuclear dissociation 419 – n/a	
	42 – Visual nucleus-satellite relations	421 – nucleus-satellite consociation 422 – nucleus-satellite dissociation 429 – n/a	
	43 – Visual satellite relations	431 – satellite consociation 432 – satellite dissociation 439 – n/a	
	44 – Signaling principle	441 – yes	4411 – visual (popups, callouts, arrows) 4412 – textual (hyperlinks, headings) 4413 – mixed
		442 – no	
	45 – Signaling orientation	451 – mostly internal 452 – mostly external 453 – mixed 459 – n/a	

the signaling (internal, external, or mixed) is logged. The goal, however, is not to help a given website hierarchy flesh out (Djonov's aim) but to uncover each webpage's hyper-nodal nature.

The first coding category refers to nuclear visual relations. This covers the semantic relationships between the major visuals present on each webpage. To be considered nuclei, the images have to be *similarly prominent* and of *comparable size and placement*. Additionally, each of these images needs to be *semantically independent;* its correct interpretation must not depend on another visual. When two or more such images coexist in the same webpage and their contents converge to a discernible visual narrative, this is a case of "411-nucleus-nucleus consociation." This signals that the visuals' apparent meanings cohere. It is crucial to still remain on the visual level in this layer and not to refer to the accompanying text for help with bridging seemingly divergent image narratives.

For instance, a news story with two main visuals, one showing an erupting volcano and another one showing refugees fleeing a burning town, would receive this code. On the other hand, a photo of the volcanic eruption followed by one of a bird would be an example of "412-nucleus-nucleus dissociation." Although it might be that the eruption is endangering the bird species' natural habitat and this is why the two photographs appear with equal prominence, the visual narrative is not clear without the accompanying textual information, and the second coding option is the appropriate one. "419-n/a" is reserved for webpages without any visuals or with only one visual nucleus.

The second visual narrative category covers the relationships between main and secondary images, that is nucleus-satellite relations. As we clarified above, nuclei are images with prominent placement in the webpage's layout and direct involvement in the main story. Satellites, on the other hand, are of smaller size and either slightly detached from the main story (e.g. illustrations in boxes of additional information or visual hyperlinks to other stories), or they appear as secondary illustrations embedded in the main text. In the case of multiple satellites, the sum total is taken into account, and the codes should be read as "*mostly* consociation" or "*mostly* dissociation" between the nuclei and each satellite. Going back to the volcanic eruption example above, the lead photograph of the cataclysm combined with a small photograph of a destroyed city landmark and a mug shot of a casualty would present such a harmonious nucleus-satellite relation. Recognizing the person in the mug shot as victim of the volcanic eruption depends on perceiving the main photograph first. Only then do the two produce a consistent visual narrative, which would be coded as a case of "consociation." In the absence of such consistency, the nucleus-satellite relationship is determined as dissociative. The "n/a" code is reserved for webpages without identifiable satellite visuals.

Finally, the last visual narrative category here checks the satellite relations as well. The same two main options and respective decision guides apply as above. The "n/a" code applies to examples of a single visual satellite or none at all. The reasons behind delving into the satellite semantic relations have to do with the fluidity of the Internet as a communication medium. It gives significant freedom of information consumption and perception. Therefore, comprehensive analyses of all meaning-bearing elements pay off, especially at the early stage of testing a new analytical tool. At the same time, the thorough visual analysis of satellites is still not a viable option due to their characteristic low-definition structures. The general meaning they convey is sufficient for the narrative research purposes of ICON's fourth layer, and for determining their contribution to the visual storytelling of each webpage.

After considering visual narratives in detail, here we also focus on the webpage layout with the help of Holsanova and colleagues' (2006; 2008) work on eye tracking. The application of the signaling principle serves the double purpose of systematizing the design annotations with the help of confirmed preexisting theories, and at the same time testing the goodness of fit of those same theories for research into online documents. The original concept is based on studies conducted with physical newspaper broadsheet spreads (e.g. Holmqvist, Holsanova, Barthelson, & Lundqvist, 2003; Holsanova, 2008, 2012). The main purpose of this annotation level is to shed light on the intended organizational and reading logics of each page. Therefore, visual-verbal relationships already come into play here.

The first stage is determining whether there is any evidence of the signaling principle at all. A "yes" leads into a sublevel that logs the nature of the signaling—is it through visual layout elements such as pop-ups, callouts, or arrows, through textual means such as subheadings, numbered lists, or hyperlinks, or through both visual and textual signaling elements? Additionally, it is worthwhile to verify the direction of that signaling (as others, e.g. Djonov, 2007, have done in previous studies)—does it guide the readers through the webpage, or does it direct them to another online document?

Wherever signaling appears, we also look at its orientation. "Internal signaling" describes navigation devices which guide attention *within* the given document—such as headings, arrows, callouts, etc. "External signaling," on the other hand, refers to prominent layout elements that direct the user to other webpages. These are usually hyperlinks, visual or textual. "Mixed signaling" refers to an even ratio between in-document navigation elements and external links. While most of the webpages in the sample are likely to show mixed signaling, the tendency towards internal or external is still an important finding that reveals how thorough the communicative effort in each particular document is. The visual or textual nature of that signaling and its placement within the page, in turn, provide additional information about the layout and intended reading paths, which may lead users through the semantic constructs or direct them to another document on the highway of hypermodality.

CONTEXT (MULTIMODAL LAYER)

This is the layer that covers visual-verbal semantic interactions. It scrutinizes the whole webpage document and qualifies the visual-text relationships within it as "consonant," "dissonant," or "disjunctive," depending on the connection between the visual motif(s) and the verbal message(s) identifiable therein. For this purpose, it relies on the accompanying caption and pays close attention to its verbalization of the visualized event. It also connects the major visual(s) to the headline and lead (if applicable). In the absence of dedicated captions, the surrounding text is taken into account. Finally, the article's complete verbal content is taken into account and its major identifiable themes are set against the visual depictions analyzed previously. Therefore, the visual and textual narratives are put side by side here, and their interplay is fleshed out. Hence, all information generated in the previous layers is integrated here, at the highest level of analytical and modal complexity. At this stage the synergetic benefits of the transdisciplinary approach become apparent, as the information generated through different methods (and, in fact, different reading logics that are characteristic for each discipline) fuses into one unified account of the semantic qualities of the communication artifact.

The visual-text narrative relationship is coded as "consonant" whenever the two communication modes work in harmony to create consistent

48 *Analytical Levels and Procedures*

Table 3.5 The coding options for ICON Layer 5 consider the visual-verbal narratives as well as the principles of spatial semantic organization in each webpage.

5 – Context (multimodal layer)	51 – Visual-textual narratives	511 – consonant 512 – dissonant 513 – disjunctive 519 – n/a
	52 – Spatial semantic relations	521 – spatial contiguity 522 – split attention 523 – misc 529 – n/a
	53 – Dual scripting	531 – yes 532 – no 539 – n/a

common meaning. Texts and visuals that send conflicting messages are characterized as "dissonant"—for instance, a photograph of people in a peaceful everyday setting accompanying an article about civil war, as in the sample of Mellese and Müller (2012). A "disjunctive" image-text relationship refers to disconnected image and text meanings, where no clearly and reliably deducible relationship between them can be formed. For example, a disjunctive multimodal narrative can be found in an article about civil war in the Sudan accompanied by a photo of an elephant, without any explicit link between the two presentations.

It is important to note that some of the findings from Layer 4, which deal with purely visual narratives, inform but do not constrain the analyses conducted at this level. Some instances of visual nuclear-satellite dissociation might be explained once the verbal elements come into the analysis, and consistent visual narratives might go in a completely different direction than the text that runs beside them. Thus, Layer 5 makes the most out of the integration of visual and verbal semantic cues, and the comparison between Layers 4 and 5 can give important clues as to how much multimodal meaning making adds to the purely visual narratives analyzed previously.

Going further into Layer 5, we log the semantic and proximal relationship of visual and verbal elements by assigning either a *spatial contiguity* or *split attention* tag to each document. The classification is based on prominent eye-tracking research (e.g. Mayer, 2005; Sweller, van Merrinboer, & Paas, 1998) and describes the spatial organization of ideas. Congruent multimodal messages reinforce each other in close proximity and create a sense of cohesion. They are also much more persuasive. Spacing them out, on the other hand, breaks the logical flow of the document's multimodal text and places a higher demand on the recipient to put the pieces together. The presence or absence of the *dual scripting principle* (Holsanova, Holmberg, & Holmqvist, 2008) is also noted in order to ascertain the level of semantic and

Analytical Levels and Procedures 49

design integration between the document's visual and verbal components. In this step, the levels of multimodal organization and design are used as a final proxy for intersemiosis in the sample of online political communication artifacts. The code reflects multimodal semantic relations across the web document as a whole.

The coding options for the spatial semantic relations come from previous eye-tracking research into newspaper spreads. The "spatial contiguity" code applies to cases where visuals and text of similar content are placed in close proximity. For example, if a photograph of citizens clashing with police appears right above the paragraph that offers details on a civil war breaking out, and a casualty's mug shot is next to the paragraph that describes the violence, there is clear evidence of "spatial contiguity" there. If, on the other hand, the images appear at various other places in the layout, away from the verbal content they illustrate or enrich, the "split attention" code applies. The "miscellaneous" option is reserved for more unorthodox layouts, which the World Wide Web supports but which are less likely to appear in most of the serious websites in the sample. Finally, "n/a" is reserved for the examples without any clear organizational principle and for mono-modal designs, which are both expected to be rare.

At the end, we check for the presence of "dual scripting" because it offers the highest level of visual-verbal integration and clear semantic organization. It refers to a near-perfect synergy between form and content and between message and layout. Therefore, it can only exist as an extension of the spatial contiguity principle, so a code other than "spatial contiguity" at the previous sublevel automatically leads to a "no" code here. Dual scripting is operationalized here as the layout integration of text and visuals in such a way that a consistent, uninterrupted line of information forms and each semantic element is in a clear and logical place within the complete document. This is different from simple spatial contiguity. It involves the purposeful creation of an uninterrupted flow of multimodal meaning, where visuals and texts repeat and reinforce each other's messages. For instance, captioned photos of refugees above the paragraph telling about the civil war would be an example of spatial contiguity but not of dual scripting, since the photos come ahead of the text and, thus, interrupt the natural flow. If these photos are embedded into the paragraph or split at appropriate intervals, which are consistent with the text flow, dual scripting is evident and a "yes" code should be assigned.

The principle would also be evident in an election platform that presents individual policies sequentially with relevant illustrations, to which the accompanying text refers explicitly. It is difficult to come up with precise cut-off points between the two levels of image-text integration, but this provides a general idea of how fine the distinction can be. It is also unnecessary to give ideal examples here, since dual scripting is a somewhat fluid construct and pinpointing it still involves a touch of intuition on top of the positive empirical data. To avoid reliability issues, there are several thresholds a document has to pass through to achieve a "yes" code here: 1) spatial contiguity as a general organizational principle; 2) multiple visual nuclei; and 3) consonant relations between the visuals (nuclei or satellites or both). Satisfying all of these conditions leaves considerably less to intuition and provides solid ground for the decision to characterize a page as employing dual scripting. Again, whenever intuition is involved, questions of reliability arise, but the relevant analyses in Chapter 8 leave little room for doubt.

A "no" code, naturally, means dual scripting is not involved, and it can only be assigned in conjunction with a "spatial contiguity" code at the previous sublevel. The "n/a" code is reserved for webpages without any visuals at all or for ones that employ "split attention" or "miscellaneous" layout principles. The investigation of dual scripting goes back to the discussion of convergence and fragmentation in previous chapters, and it adds a palpable empirical component to the more theoretical discussion of these two opposing but related phenomena. The semantic flow and sequentiality of each webpage present concrete manifestations of convergence, and the presence of dual scripting is its purest instantiation.

This concludes the discussion of the visual-verbal analyses located at ICON's highest level. Although at least two of the other layers also cross modalities and disciplines, Layer 5 truly deserves the label "multimodal" because it finalizes the task of exploring the image-text relationships and integrating the approaches utilized at earlier stages into an overarching semantic account. In this layer, some of the purely visual findings generated at earlier stages undergo review and reinterpretation, and this demonstrates the considerably greater potential of a multimodal approach to uncover connections when it comes to document semantics. The conclusions drawn here are also the results of the empirical portion of this book, and they stand as a first attempt at using this novel integrated approach, open for evaluation, critique, and improvement.

DATA, SAMPLING, AND COMPARABILITY

The data for ICON's pilot test come from a variety of sources that aim to encompass the richness of the Internet as a new medium. The choice of sources reflects the expansion of political communication as a research and professional field. The four genres of websites sampled represent political campaigning, political news, NGOs related to politics and mass media, and citizen movements. Each website genre exemplifies one or more of the media phenomena relevant to political communication's online move: convergence, hybridity, prosumption, intersemiosis, multimodality, etc. The characteristics of each strand of online political communication stem from these phenomena, and the empirical study that follows takes on the task of uncovering their semantic realizations and describing them comparatively. The sample, thus, aims at gauging major multimodal communication structures and styles of different classes of political communication. The data are collected in a one-shot sampling effort on June 21, 2012. The time window of the webpage harvesting is deliberately as tight as technological time allows (grabbing, processing, and referencing each webpage image) in order to truly deliver a one-shot comparison, both across and within the four subsamples. This timing also fits the general goal of having an unbiased sample in terms of content: no major national or international news stories broke on that day, and no major conflict was ablaze. Hence, there are no intervening factors to sway the established visual-verbal style of the sampled websites, and we can assume we are working with examples that accurately represent their multimodal message design practices.

The comparative design juxtaposes several genres of online political communication in an effort to uncover the differences between them as well as to underscore the similarities, which stem from the common positioning of these communication genres in an online media setting. At the same time, it provides useful information about the actors and stakeholders behind these communication channels. One important aspect is the level of professionalism and access to information, the technical know-how, and other vital resources for political communication to occur. Each website genre's characteristics are determined equally by its target audience and by its producers, and their access to the abovementioned resources. This theme informs the discussion of the results. Being aware of the stakeholders as well as the production values and possibilities is of central importance to conducting telling analyses of the communicative artifacts.

The data described below are innately comparable for a number of reasons. Most generally, they are all examples of political communication online. While there are increasingly less constraints as to layout, design, and other relevant message formulation parameters, there are still conventions for authoring and organizing webpages, which ensure that the sample is formally homogeneous to a reasonable extent. Furthermore, a certain congruence of topics is targeted by retaining the focus on US politics. This was achieved by selecting the "Politics" sections of the US news websites CNN and NBC, the "U.S. and Canada" section of BBC News, and the "Americas" section of Al Jazeera English. The specific stories that come under scrutiny were not sampled according to topic, though, so as to avoid a comparison of convenience. Instead, the first five stories related to US politics were selected from each of the abovementioned websites in the sampling window between 1:00 and 4:00 P.M. CET on June 21, 2012. This resulted in a total news website sample N_{news} = 20 webpages.

The sampling from the Obama and Romney campaign websites keeps the focus on politics by going to the "Issues" sections of each site and taking all major issue positions, which appear in a webpage of their own. The sampling was conducted on June 21, 2012, between 4:30 and 6:30 P.M. CET. The Obama campaign comes up with eight core policy issues which stay on a general level (e.g. the economy, foreign policy, taxes), while the Romney campaign tends to break issues down to specifics (i.e. there is no comprehensive foreign policy page, but specific pages are dedicated to relations with Russia, Iran, the EU, etc.). To ensure comparability within the campaign subsample, wherever possible the general issue pages from the Romney campaign were selected. This decision did not result in any notable data loss since all of the issue-specific policy pages on the Romney campaign website follow one and the same stripped-down format: exposing Barack Obama's failure in the specific instance (e.g. not being firm enough with Iran), and outlining Mitt Romney's plan on how to improve the situation. All of these pages are realized in the same text-dominant fashion and are not discernible from one another in terms of multimodal design and narration. Therefore, covering one of them is sufficient to ensure an informative comparison of the two political websites. This resulted in a total campaign website sample $N_{campaign} = 16$ webpages.

When it comes to NGOs, both Freedom House and Reporters Without Borders offer regional foci of their content, allowing a focus on North American media and political issues. From these sections, the five most recent items from each NGO website were sampled between 6:30 and 8:00 P.M. CET on June 21, 2012. This too keeps the policy and issue-specific focus of the sample. This sampling decision comes with the general warning, however, that Freedom House's forte lies in country reports. This is where the crux of the organization's efforts go, and its focus is not so much on providing daily updates, although a dedicated website section for this exists as well. The choice to focus on such news-type sections is a conscious one because it uncovers how NGOs that actively work in the field of political communication address issues such as media freedom, Senate bills that affect journalistic practices, and other relevant developments as opposed to expert reports, which are often intended for print publication and abide by different layout and organizational rules altogether. Thus, the final NGO sample is $N_{NGO} = 10$ webpages.

Finally, the sample of the Occupy Wall Street movement features the five most recent entries at the time of sampling: June 21, 2012, 8:00 to 9:00 P.M. CET. Since the movement is based in the US and all issues it tackles are local, there is no need for any content filtering to ensure comparability with the rest of the sample, and the five most recent stories at the time of sampling were harvested. Apart from being the primary example of prosumption, or at least of semi-professional information design online, this subsample also provides great insight into movement organization at the grassroots. The majority of the contents that come in the sample are announcements for local events, complete with poster and flyer designs, which are of great interest for the multimodal political communication researcher. This clearly more sophisticated web presence finds a good counterpart in the original "protest website" entitled "We Are the 99 Percent." It follows a typical blog structure, where users and visitors get to post their stories in pictures and words. Since the format and realization remain almost constant, a screenshot of the first page of the blog is sufficient for the analytical purposes of this project. This makes for a final sample size of $N_{citizen}$ = 6 webpages.

The total sample, therefore, adds up to N_{total} = 52 webpages. As described above, they all share a political communication background and a focus on US issues and policies. Each specific subsample presents an interesting case of political communication bound by slightly different rules, expectations, and overt and covert purposes. Therefore, both the findings about the overall sample and the comparisons between subsamples have the potential to generate relevant new information about political communication processes online, their structures and functions as well as the challenges they face. As in any example of comparative research, equivalency is a major point of interest. Van de Vijver and Leung (2011) provide a definition of equivalence as "the level of comparability of measurement outcomes" (p. 19). Given that most materials under scrutiny originated in the same country, and, arguably, all material originated in the same culture, both "construct/item equivalence [. . .] and method equivalence" (e.g. Rössler, 2012, p. 460) can be considered sufficient, also because of the high chances of "random sameness" (Wirth & Kolb, 2004, pp. 101–104). The sample does not make any claim to being representative, but the subsamples are systematic in the sense that they enjoy wide distribution and are of particular relevance to the project at hand (Rössler, 2012, p. 462). Wirth and Kolb (2012) provide an extensive discussion of cross-cultural equivalence establishment, but given the predominantly intra-national character of the sample and the scarcity of abstract concepts within the research design, it is safe to assume that the levels of equivalence are more than sufficient. The project deals with political communication that takes place in democratic environments and on the same media platform—the World Wide Web, with roughly the same affordances available to all producers. Furthermore, it is reasonable to take for granted that both the producers and consumers of the multimodal documents in the sample are familiar with the semantic conventions of the West and use the presentation capabilities of the medium as best as their resources and skills allow them. Therefore, applying the same analytical tool to each case indeed sheds light on identical constructs and concepts in action, and the measurements in each case study are highly comparable. Under these conditions, equivalence is guaranteed and the analyses may move forward, starting off with a brief overview of the four subsamples.

METHODOLOGY, CONTENT ANALYTICAL SCHEME, AND PROCEDURE

The content analytical categories are layers of ICON presented above. They stem from the theoretical and practical considerations that make up the bulk of the preceding chapters and cover a varied scope of previous research and conceptual approaches dedicated to the study of political communication, on- and off-line. The result of this discussion is the five-layer ICON construct, which combines visual and multimodal research foci in order to explore the visual-verbal narratives created by each sampled webpage. Of course, all this empirical work is done with the main topic of this book in mind, namely the structures and functions of political communication online as well as the challenges it faces. A summary of the coding frame in one uninterrupted sequence appears in Table 3.6.

The boundary between structures and functions is not as clear as one would imagine. Oftentimes structures evolve because specific functions necessitate their reshaping. This is best exemplified by the technological innovation on the Internet, which was addressed in the opening chapters of this book. The possible content realizations grew in number and kind in order to serve the function of carrying out political communication in novel settings to the highest levels of information richness and presentation functionality. Hybrid media (Kraidy, 2005) evolved according to this model of function pressing over structure. The opposite, however, can also be true: structures have the power to dominate over functions. Here it is good to remember Bateman's (2008) notion of canvas constraints, which delineate the functions and affordances of multimodal genres according to the possible content realizations they can carry out. In other words, the possible structures can determine the functional gamut.

Due to this ambivalence of the structural-functional chain of command, the categories of ICON are presented in spots along a continuum rather than in fixed camps of either "structure" or "function." For instance, a visual

Table 3.6 The coding categories embedded into ICON's five layers. The total number of content-analytical categories is 16.

1 – Motif (iconographical layer)	11 – Main motif 12 – Secondary motif
2 – Genre (material layer)	21 – Material property 22 – Media outlet
3 – Composition (production layer)	31 – Color scheme 32 – Camera distance 33 – Camera angle 34 – Visual-verbal ratio
4 – Consociation (communication layer)	41 – Visual nucleus relations 42 – Visual nucleus-satellite relations 43 – Visual satellite relations 44 – Signaling principle 45 – Signaling orientation
5 – Context (multimodal layer)	51 – Visual-textual narratives 52 – Spatial semantic relations 53 – Dual scripting

analysis that looks at the major motifs yields relevant information both for the structure of the visual message and for the function it plays in the multimodal narrative. Therefore, the placement of the categories of Layer 1 is around the middle of the imaginary continuum. The same logic governs the organization of the rest of the canvas: Each category leans towards the end it serves more or better, without denying its role in shaping the opposite end as well. Ultimately, a structural-functional "cloud" forms, which gives an impression of where ICON stands as an analytical tool in shedding light on the phenomenon of political communication online. This fluid, fuzzy representation of structural and functional analytical elements illustrates the flexibility of online communication tools and genres, but it also has consequences that reach further. As new media evolve and constantly grow their affordance base, the significance of structure and function as separate features of communication artifacts is bound to dwindle and give way to integrated ways of thinking about the building blocks of communication. These blocks can no longer be black or white, structural or functional, boxes of meaning or empty bricks; they are, rather, all of the above.

The fuzziness of the structure-function scale is the final theoretical position that needs to be considered before the commencement of the actual empirical work in this book. The evolution and placement of the content analytical categories along the structure-function continuum place the analyses in their proper context and inform the categories' manifestation and application. While ICON itself does not feature rigid hierarchies, and the layer sequence is for reasons of convenience and logic rather than importance or semantic supremacy, the structural-functional leanings of each subcategory are important road signs toward the more sound application of the annotation tool and also inform the sound interpretation of the results it yields.

Before approaching the main sample, pilot coding was conducted on a small sample of $N_{pilot} = 5$ webpages from the news website CNN collected on June 19, 2012, between 4:00 and 5:00 P.M. CET. The first five stories were selected from the "Politics" section of the US version of the website, and their full snapshots were harvested via the Abduction! Firefox add-on described previously during the discussion of the sampling. The purpose of the pilot coding was to test ICON in its then-current state and to gauge the extent to which it can accurately describe online content for the purposes of this book. The choice to test the model on different data was purposeful, with the aim of refining the annotation tool without overly biasing it against a complete, somewhat varied sample. At the time of the pilot sample's collection, the principal investigator was already familiar with the main data and with the degree of variation within the sample in particular. This provides additional justification for the limited, convenient sample for the pilot coding. The upshot of the pilot coding was instrumental for revising ICON in subtle but important ways to prepare it for the task of the main coding. The revisions that resulted from the pilot coding are described below.

Text in image: The necessity to include the text integrated into visuals as a secondary motif became apparent during the pilot coding, which featured a number of such examples in visual nuclei and satellites alike. Often the text played the most important role in narrowing down the visual's meaning, and it was also the most prominent element apart from the main actor(s) or event(s) depicted. Although the analyses in this ICON layer are visual, whenever the text appears as an integral part of the image, it receives its deserved attention.

Material property: The list of possible material properties was augmented with "maps" since several stories featured this kind of visualization either as main or secondary motif, and it was important to single it out as opposed to filing maps under "miscellaneous." "Drawings" were also added to "caricatures" to cover all kinds of artistic visualizations (as opposed to data visualizations) in a single category. Thus, the list of kinds of visuals now covers all frequently occurring types, and very few visuals fall under "miscellaneous," if any.

Visual consociation/dissociation: The original plan was to record the semantic relationships between all visuals on a webpage within a single, dichotomous category. During the pilot coding, it quickly became apparent that such a general approach does not generate useful information about the actual visual semiosis that is taking place. Therefore, the linguistic notions of nucleus and satellite came into play, and the general category was broken down to measure the semantic relationships between visual nuclei (main visuals of each webpage), between nuclei and satellites, and between satellites only. This refined coding effort provided more insight into the visual meaning making within the specific article, and also shed light on the relationship between the main visuals there and the accompanying images on the side, in the navigation, and elsewhere on the page. Since many of the satellites were not directly embedded in the article, this separation eliminated a number of false negatives (i.e. "visual dissociations"). The focus on satellite-satellite con/dissociation has the additional advantage of tapping into the hypermodal structures of each page: How similar are the external links to one another visually? How, if at all, do they relate to the main story?

Visual-text narratives: The original dichotomous "consonant vs. dissonant" had to be augmented with a third option, namely "disjunctive." This was done for the sake of accuracy, since "dissonant" holds in itself a connotation of friction, of inharmonious discord—of conflict. This was not always the case when it came to visual-text narratives that could not be classified as "consonant." A visual narrative could be detached from the textual one without giving conflicting cues to the reader; it could simply be not relatable to it. Such detachment is not a good condition for dissonance, which implies discord within a unified whole. A complete musical chord can sound dissonant; separate notes and melodies cannot, if we permit ourselves

Analytical Levels and Procedures 57

a short musical metaphor. To allow for the latter case and to avoid false dissonances, the third option of "disjunctive visual-text narratives" was added here. It applies to cases where the visuals and the text tell seemingly unrelated stories as opposed to sending conflicting or mixed messages about one and the same story. Though rare, such occurrences deserve special attention, and this revision ensures it.

After these revisions were incorporated into ICON, it was considered ready for the main empirical study in this book, which is the subject of the following chapters.

4 Political Communication Online at a Multimodal Glance
General Trends and Characteristics

The first practical application of the ICON annotation scheme centers on description. It can be used as a tool for gathering information about a multimodal data corpus and synthesizing its main features. The following chapter presents the findings based on the relatively small sample (N = 52) of webpages described previously. Given the sample size and the one-person content-analytical effort, the results are not meant to be generalizable or conclusive; rather, they demonstrate the applicability of ICON to the task of describing multimodal datasets meaningfully. When applied to a larger corpus, the analysis will greatly benefit from additional personnel who have undergone extensive training. As the sample gets extended, questions of construct validity (e.g. Yin, 2009), internal validity (e.g. Cook & Campbell, 1979), external validity (e.g. Kidder & Judd, 1986), and equivalence (e.g. van de Vijver & Leung, 2011) become even more prominent. They have already been discussed in the preceding chapter as well.

Even though we are working at the descriptive level here, ICON's results are still quite complex. For the sake of clarity, the results are initially summarized by analytical layers, first visual and then multimodal. Keep in mind that despite the positive formulation of trends, this is not a full-fledged empirical study but rather a pilot test of the novel multimodal annotation scheme. The goal is not to postulate trends but to assert the possibility of uncovering them in a large-N follow-up study. After the layer-by-layer discussion of ICON's capabilities, a more general evaluation of its application on the aggregate scale concludes the chapter.

VISUAL LAYERS

Looking at the first stage of ICON analysis, "*Motif (iconographical layer),*" we should reiterate that it deals exclusively with the visual nuclei of each webpage. It follows in a rich tradition of visual analysis using political iconography (Müller, 2011a; 2011b) and considers all "main visuals" which are embedded in the multimodal narratives. These add up to a total of 98 visuals of various genres, or an average of 1.9 visuals per webpage. The majority of depictions focus on people. The undisputable focus on depicting people confirms the basic principle that media tend to use photographs of people to illustrate news more often than any other visual motif, simply because human attention is drawn the most by other humans. "Persons" are also a viable secondary motif although they are second to "text-in-image." Therefore, the most common visualization schemes involved humans and text, closely followed by objects; actions were rarely depicted in a clear way. Only about 3% of all webpages did not feature a visual at all.

ICON's second stage of analysis, "*Genre (material layer)*," focuses on the material properties of the visualizations under scrutiny. As discussed above, each visual genre carries specific semiotic affordances, and it also has different interaction mechanisms with other communication modes. Therefore, mapping the genre structure of the sample is of primary importance for all further investigations. The supremacy of photographs and drawings/caricatures probably relates to the nature of the websites in the sample. They are mostly professionally done (only 11.5% can be considered amateur) and need to communicate their messages in a straightforward and effective way, which is best achieved via the most typical and easily digested visual genres. This need goes, perhaps, even further for the unprofessional communicators who are likely to have a limited scope of communication means and, therefore, more prone to using traditional and well established visual genres.

The "media outlet" dimension makes clear which genres were represented more or less in the sample. News and campaign webpages account for more than two-thirds of it, while NGOs and citizen websites contribute the other one-third. This has implications for the interpretation of the preliminary frequencies and results, of course. One is that the overall level of professional PR and know-how in the sample is expected to be quite high, since both political news and campaigns involve dedicated professionals in their production cycles. The same is true to a lesser extent about NGOs, while social movements rarely have the means or central organization and present a slight contrast. The sample sizes also reflect the ubiquity of information in each website genre: naturally, campaigns and news had much more material to offer; therefore, they received more attention. This should not be taken as a value judgment, of course; it rather reflects the realities of political communication online, the output of its different genres and the corresponding attention they garner.

ICON's third layer, "*Composition (production)*," looks at the technical parameters of the visuals, which were extracted from the webpage snapshots, and also considers the spatial relationship between visual and verbal elements on the whole webpage, without going into their semantic contents as of yet. The previous layers established the dominance of "normal" visualizations in terms of genres and subjects as opposed to more outlandish or untraditional visual compositions. Therefore, a good deal of additional information is readily available through the analysis of the standard visual properties that are embedded into Layer 3. It is notable that the trend toward visual normalcy continues at this level, too. The most common visual traits are

Table 4.1 Coding results from ICON's visual layers based on the whole sample.

1 – Motif (iconographical layer)	11 – Main motif	111 – person(s) = 52.04% 112 – actions(s) = 5.1% 113 – objects(s) = 39.8% 119 – n/a = 3.06%
	12 – Secondary motif	121 – person(s) = 25% 122 – object(s) = 18.75% 123 – text in image = 39.58% 129 – n/a = 16.67%
2 – Genre (material layer)	21 – Material property	211 – photograph = 61.46% 212 – cartoon / caricature / drawing = 14.58% 213 – infographic = 6.25% 214 – map = 4.17% 215 – misc = 11.46% 219 – n/a = 2.08%
	22 – Media outlet	221 – news = 38.46% 222 – campaign = 30.77% 223 – NGO = 19.23% 224 – social movement = 11.54%
3 – Composition (production layer)	31 – Color scheme	311 – warm = 19.39% 312 – neutral = 42.86% 313 – cold = 31.63% 314 – grayscale = 2.04% 315 – rainbow = 1.02% 319 – n/a = 3.06%
	32 – Camera distance	321 – close-up = 13.4% 322 – medium shot = 28.87% 323 – long shot = 18.56% 324 – panorama = 1.03% 329 – n/a = 38.14%
	33 – Camera angle	331 – high = 7.22% 332 – level = 46.39% 333 – low = 8.25% 339 – n/a = 38.14%
	34 – Visual-verbal ratio	341 – visual = 9.62% 342 – verbal = 71.15% 343 – even = 19.23%

neutral color scheme, medium shot distance, and level camera angle. Outside this area, cold color schemes are twice as common as warm ones. This might have implications both for the content of the multimodal messages (negative information or creating a stern visual presence), as well as for the intended emotional charge of the visuals. The 38.14% of "n/a" refer to the

Multimodal Trends and Characteristics 61

non-photographic cases in the sample whose production does not involve a camera and, therefore, the notions of angle and distance are not applicable indeed. Even those visuals, nevertheless, continue the trend of mostly neutral or cold color schemes, which are characteristic of the overall sample.

The visual-verbal ratio of the overall sample is overwhelmingly in the ballpark of the verbal, with only 9.62% visual dominance and 19.23% even visual-verbal distribution. This, too, can be attributed to the nature of the websites in the sample where coherent, clear messages need to come forth, and the best way to formulate such unambiguous narratives is to rely on textual formulations with visual illustration. The pursuit of message clarity also relates to the findings from the previous Layer 3 subcategories, which establish a visual normalcy in the sample: On top of spelling out the major points in writing, the websites illustrate them with standard visuals, mostly photographs or drawings, which tend to present balanced, unimpassioned depictions of persons or objects and also often feature text themselves to assist in meaning attribution. The neutral or cold color schemes imbue the visuals with additional clarity and deprive them of strong emotional charge, and the level camera angles and medium distances lend neutrality and inclusiveness to the photographic subjects.

NARRATIVE AND MULTIMODAL RELATION LAYERS

The fourth layer of ICON, "*Consociation (communication),*" goes beyond the level of individual images and checks for the visual narratives, if any, present in the webpage snapshot as a whole. By checking the meanings of both visual nuclei and satellites, it lays the foundation for the detection of more complex visual storytelling, which would then play important roles in the page's overall message. The textual dominance and visual normalcy evident from Layer 3's findings do not mean important visual messages are lacking; on the contrary, in a text-heavy environment, images garner even more attention and display their reading orientation and meaning generation qualities even better than in more nonverbal settings. The association between the predefined different classes of visuals is explored below.

The levels indicate that in more than half of the cases, there is only one major visual in a webpage, or none at all. This goes hand in hand with the observation of heightened textuality vs. visuality, which became apparent in Layer 3. Articles utilize a single main visual for illustrative purposes, or none at all, leaving the complete message formulation process to textual means alone. Wherever more visual nuclei are present, they are far more likely to form a coherent narrative than not. This, too, hints at a concerted effort towards clarity. A lack of visual coherence within a webpage immediately opens up the messages to interpretation, or at least to more skeptical reading, while a neat visual semantic chain sets the reader up for a less critical absorption of the main text. Since most of the sample—some might argue all

62 *Multimodal Trends and Characteristics*

Table 4.2 Coding results from ICON's multimodal layers based on the whole sample.

4 – Consociation (communication layer)	41 – Visual nucleus relations	411 – nuclear consociation = 32.69% 412 – nuclear dissociation = 9.62% 419 – n/a = 57.69%	
	42 – Visual nucleus-satellite relations	421 – nucleus-satellite consociation = 18.87% 422 – nucleus-satellite dissociation = 18.87% 429 – n/a = 62.26%	
	43 – Visual satellite relations	431 – satellite consociation = 12.07% 432 – satellite dissociation = 25.86% 439 – n/a = 62.07%	
	44 – Signaling principle	441 – yes = 99.07%	4411 – visual = 1.89% 4412 – textual = 77.36% 4413 – mixed = 20.75%
		442 – no = 0.93%	
	45 – Signaling orientation	451 – mostly internal = 19.23% 452 – mostly external = 65.38% 453 – mixed = 13.46% 459 – n/a = 1.92%	
5 – Context (multimodal layer)	51 – Visual-textual narratives	511 – consonant = 73.08% 512 – dissonant = 3.85% 513 – disjunctive = 11.54% 519 – n/a = 11.54%	
	52 – Spatial semantic relations	521 – spatial contiguity = 65.38% 522 – split attention = 19.23% 523 – misc = 13.46% 529 – n/a = 1.92%	
	53 – Dual scripting	531 – yes = 28.85% 532 – no = 59.62% 539 – n/a = 11.54%	

of it—includes different extents of persuasion, the lack of ambiguity regarding visual nuclei is no surprise.

Looking beyond visual nuclei alone, a lack of visual nucleus-satellite cohabitation is the leading trend here, with 62.26% of all webpages not featuring this kind of visual relationship. The remaining examples are evenly distributed between consociation and dissociation. The most important conclusion here is that visuals are clearly used sparingly within the sample, and more often than not single ones are placed center stage without further distractions. The identical levels of consociation and dissociation are a bit more puzzling and possibly hint at a lack of concern over this kind of relationship, since most visual satellites are not part of the main page's content focus and serve the purposes of hyperlinking. The examples of nucleus-satellite consociation all come from webpages where the satellites are specifically integrated into the main text, which points towards semantic coherence as a value and a goal of political communication online.

As above, the typical case with satellite relations is "none," due to the presence of either one or no visuals that fit the classification. In the other instances, dissociation is twice as common as consociation. This has to do mainly with the role that satellite visuals normally assume in the sampled webpages, namely of visual or integrated visual-verbal hyperlinks to other pages, which may be related to the topic of the main page (which brings higher chances of consociation), or which may simply be a compilation of the most read or most recent pages in the website (which is more likely to bring visual dissociation along, given the diversity of topics). It is important to keep in mind that these cases, however, were in the minority, and that more than half of the webpages did not employ multiple visual satellites and rely on text-heavy, unambiguous expression. Apart from visual narratives, Layer 4 also considers the presence and types of reading attention guides. On one hand, this relates to the previous topic of visual consociation and dissociation because images also routinely serve the purpose of attracting attention and are the first point of contact between the reader and the document. On the other, it serves as a smooth transition into the multimodal analytical realm because it considers layout elements that stand out visually in one way or another without necessarily *being* visuals proper.

As was expected due to the sample's online focus, less than 1% of the webpages do not utilize any kind of attention guide or hypermodal element. In absolute numbers, this means one webpage. All others in the sample feature attention and reading guides of various kinds. The most common types are textual, either hyperlinks to other online documents or headings and passages in bold or italics, which help organize the text and emphasize important content within it. Visual-verbal attention guides are a far second, with almost four times less occurrence, and they mostly take the form of hyperlinks to other documents on the side of the main material. Purely visual attention guides are the least common attention guide, with two occurrences in the whole sample in absolute numbers. The lack of visual attention guides can be attributed to their higher ambiguity when compared to textual or mixed-mode guides. Unless they serve the blunt purpose of pointing the reader to a certain block of content via arrows or circles, visual guides cannot create a clear meaning in the little space they occupy in the global layout of the webpage. A minuscule photograph as the sole link to another article, for example, would make little or no impact on the reader, especially on the increasingly smaller screens, which serve the modern media consumer's needs. Therefore, multimodal or purely textual attention guides remain the norm here.

After checking for the presence and nature of signaling, the orientation of that signaling is also telling about the semantic structures and intended meanings which different webpages display. The numbers here reveal high levels of hypermodality, with more than 65% of the signaling directing the reader to other online documents. This has implications for the sampled webpages' nature and standing in the cyber-world. To coin a new term, it reveals their hyper-nodality and their connections to other pages, or "nodes," near and far. This finding also harmonizes with the prevalence of textual hyperlinks, which were and still are the primary way of connecting the nodes of the World Wide Web. Despite developments in design, layout, and server storage, the traditional, "low-tech" option of embedding text links into online documents remains the norm within the sample.

The cases of mostly internal signaling, less than 20% of the sampled webpages, refer to reading attention guides embedded into the layout. About 13.5% of the webpages employ mixed signaling—both reading attention guides and hyperlinks to other pages. The textual focus in all of these instances harmonizes with the observation of layout simplicity, coherence, and clarity from ICON's previous analytical layers. Textual hyperlinks are arguably the least invasive manifestation of hypermodality: they do not offer flashy visuals which might deter reading attention from the document at hand; they merely signal that additional information is readily available if and when it is needed. Because of this reliance on least invasive and ambiguous external signaling, the semantic coherence of the document under scrutiny is not jeopardized by possible alternative interpretations, and the proper sequential consumption of the text is often assisted by embedded layout help. Therefore, the conclusions from Layer 4 point towards visual clarity and pleasantly unified multimodal texts. Whether this is indeed true depends on the findings from the last annotation level, which follow below.

"*Context (multimodal layer)*" is the fifth and final level of analysis, which integrates visuals and text into complete multimodal narratives. It checks for the consonance of the visual and verbal narratives and can explain the possible visual dissociations registered at earlier levels of analysis. Given the current sample, however, it is more prone to explaining the roles of individual images in the complete page's meaning structure, since the majority of examples were not too visual. In such environments, taking text into account becomes even more important for the proper understanding of visuals and of communication in general.

It is clear that consonance dominates the sample with a little more than 73% occurrence. This means that visuals and texts presented a harmonious message and, in the most typical case, the visuals illustrated the textual information or expanded it meaningfully. Dissonance occurred most infrequently—only in two cases altogether. Within the current sample, a page was three times more likely to display disjunctive image-text relations or not to feature any visuals at all than to show dissonant visual-verbal semiosis. This clear effort towards consonant image-text relationships is also a continuation of the trend towards clear information design that is easy to assimilate with little deviation or doubt. In light of these data, the dissonant examples become even more intriguing and deserve special mention here.

Multimodal Trends and Characteristics 65

Both cases of dissonant multimodal narratives come from Al Jazeera's English website and, as clarified in the sampling section, discuss political news from the United States. Fragments of their visual nuclei and surrounding text can be found in Figure 4.1. The example on the left relates the story of a group of Catholic nuns who are protesting budget cuts by the US government, which they believe are harming low-income families. The video still that serves as the page's static illustration, however, features an embrace: an action quite the opposite of protest. Furthermore, none of the depicted persons has the typical visual characteristics of a Catholic nun, such as black-and-white attire or Christian insignia. The incongruence between the verbal message of nuns protesting and the visual content, which shows secular persons hugging, leads to the qualification of this image-text semiosis as "dissonant." The other example talks about a decision by US President Barack Obama not to deport Latino youth who entered the country illegally but who stayed in or finished school there and who are not convicted felons. The new policy has the auspicious title DREAM ("Development, Relief, and Education for Alien Minors"), and the positive message of the article comes in sharp contrast with the visual illustration of a Hispanic man, visibly older than the age group considered in the text of the article, being arrested by a US Marshall, as two more officers look on, while a Hispanic lady is sitting

Figure 4.1 Fragments of the two Al Jazeera webpages that feature the only cases of dissonant image-text relations in the sample

(*sources:* "Catholic nuns protest . . ." <www.aljazeera.com/video/americas/2012/06/2012 620142917511451.html>; "US police to halt deportations . . ." <www.aljazeera.com/ news/americas/2012/06/20126151454465521318.html>).

down on the ground and observes the scene while resting her chin on her hand. The verbal message of hope and acceptance clashes with the visual message of government crackdown and possible deportation. The position and gesture of the woman in the background imbue the image with additional feelings of sadness and helplessness at the hands of the law.

Both of these cases provide interesting examples of multimodal dissonance. While there is no doubt about their semantic relationship's classification, there is additional room for interpretation regarding the purpose of this dissonance. The embrace in the first example, though ill fitting with the protest theme of the text, invokes the peace and love associated with Christianity and its clerics. The arrest of the Hispanic man is oriented towards the past or the present, when the DREAM act is still not enacted and illegal immigrants are in constant danger of apprehension and deportation. Hence, both visual cues are closely related to the textual content and cannot be classified as "disjunctive" with it. They are also not "consonant" because their messages are too divergent, and the road to multimodal coherence is too long and filled with variables. It is important to note here that both visuals are the opening frames of video sequences embedded into the articles. A complete analysis of such videos was not possible due to the additional effort and expertise involved in analyzing moving images with their corresponding visual, audio, verbal, and editing features. From its inception, ICON was meant to analyze still images and multimodal documents. Therefore, the visual element of a video still acts as a visual nucleus and is treated as such in all of its occurrences. This is a detail that receives attention in the end discussion as well.

After delving a little deeper into the image-text relationships and discovering the stable trend towards multimodal consonance, Layer 5 also involves a more thorough analysis of the webpage layout's semantic organization based on previous research of newspaper spreads. The two main options were "spatial contiguity" and "split attention" designs, which involve the placing of mutually relevant information close or far apart, respectively.

More than 65% of the webpages rely on spatial contiguity, which is the most logical and convenient principle for content organization due to its ease of perception. This design model also makes multimodal consonance more achievable since proximity of similarly themed content elements reinforces their relationship to each other. Nevertheless, when comparing the consonance/dissonance and spatial contiguity percentages, it becomes evident that some examples of visual-verbal consonance must have employed another information design principle, too. The examples of this "consonant split attention" are discussed later on. For the time being, it suffices to note that physical (or here, virtual) proximity is not the sole determinant of multimodal agreement, and the evolution of layout structures and strictly virtual content organization paths will likely make physical proximity a measure too crude to be precise and useful in multimodal analysis. Nevertheless, it still retains its significance nowadays, and examples like the one below are merely the harbingers of future trends towards "unfettered" consonant multimodality.

Multimodal Trends and Characteristics 67

In Figure 4.2, we see a CNN article about the financial side of the US presidential race. In it, an Obama campaign official shares the concern that the Republican campaign will raise more money for the month of June 2012. The element of split attention comes into play because the first few paragraphs are dedicated to campaign fundraising, but the image of President Obama seemingly scolding someone from his lectern on the White Houser lawn becomes relevant when the article's second point comes along: The Romney campaign has relied on dubious funds from an organization not authorized to support political candidates according to the US presidential race's numerous intricate regulations. The visual nucleus and its satellites, therefore, congeal in their focus on the presidential campaigns of the two major candidates; Barack Obama's solemn expression and raised finger point towards an unpleasant topic for him. The fundraising issue is presented textually by a campaign official, not by Obama himself, which brings certain dissonance into the image-text relationship. However, this dissonance

Figure 4.2 A fragment of a webpage with split-attention design that still maintains a consonant image-text relationship from CNN's US edition

(*source*: <http://politicalticker.blogs.cnn.com/2012/06/20/massive-money-being-raised-by-republican-side-worries-top-obama-campaign-officials-2/>).

is righted when the additional topic of illegitimate funding comes along, as President Obama speaks against it, both in his role of political opponent as well as acting president and embodiment of the state and the rule of law. The distance between these themes in the article's arrangement and design make it a classic example of split attention; the content, however, is decidedly consonant, and this proves the dominance of substance over structure, at least in this sample of political communication webpages.

After determining the dominance of spatial contiguity designs in the sample and considering a counterexample, the study goes one step further and checks for the presence of an even more sophisticated content organization mode: the dual scripting principle, which offers both verbal and visual cues for reading attention, places mutually relevant content in close proximity, and organizes the document's overall message exclusively according to these guidelines. Pages that employed split-attention or miscellaneous content organization principles were automatically coded with "no" on dual scripting.

The overall sample displays relatively low percentages of dual scripting—28.85% versus almost 60% of less sophisticated content organization. This is easily attributable to the high "cost" which this principle's application involves: visuals and texts need to overlap semantically to great extents, verbal phrasing must double visual expression, mutually relevant content elements need to be arranged in close proximity, etc. This involves much more effort on the part of the message producer. Additionally, the spatial contiguity design offers sufficient levels of clarity for most general communicative purposes, and dual scripting is more of a specialized version of it. Within the sample, it is mostly applied to episodes of more complex message relay, which require intricate facets of a bigger problem to be explained and understood on their own first and then in mutual relation, like in the example of President Obama's record of fighting for equal rights, which is discussed in detail further on.

Finally, it is also important to note that the occurrence of dual scripting in the overall sample might seem low, but within the subsample of pages that display spatial contiguity it hovers around 44%. Therefore, almost half of the webpages that employed spatial contiguity moved to the next level of semantic content organization. This is one trend which communication research should definitely take into account in the future as well.

It is only logical to assume that, with the evolution of communication technologies and layout options in particular, the application of dual scripting will become more easily attainable, and the production costs for it will also fall. Another factor that speaks in favor of this information organization principle is already evident nowadays: attention spans are decreasing, and persuasion has to happen more quickly than ever before. A clear organization which allows maximum information effect at high reading speeds and skimming through is very likely to become the norm in political communication, just like it happened in commercial advertising earlier. The long, cleverly written advertorials and pamphlets that made names like C. C. Smith and David Ogilvy advertising legends in the first half of the 20th century are now a thing of the past. They displayed a gradual reduction in length and complexity and finally reached the stripped-down, slogan-only form they commonly take on nowadays. A similar fate likely lies ahead of the elaborate campaign platforms and statements that are now abundant on- and off-line. Initially complex messages will be broken down more and more often in order to make the chunks more palatable, and after a while the messages themselves are likely to become simpler as well. The rise to prominence of dual scripting in the coming years can reliably signify a move in this direction and, therefore, should be on communication scientists' radar from early on.

An early example of the possible trend towards message fragmentation and simplification comes from the Obama campaign, which is a constant source of new know-how since its historic success in the 2007–2008 battle for the US presidency. The webpage above presents Barack Obama's record on protecting and enforcing equal rights. It is an excellent example of dual scripting because it employs numerous layout tools and content organization principles in order to create a complex, coherent narrative. The opening paragraphs feature many sentence fragments in bold, which emphasize the key message of the webpage, and the accompanying photograph shows Barack Obama as he signs the revocation of "Don't Ask, Don't Tell" into law as an illustration of his dedication to granting equal rights to a prominent group—homosexuals—who used to be discriminated against in the US army. Another aspect of the dual scripting principle is the clear semantic overlap across semiotic modes: The image of Barack Obama signing a bill is accompanied by phrases in bold such as, "President Obama repealed 'Don't Ask, Don't Tell'" and "The President signed the Lilly Ledbetter Fair Pay Restoration Act," which create a reference feedback loop to the visual in that content box. The rest of the page's content is organized in similar clearly delineated boxes, each of which adds a discrete fragment of visual and verbal information to the complete webpage's message: Barack Obama's policies enforce equal rights, and he has a proven track record of working towards this high goal. Like in the example above, there are recurrent direct textual references to the visual illustrations, which guide attention and create semantic cohesion across the semiotic modes. Therefore, the dual scripting design that the page employs lends the message additional credence with its clear and logical organization. This is indeed the essence of the dual scripting principle.

Another important goal of the application of Holsanova and colleagues' (e.g. 2006, 2008) findings to online information sources was to test their usefulness in a new context. The results are more than hopeful, with 84.51% of the whole sample fitting into either one of the two major classifications, and a fair amount of pages also displaying the highest multimodal cohesion levels the authors identify. The remaining cases of "miscellaneous"

Figure 4.3 A policy page from Barack Obama's campaign website as an example of dual scripting design

(*source:* <www.barackobama.com/record/equal-rights?source=primary-nav>).

classification do not display traits of either model clearly and, therefore, will require the development of another possible layout classification. This, however, is beyond the goals and capabilities of the current dissertation and will have to involve the use of eye-tracking technology to ensure comparability with the previous two models. Expanding the array of semantic layout models is, therefore, one viable direction for further research and will be addressed later on in this dissertation as well. For the time being, it is sufficient to note that the pre-existing theory is strong enough to describe online layouts reliably and to shed light on constructs and meanings from political communication in this mediatization context.

STRUCTURES, FUNCTIONS, AND CHALLENGES: A GENERAL OVERVIEW

Now that the overall frequencies have been presented and some examples already discussed, a preliminary discussion of structures, functions, and challenges pertaining to political communication online is in order. Specific analyses of the respective subsamples follow in the upcoming chapters; however, they can only benefit from a general overview of emerging trends after the initial frequency counts. The general findings summarized here can then be set against the specific subsamples' idiosyncrasies, and more informed conclusions about aspects of political communication online can emerge at the very end.

The leading trend that recurs throughout all five ICON layers is that of clarity and coherence. More than half the webpages in the sample display visual austerity and multimodal consonance. Conflicting messages within and across semiotic modes are a rarity that deserves special attention and interpretation. The structures that support this message relay can be best characterized as standard, ordinary, or nondescript. In the typical case, the visuals are produced without multiple layers of meaning, in neutral colors, from level angles; visualization is sparse and to the point; the accompanying text is related to the visuals and often even retells their stories. Text dominates imagery, which is another check against ambiguity. Hence, the dominant structures are multimodal, with a clear emphasis on text, and the narratives are organized according to the verbal rather than the visual flow of information and meaning. All webpages except one employ attention guides, where text dominates again. These guides extend the meaning structure by emphasizing and organizing the concrete page's content, and by providing meaningful hyperlinks to other relevant documents.

When it comes to functions, the major function evident in the current sample is to inform. The emphasis on clear formulations and consonant multimodal narratives speaks of a focused effort towards coherence and transparency. The visual analyses reveal mostly unimpassioned, illustrative imagery that is characteristic of professional news media, as they tend to strive for objectivity. Given that such media provide less than half of the overall sample, this finding is surprising, at least at face value. Campaigns and NGOs usually aim to persuade and do not refrain from using irrational, emotional appeals, which is best done with ample visualization. Contrary to this established practice, the overall sample features close to no such affective imagery. The main function which visuals take on is to illustrate and reinforce the verbal information, and less often to fulfill the World Wide Web's hypermodality standards by serving as attention-grabbing hyperlink illustrations. It is quite intriguing to check whether this visual "subjugation" appears across the subsamples consistently.

The goal to inform finds expression in the content organization as well. As discussed previously, the arrangement of multimodal texts (verbal and visual) also conforms to the trend of clearly presented information. A large portion of the overall sample obeys the content organization principle of spatial contiguity and, as an extension of it, dual scripting, which pairs visuals and texts in cohesive, self-referential semantic units. This shift towards clearer content organization and "serving" complex messages in neat visual-verbal portions is a projected future trend in political communication in general. Together with the scarcity of emotional appeals, it may signify a move towards reasoned argumentation rather than emotionality and manipulation, which have allegedly been plaguing the political process ever since campaigning was invented in the nineteenth century. In light of this hopeful opportunity, it is especially relevant to go into the specific subsamples and to identify the genres that display the highest and lowest levels of dual scripting. Such knowledge will shed additional light on the phenomenon of information-centered political communication we are witnessing in this sample. A positive conclusion about a uniform shift in this direction will be another confirmation of the importance of this development for both the structures and functions, which characterize political communication online in its many forms. It is important to keep in mind, however, that the functions discussed here are the deducible intended functions, which the website makers and owners put into place.

As far as challenges are concerned, there is little that can be said at this general point in the analyses. The reliance on neutrality and rationality can be applauded, but it might prove to be an issue for the persuasive genres, such as campaign and citizen websites, whose very reasons for existence are to draw attention to their messages and to convert the highest number of people possible from onlookers to active supporters. There are campaign strategies based on reason and argument, of course, (e.g. Brader, 2005; Müller, 1997), but they are rarely the sole approach in use. Modern campaigning and battling for hearts and minds, whether for political, social, or commercial reasons, tends to grow *more* impassioned and targets feelings more often than reason, not less. In that sense, the trend that can be observed across the sample here is unexpected, since reliance on argument rather than emotional connection comes with the risk of not reaching or converting audiences who have firm rational beliefs in the direction opposite to the sponsor's message. Emotional campaigning is particularly effective on this audience segment (e.g. Brader, 2006). Whether this issue is indeed looming over the persuasive genres in question or not will become clearer in the following chapter, which gives an in-depth look into each separate subsample with the same analytical foci, namely structures, functions, and challenges of political communication online as identifiable via the ICON analytical tool.

ICON's CONTRIBUTIONS TO INNOVATIVE AND THOROUGH MULTIMODAL CORPUS ANALYSIS

The analytical model presented in this book has the comfort of relying on a number of different fields and research traditions. It clearly relies on previous knowledge and expertise generated therein and often goes beyond these fields' various limitations and idiosyncrasies. This section reviews some of the influences in ICON's development and some specific improvements it presents.

The results presented here compare most readily to previous research from visual communications studies. By default, visual research in political science remains sparse even though we may well speak of a recent visual turn in the field. A deficiency in visual political communication research was already identified years ago by Griffin and Kagan (1996). A major reason visuals should not be neglected is their uncanny ability to transcend the usual limitations of verbal communication. Doris Graber conducted numerous studies attesting to the ability of photographs to "make information transmission more realistic, accurate, and touching than is possible in purely verbal messages" (Moriarty & Popovich, 1991, p. 372). This comes in sharp contrast to the prevailing Western practice of achieving proficiency in reading and producing verbal rather than visual communication artifacts. Therefore, despite the ubiquity of visuals, there is a scarcity of research done on their meaning-making potential and actual effects. Furthermore, as Blackwood (1983) asserts, "in some cases the photos are the only representation of an event. Visuals are important as conveyers of information and shapers of attitudes" (p. 712). Adds Harding (2003): "In order to construct an image of some place, person or thing of which we have no direct experience, we rely heavily on visualization presented by others and made available to us" (p. 69). It is, therefore, of considerable importance to document and better understand the ubiquitous use of political communication visualizations and their relationships to other modes of communication.

This, however, should never be done at the expense of the other concurrent communication modes running through the document under scrutiny. Doing so would merely repeat the same mistake—giving primacy to one communication mode and belittling all others—just from a different starting point. Luckily, the current level of technological development rarely allows for the instances Blackwood refers to above: visuals are very rarely displayed alone, and they are in a complex interplay with their context (e.g. Müller, 2007), which needs to be taken into account when conducting any sort of analysis that pretends to be exhaustive and revealing. ICON demonstrates one such reliable and reproducible approach by keeping visual analyses pertinent and down to objective, easily measurable variables. It then considers the contextual embedding and tracks the image-text relationships in order to map out the final message.

One cannot talk about meanings without considering the media's central role in shaping reality. Digging deeper into the definitions and varieties of media content reveals a complex interplay between political reality and how it appears in and across media. Boczkowski and de Santos (2007) address the issue of content homogenization across news media (which was already covered in our discussion on convergence). Wolfsfeld and Sheafer (2006) and Bennett and Livingston (2003) get into the reality-construction function of news media, already identified by Kaid et al. (1991), in the specific context of an Israeli social issue. Ryfe (2006), Benson (2006), Lawrence (2006), and Entman (2006) put news production in the theoretical framework of new institutionalism to explain the contemporary convergence of Western news media. Callaghan and Schnell (2001) look into how news media frame the elite policy discourse and how they reinforce or moderate social distinctions. Liebes (2000) also considers framing as part of each news item's agenda-setting function. This strand of research, therefore, deals with the way political communication shapes both the political and the social realities and how it interacts with its audience as a society. The social and society-bound aspects of communication are also an important branch of linguistics, another discipline of central importance to this book. While for many branches of linguistics the social order plays out in language and its rules and conventions, political communication is often granted the powers to shape and reshape society and social order through framing and agenda setting. These are two complementary views on communication as both an agent and an object of social order; indeed, one cannot have one without the other, and this is an important interdisciplinary insight.

Framing as a concept and analytical approach deserves a little extra attention in this overview. On the most general level, framing has to do with media's primary social function of informing the audience, defining salient issues in specific ways, and ultimately inspiring and directing social actions (e.g. de Vries, 2008). This entails a news selection process, which is based on events' so-called "newsworthiness"—a concept already tackled by Galtung and Ruge (1965) in their seminal study on foreign news. Once an event has been deemed newsworthy, specific features are made salient in a process of organizing "life experiences to make sense of them" (Goffman, 1974, p. 21); in other words, to direct audiences in their decoding and interpreting of news. This is what constitutes framing in the most general sense. Robert Entman provides the definition that by now has become classical:

> To frame is to select some aspects of a perceived reality and make them more salient in a communicating text, in such a way as to promote a particular problem definition, causal interpretation, moral evaluation, and/or treatment recommendation for the item described. (Entman, 1993, p. 52)

So defined, framing rests on two key concepts, namely selection and salience, and studying them implies casting a gaze both at production processes (e.g. journalistic routines), as well as reception (e.g. audience studies) (Mellese & Müller, 2012). Although the above definition focuses on text, framing is applied with equal force to visuals, too. Messaris and Abraham conceptualize visual framing as:

> [C]hoosing one view instead of another when viewing a photograph, cropping and editing the resulting image in one way or another, and/or just to show one image out of many images that may have been produced at the same time and place. (Messaris & Abraham, 2003, p. 218)

In other words, selection and salience remain the defining features of visual framing as well. While framing is a favored research angle, and visual framing analyses remain scarce, this book chooses a different course. Nevertheless, its focus on multimodal narratives and the interplay between different communication modes is in the spirit of framing analysis, given the influence text and visuals exert on each other.

Since ICON's goal is to talk about meanings in the multimodal context, it automatically enters the field of semiotics, too, and social semiotics in particular. It is the branch that investigates sign usage in social contexts, which come with specific meaning-making implications and affordances (e.g. Kress, 2010). Semiotics as we know it today is greatly influenced by two 19th-century scholars: American philosopher Charles Peirce and Swiss linguist Ferdinand de Saussure, whom Kress (2010) singles out as the formative figures in the field. Peirce defines a sign in the following way:

> A sign, or *representamen,* is something which stands to somebody for something in some respect or capacity. It addresses somebody, that is, creates in the mind of that person an equivalent sign, or perhaps a more developed sign. That sign which it creates I call the *interpretant* of the first sign. The sign stands for something, its *object*. (Peirce, 1931–58, §2.228)

This complex process of perpetual sign creation which happens instantaneously upon perception is what Jensen (2010) calls a "three-way interface for maintaining our contact with reality" (p. 29). Peirce's is a semiotic framework that clearly puts the interpreter (and hence, the individual) in a position of unprecedented power. As new interpretants are born, they in turn become the objects of new signs, and the cycle goes on for as long as human communication exists in any shape or form. This model of semiosis bears remarkable similarity to the prosumption model of mediatization that is valid nowadays, where once again individual actions prompt revisions and reinterpretations of reality by reshaping and augmenting media content through the active prosumer's prism.

In contrast to this fluid three-way model, Ferdinand de Saussure (e.g. 1959 [1916]) presents a rigid two-part system of a *signified* and its *signifier*. An individual's actions do not have the capacity to modify this relationship (e.g. Hodge & Kress, 1988), which is characterized by arbitrariness and determined by stiff convention. Kress (2010) notes that "*arbitrariness* [is] an indication of a social power that is sufficiently strong to tie any form to any meaning," while *convention* presents itself over time and acts "as a social force which acts to keep signs *stable*" (p. 63). Perception and interpretation are, therefore, not a source of empowerment and individualism. Rather, they testify to the centrality of social power in meaning making and, ultimately, in communication. Furthermore, it follows that successful communication and meaning attribution depend on *shared* conventions, that is on mutual subscription and obedience to the same set of socially enforced semantic rules and regulations. ICON shares both of the models' focus on meaning creation as a process closely related to shared social conventions, and it is also a useful tool for uncovering such principles as they evolve online. Its descriptive application in the previous sections of this chapter shares in the spirit of "meaning as use" and presents a hands-on application of a fluid annotation scheme that matches the World Wide Web's constantly evolving means of expression.

This review of previous theories and methods once again confirms the need for an integrative approach such as the one ICON presents. The findings based on the general sample bolster the argument for thorough multimodal annotation analysis: the level of detail they offer when it comes to both visual and multimodal narratives is higher than any other single method could deliver. The incorporation of social semiotics in the mix raises an important point that the present analysis does not take up, namely the role of the interpreter in the meaning-creation process. This also points to one of the major challenges in front of political communication research today, especially in its novel online incarnation: the lack of reception studies. Any follow-up study along the lines of ICON's application here must incorporate an audience study in its design.

Before we go into the audience side, however, it is paramount to at least map out the subgenres of political communication online. Knowing how each of them makes use of the rich semiotic affordances of the World Wide Web is a prerequisite for effective semantic and reception analysis. The following two chapters consider the use of multimodal meaning-making resources across the four subgenres that are at the core of this book's empirical portion. Although the general portrait of political communication on the Web appears quite uniform and bland, going into genre specifics promises to reveal a different picture.

5 News and Campaigns
Findings From Two Traditional Genres of Political Communication

The discussion of the general results uncovers a few intriguing trends and overall characteristics of the political communication sample under scrutiny here. When staying on the general level, these conclusions add up to a somewhat unorthodox communicative model, given the makeup of the sample, and it is tempting to ring the bell of novel approaches and practical breakthroughs. However, before going into debates that dig deeper and go further into analyzing the findings' implications for the field and practice of political communication online, it is paramount to discuss the extent and relevance for each subsample. The overall sample's makeup includes four major genres of political communication. Although they share this common label, each of the genres has specific characteristics, tried and tested features that set each apart from the others. Therefore, a cumulative analysis and discussion of the results are useful for the purposes of circumscribing the field; yet bolder conclusions about the structures that support each genre of political communication and the functions that each genre assumes in serving its audiences have to be informed by subsample-specific analyses. This is the purpose of the two specific-results chapters of this book, which consider each subsample in its completeness and discuss the subsamples' features as the ICON framework describes them. For convenience and clarity, the particular analyses are grouped in traditional political communication (this chapter) and social political communication sections (Chapter 6).

Before delving into the subsamples, it is important to reemphasize the exploratory nature of the current project. The conclusions drawn here are not meant to be representative. Rather, they uncover trends that need to be verified through a more comprehensive follow-up project, involving sample sizes suitable for robust quantitative statistical analysis. The contribution ICON makes to this endeavor is to provide the methodological toolbox for a thorough analysis of multimodal page-based documents, with the possibility of making the analyses semi-automatic as discussed previously. Based on the trends emerging from these initial explorations, each of the following sections offers a typical genre framework, against which future research endeavors can be compared and which is bound to evolve as new information becomes available.

NEWS WEBSITES

When it comes down to studying political communication, there is a long research tradition dedicated to political news, which also figures prominently in the preceding literature reviews. This thesis makes no exception and acknowledges the primary importance of news media in the political communication process, namely the relay of political information from political actors to citizens and, more recently due to the relevant developments in the World Wide Web, vice versa. The choice of media aims at an international sample of prominent news sources. From the US, the websites of CNN and MSNBC are covered. Both media figure prominently in numerous studies of news, whether they were chosen for semantic analysis (e.g. Aday, 2010; Tian & Stewart, 2005) or for automatic content-analytical software testing (e.g. Nakamura & Kenada, 1997; Qi, Gu, Jiang, Chen, & Zhang, 2000). On both websites, the "Politics" sections are taken into account so as to keep the semantic focus on US domestic political matters. The US webpages' layouts and multimodal structures are compared with BBC News, which is another common comparative choice, and with Al Jazeera International. To ensure the topical comparability, the "Americas" sections of both extra-US news outlets are considered, and only stories pertaining to US politics appear in the final sample.

The political news websites are the largest subsample in this empirical study. They also represent the most widespread genre of political communication: offering 24/7 updates and staffed by a host of professional reporters and technical personnel, modern news websites have the highest incentive to be at the helm of all information flows and design innovations. This has implications for the expectations and the actual findings of the ICON analyses conducted here. On the one hand, in terms of design and technical know-how, all websites under scrutiny are likely to display considerable similarities since they all strive towards the same standard of effective and up-to-date online communication. This trend will likely be reinforced by the similarity of content as well, since the new sample focuses on US news or news about that region in the case of BBC and Al Jazeera. This gives good grounds for speculations about the influence of content over communication structures and designs: Will the reporting on similar events overlap multimodally across the different websites? If yes, what implications does this have for the field of multimodal political communication research?

On the other hand, mass media serve the interests of their stakeholders, in practice and most often also by design. Semblances of objectivity and visions of purely factual reporting are part of almost every mass medium's public image, but any mass communication system is fraught with political and economic interdependencies (e.g. Hallin & Mancini, 2004) which exert influences on news content selection and presentation. Keeping this in mind enriches the above multimodal analysis and helps explain the similarities and differences that occur in reporting similar or identical events across different news media. This view also helps imbue the overall structures with additional meaning and enhances the interpretive powers of ICON beyond describing structures and functions. It empowers it to uncover the implications of these for message framing and transfer.

Going through the five ICON layers, visuals appeared in a stunning 96.7% of all news webpages. The main visual motifs present in online news stories are people, taking up 63.33% of the sample, followed by objects with 23.33%. Actions are rarely in the visual focus. The accompanying motifs are much more diverse, with other persons and objects taking 30% each. Another 30% of the visuals in the sample do not have a discernible secondary visual motif and place the focus solely on one depiction. Text in image occupies the remaining 10% of the sample as a notable accompaniment to the main visual focus. These data speak of a pronounced visual focus on depictions of humans. In most cases, the depiction is one well-known individual with political functions who is also the main protagonist of the article under scrutiny. The accompanying objects are most often either microphones and lecterns (typical attributes at a press conference) or artifacts with symbolic meaning (e.g. a national flag or a pen for signing bills into law). Whenever the secondary motif involves other people, they are not notables and usually play the role of living backdrop to the main character. In 30% of the cases, there is no secondary motif whatsoever, and the visual focus falls completely on the main depiction. Only 3.33% of the news webpages do not feature any visuals. Photographs account for 86.67% of the sample, which is consistent with the notion of news as representations of (political) reality (e.g. Kaid & Postelnicu, 2005) and, therefore, striving to supply as accurate and lifelike visualizations as possible. The remaining 10% of the visuals are maps of regions relevant to the article's story.

Describing the news visuals' parameters and attributes leaves a sense of normalcy and impartiality, at least for the most part. Half of all visuals utilize a neutral color scheme, and 20% go for the warm and the cold gamut each. Gray scale and rainbow color settings are rare, each showing up only once. The predominant camera distance is medium (41.38%) with close-ups (24.14%) and long shots (17.24%) not too far apart. The level camera angle is by far the most common (68.97%). Heroic depictions from a low angle appear in 13.79% of cases, while the deprecating high angle accounts for 3.45% of the sample only, equivalent to a single instance. The information extracted from the news sample so far confirms the relevance of doing visual research on political news since all but one of the sampled pages utilized at least one lead visual, most likely to be a photograph. The nature of these photographs lends some credence to news media's claim to unimpassioned, fact-oriented reporting. At least in terms of objective criteria, there is little evidence for emotionally laden visualization, as camera distances, angles, and color schemes tend towards neutrality and little built-in emotional appeal. The aim at unequivocal communication is also illustrated by the verbal dominance in terms of page space allocation: 75%

of the news webpages were characterized as "textual" and another 20% as "even." Only 5% allocated more space to visuals than to text. Despite the expanding boundaries of layout and information design, text remains the truest form of communication when it comes down to hard facts, it seems.

Looking globally at the presence of visuals in each webpage, some more interesting patterns emerge. Visual nuclei are much more likely to be consociated than dissociated (35% vs. 5%), but are even likelier to appear alone on a page. Therefore, on top of being predominantly textual, news websites prefer austere visualization. Visual satellites, on the other hand, appear in 90% of all cases, and are slightly more likely to be dissociated from the visual nucleus (50%) than in visual connection to it (40%). Satellites also tend to be unrelated among each other (60%) than otherwise (24%). This is one aspect of visual hypermodality in practice: A good chunk of the visual satellites act also as hyperlinks to other stories, related or not. Many of them come from the "Most Recent" or "Top Stories" side bars, which are almost obligatory for any news website. Since these stories do not necessarily relate to the main article at hand or amongst each other, the percentage of visual satellite dissociation is more than half. Hypermodality also appears in the coding for the signaling principle. Every single webpage in the news sample utilizes signaling of some kind, and text-only or text-visual signaling accounts for 95% of that. Purely visual signaling (arrows, pop-ups, callouts, etc.) accounts for the remaining 5%, and news websites are the only genre in the sample that utilizes purely visual attention guides. The persistence of textuality in the multimodality of online news hints at certain path dependence: Hypertext, more often than not, remains a text. This more traditional approach to hypertextuality is somewhat offset by the direction of the links: 85% of the pages in the sample direct their readers to external websites for further reading. Even though the means of hyperlinking remain "old school," its reach is quite broad.

Going into the truly multimodal analytical phase, 75% of the visual-verbal narratives are consonant, while 10% each are dissonant and disjunctive. Combined with the findings discussed above, this paints a picture of multimodal lucidity, a well-formulated textual component backed up by (usually) a single relevant visual and accompanied by hyperlinks to further reading, as well as visual-verbal attention guides to other important stories of the hour. The analysis of spatial-semantic relations in each webpage supports these impressions. In the sample, 65% utilize the principle of spatial contiguity, meaning the visual satellites stand in the immediate vicinity of the relevant chunks of text. Split attention is the organizational principle for 25% of the news websites. In these cases, usually there is a lead visual at the top of the page, and its relevance becomes apparent only after reading the complete article. The remaining 10% either do not feature visuals, or their semantic organization does not fit into a preexisting model. Only 30% of the webpages go to the next level and employ dual scripting for achieving ultimate lucidity and visual-verbal agreement, both structurally and semantically.

82   *Findings from News and Campaignse*

The overall picture of political news websites, therefore, is one of clearly organized content with sparse but to-the-point visualization, which tends not to employ emotional gimmickry but rather to illustrate.

TYPICAL EXAMPLES FROM THE ONLINE NEWS SAMPLE

The examples at which we will look closely come from each of the news sources and are chosen to be more or less representative of its multimodal style. The final example makes for a comparison of how several sources covered the same story, which happened to be serious enough to draw the attention of all four of the websites. The purpose of this and all following example sections is twofold. First of all, it breathes much-needed life into the numbers above and attaches real visual-verbal experience to them. Second, it helps pinpoint concrete multimodal structures and functions that become evident upon close inspection of the webpage materials at hand.

Starting out with CNN, the example in Figure 5.1 presents a design that is typical for the news network's website: A lead image followed by a long text-flow composed of short paragraphs, a short list of highlights on the left-hand side, and visual hyperlinks to several videos. A self-promoting ad in bright green is directly on the right of the lead image, and a list of related articles from "The Complete Coverage of Election 2012" is promoted visually and verbally for the entire length of the webpage. This article is a good representative of the news sample, with its visual focus on persons, the prominence of text-in-image, the neutral-to-cold color schemes that dominate the visuals, and the presence of a single visual nucleus. It is remarkable that the satellites consociate both with that nucleus and among each other. This hints at the embedding of the article at hand into a large network of Election 2012 pieces. The multimodal narrative is characterized as consonant: The news story deals with the battle that Obama and Romney will lead for the Latino vote, and the visual shows groups of Hispanic people registering at a booth with a banner reading, "Latinos for Obama." The visual focus on Latinos supporting Barack Obama comes in contrast with the content of the article; therefore, the semantic organization principle registers as "split attention": The visual and its subtitle inform the reader that Latinos supported Obama in 2008, but the article emphasizes the almost-equal efforts both candidates are putting in attracting the Latino vote again in 2012. An indirect reference to the 2008 visual appears in paragraphs 6 to 8, which recount the decisive victory Obama held against Republican John McCain in the infamous battleground Orange County, Florida, in 2008—a county where, historically, margins between Democrats and Republicans used to be too close to call.

The main visual satellites on the left-hand side of the text redirect to videos, which are also directly related to the news item and which document Obama's reliance on Latino celebrities, both presidential hopefuls' counting on the Latino vote, and the weight of this ethnic group's ballots in

Findings from News and Campaigns 83

Election 2012. The article goes on to break down the Latino voter segment into Puerto Ricans, Cuban-Americans, etc., without relating visuals. This, therefore, makes for a split-attention design, which clearly does not feature dual scripting but still manages to present information coherently and thoroughly. An interesting aspect of this case is the uniform context embedding which partially makes up for the slight incoherence that might be associated with split attention designs.

The coherence and consociation of the satellites, visual and otherwise, imbues the whole webpage with a sense of completeness and allows for the smooth perception and appraisal of information in the context of the

Figure 5.1 CNN's Web article "Latino boom makes Orlando proving ground for Obama"
(*segment; source:* <http://us.cnn.com/2012/06/21/politics/florida-hispanic-vote/index.html>).
ICON codes: 111 – persons | 123 – text-in-image | 211 – photograph | 221 – news | 312 – neutral | 322 – medium | 332 – level | 342 – textual | 419 – n-a | 421 – nucleus-satellite consociation | 431 – satellite-satellite consociation | 4413 – visual / textual signaling | 452 – mostly external | 511 – consonant | 521 – spatial contiguity | 532 – no dual scripting.

US presidential race. This context embedded-ness lends additional credence to the lead visual and allows it to make sense immediately, even before the reader reaches the sixth paragraph, which then makes the reference to the 2008 vote explicit. In that sense, this CNN webpage, although it does not tell its main story as clearly and fluently as possible, demonstrates how larger-scale context dependence can be a viable substitute for crystal-clear multimodal layout. It is also an example of subtle cuing: While the article questions both candidates' chances to attract Latino voters, the lead visual clearly favors Barack Obama.

The example from MSNBC's news website also relates to the presidential candidates' struggle to win over the Latino vote in Orlando, Florida. This article, however, focuses on Republican contender Mitt Romney and discusses the difficulties he will face when trying to gather the Latino vote after illegal immigration has been a steeple of his campaigning for years. It can be found in Figure 5.2.

In comparison with the CNN example discussed above, MSNBC takes a very different spin on virtually the same topic. The lead visual is a close-up of Republican candidate Mitt Romney seemingly caught mid-sentence, holding a microphone, his eyebrows lowered. The microphone and the usually favorable low angle seem to put him in a position of power, enhanced by the sleek, neutral color scheme. However, these generally flattering visual composition elements are turned around: Although in close-up, Romney shows his profile to the viewer, which increases the perceived social distance between them, and his solemn expression amplifies this effect. Under these conditions, the "heroic" low angle becomes just another aspect of the photographic subject's alienation from the audience. The sole lead visual, therefore, paints Mitt Romney as an alienated leader facing a conundrum that requires him to explain himself in public, via a microphone. This visual message is in unison with the verbal portion of the article, which outlines the difficulties the Republican presidential candidate will have in convincing Latino voters he is on their side. In several paragraphs, considerably longer than the choppy CNN model above, the article describes Romney's consistent anti-Latino policy positions and his most recent lack of opinion on the groundbreaking DREAM act signed by Barack Obama, allowing Latino youths who entered the US illegally to receive legal status, provided they maintained clean records and good social standing throughout their residence in the US so far. Since this lack of position is only the latest in a string of flip-flops or downright unfavorable actions in Romney's record, the solemn expression and alienation that characterize his portrait are appropriate.

Compared to CNN, MSNBC utilizes several fewer attention guides, and they are mostly textual and internal. There is a form of contextual embedding in the overhead banner, which serves as an Election 2012 hub. This is made prominent by the Capitol's dome in the "First Read" logo. There are no prominent visual satellites that lead to other articles, unlike the CNN example. The page displays a definite consonant multimodal narrative,

Figure 5.2 The MSNBC online article "First thoughts: Romney's immigration challenge"

(*segment; source:* <http://firstread.msnbc.msn.com/_news/2012/06/21/12337055-first-thoughts-romneys-immigration-challenge?lite>).

ICON codes: 111 – persons | 122 – objects | 211 – photograph | 221 – news | 312 – neutral | 321 – close-up | 333 – low | 342 – textual | 419 – n-a | 422 – nucleus-satellite dissociation | 432 – satellite-satellite dissociation | 4412 – textual signaling | 452 – mostly external | 511 – consonant | 521 – spatial contiguity | 532 – no dual scripting.

although much more austere than its Cable News counterpart. The organizational principle is spatial contiguity, but it does not go into dual scripting, mainly because the simple layout does not allow for the twofold attention guiding that this principle requires.

Nevertheless, the organization of the piece is clear and logical, and its visual and verbal elements coexist in a harmonious way, painting a clear picture of the difficult road ahead of Mitt Romney into the hearts of the Latino community in the US. It also provides a good example of the synergetic powers of good visualization and lucid writing. The seemingly favorable visual elements combine in a way that leaves a clear doubt as to the heroic image of Romney, and the text confirms these doubts from the outset, helping us turn the visual convention around and attribute the right meaning to the photograph before us.

The BBC chimes in with a different topic and yet another approach to multimodal layout. It presents a story coming from North Carolina, where the state Senate rejected the plan to offer monetary compensations to victims of forced sterilization during the period of 1929–1974. The snapshot can be seen in Figure 5.3. There are two visual nuclei, both close-up shots of Elaine Riddick, an outspoken victim. They both show her at a 3/4 angle, once crying, looking away from the camera and the second time gazing directly at the viewer. There are no secondary motifs apart from Riddick's face. This creates a powerful emotional impact, which goes in hand with the tragic topic of the article.

The material properties of the two photos add to that impact. The first close-up visual shows Elaine Riddick crying in warm color and at a level angle, breathing life into the still depiction of her victimization and establishing an immediate connection with the viewer: We see a living woman who has been wronged and who cannot hold her tears anymore. The second photograph shows a resigned, melancholy Riddick looking directly at the camera from a high angle in gray scale. The often-demeaning depiction from above, which belittles the photographic subject, pours additional sadness into the mix. Instead of feeling superior to her, the viewer is much more likely to experience pity and compassion. Her lower position relative to the viewer's eye level also frames Riddick as a lesser human—not in a degrading way, but emphasizing the fact that her forced sterilization at age fourteen took away one of the most important human biological functions: reproduction. While this is a non-traditional effect of the particular visual composition choices here, the end result is a powerful multimodal narrative, which blends harmoniously.

The two visual nuclei are in consonance, while the satellites are dissonant, being links to unrelated popular pieces on the BBC News website. There is much attention guidance, which finds mostly textual realization and directs the reader to other pages. The semantic organization principle is dual scripting, the highest level of multimodal and semantic cohesion. This is pinpointed by the emotionally charged photographs, which find themselves in direct proximity to the sentences and paragraphs that document Elaine Riddick's tragic loss and the doubled humiliation she has to endure after

Findings from News and Campaigns   87

her long-fought battle for compensations for herself and many other victims was overturned by the North Carolina Senate. This is an example that is somewhat untypical of serious news media due to its emotional charge. Nevertheless, it is also characteristic of the BBC's multimodal style: It presents the story in clear, short paragraphs, much like CNN, but it carefully embeds its visualizations in the textual "nests" where they belong in the overall document's body and line of thought. The end result is a deservedly emotional piece, which presents the straight facts just the same, but which also recognizes the human suffering and the tragic element in the story. Thus, the BBC demonstrates how "objective" reporting does not have to be cold and unfeeling and how it can retain its professional values without sacrificing humanity.

Figure 5.3   The BBC news article "North Carolina rejects funds for sterilization victims"
(*segment; source:* <www.bbc.co.uk/news/world-us-canada-18529735>).
ICON codes: 111 – persons I 129 – n-a I 211 – photograph I 221 – news I 311 – warm & 316 – gray scale I 321 – close-up I 332 – level & 333 – low I 342 – textual I 411 – nucleus-nucleus consociation I 422 – nucleus-satellite dissociation I 432 – satellite-satellite dissociation I 4412 – textual signaling I 452 – mostly external I 511 – consonant I 521 – spatial contiguity I 531 – dual scripting.

88 *Findings from News and Campaignse*

Al Jazeera English is the source furthest removed from the Western cultural context. Nevertheless, the Qatar-based news network's international edition was founded with the explicit purpose to serve Western audiences and, as such, took its cues largely from the BBC's online presence. The article under scrutiny here discusses the death of Rodney King, an African-American man whose videotaped beating by the Los Angeles Police Department in 1991 unleashed a series of racial riots in the city.

Figure 5.4 The Al Jazeera English news story about the death of Rodney King (*segment; source*: <www.aljazeera.com/news/americas/2012/06/201261716454859368.html>).
ICON codes: 111 – persons | 122 – objects | 211 – photograph | 221 – news | 311 – warm | 321 – close-up | 333 – low | 342 – textual | 419 – n-a | 422 – nucleus-satellite dissociation | 432 – satellite-satellite dissociation | 4412 – textual signaling | 452 – mostly external | 511 – consonant | 521 – spatial contiguity | 532 – no dual scripting.

The lead visual is the opening frame of the embedded video. It shows Rodney King in a close-up shot with magazines or books in the blurred background. The color scheme is warm and combines well with the short-shot distance and the low camera angle, making King relatable and respectable in the viewer's eye. His depiction is the single visual nucleus in the page, making it a predominantly textual piece with dissociative visual satellites (hyperlinks to other, unrelated stories). The nature of the signaling is also textual, in the direction of external pages. The multimodal narrative is consonant: the piece commemorates the passing of Rodney King, 47, and reminds the readers of his historical significance for the Los Angeles riots at the beginning of the 1990s. The page's organizational principle is one of spatial contiguity, as the visual featuring King is in direct proximity to the text that focuses on him and his personality, while the second half of the text flow relates the story of the riots and does not feature the police brutality victim at all. Due to this division in the article's content, which is not accompanied visually, dual scripting is not an option. Compared to the BBC or CNN examples, this news story is considerably shorter, and the paragraphs it features are less extensive. This might be attributable to the video that is embedded in the article, and which is the main information carrier here. Still, brevity is a characteristic of the Al Jazeera English news website overall, and this example is no exception. It is also interesting to note that the visual component of the page alone does not go with the message it is transmitting: It features Rodney King very much alive, and it presents him textually as "victim of police beating." The mentioning of his passing is evident only in the text, as are the historical events from the 1990s. Hence, this webpage truly gives text precedence over visuals and is the only one among the specific examples in this subchapter to do so.

COVERING THE SAME STORY: BACK-TO-BACK COMPARISON

Luckily, during the sampling period there was an event in US politics big enough to garner the attention of three out of the four online news websites: The vote by the House Oversight and Government Operations Committee to charge Eric Holder, US attorney general, with contempt of Congress. Evidently, this is a scandalous story that would attract media attention easily. It focuses on one person who has likely committed malpractice and who will face punishment for his actions. The US presidential administration and the House of Representatives are against him and support the plans of exposing him and starting a penal procedure against him. All these story elements already hint at the possible multimodal makeup of the articles dedicated to this case. The analysis below considers CNN, BBC, and Al Jazeera English's coverage of this story in direct comparison. MSNBC did not run this as a top story at the time of sampling. The three news stories are displayed in Figure 5.5.

90 *Findings from News and Campaignse*

Visually, the three news websites paint a rather uniform picture, and their depictions of Eric Holder are mutually consonant. All three photographs show him at medium to close-up range, with neutral colors, and from a slightly low angle. In all cases, Holder is caught explaining himself and seemingly having a hard time at it. CNN enhances that impression by picturing him with his left hand extended—a gesture of deterrence, as if he tries to convince his off-camera opponent to pause his attack and to let him speak. The attorney general is the clear visual focus of the depictions, although both CNN and Al Jazeera feature photographs of him with other men sitting behind him and slightly out of focus. The color schemes of all three pictures are neutral, with a hint of warmth. The features above combine to paint a picture of a person of admitted authority (low angle, serious color schemes) who has fallen from grace (shown at close range, apologetic expressions and gestures). Despite Holder being elevated above the viewer, his gaze directed even higher and the groups of men behind him in two out of three photographs emphasize visually that there is someone sitting even higher than him, and that he has made a mistake for which he is about to pay.

All three news websites rely primarily on text to present the story. Al Jazeera English is particularly notable here because it produces its longest verbal piece in the sample here. In terms of inter-visual relationships, the BBC keeps its style of two visual nuclei which harmonize: One features Eric Holder and the other features Congressman Darrel Issa, who chairs the committee and who put the contempt motion forth. The visual placement of Issa behind a high lectern reflects Holder's upward gaze and helps create a visual dialogue. CNN also repeats its practice of consociated visual nucleus and satellites by providing four video links that all relate directly to the story. The visual satellites in the other cases are dissociated, both from

Figure 5.5 US Attorney General Eric Holder's contempt charge. Coverage from (left to right) BBC, CNN, and Al Jazeera English

(*segments; sources:* BBC <www.bbc.co.uk/news/world-us-canada-18528798>; CNN <http://edition.cnn.com/2012/06/21/politics/holder-contempt/index.html>; Al Jazeera English <www.aljazeera.com/news/americas/2012/06/2012620173442995287.html>).

the respective nuclei and among each other. Al Jazeera's "leading" satellite, however, presents an interesting coincidence. On the top right from Holder's portrait is a close-up of President Obama pointing his finger, his campaign logo behind him forming a circle of stars and stripes around his head—a somewhat godly depiction. This most likely coincidental placement amplifies the sense of punishable wrongdoing in Eric Holder's ledger, and it also frames Obama (and his administration, by extension) as the punishers and bringers of justice in this scandal.

All three Web sources rely on mostly textual signal guidance, and CNN and BBC orient attention externally—to other related and unrelated news stories. Al Jazeera, on the other hand, utilizes quite a bit of internal orientation devices, such as subheadings, to help orient the reader. This might also be a byproduct of the unusual length of the article, since this particular online medium tends to keep stories short. All three stories display consonant multimodal narratives and are organized according to the spatial contiguity principle. This combination is also the most frequent choice for online news layout, it seems. The BBC article is the only one that features dual scripting: The charges against Eric Holder appear right next to his photograph, and Darrel Issa makes a visual appearance together with the first verbal mention of him. The visual composition of the two photographs, already discussed above, also binds them together and builds a virtual dialogue, much like the verbal debate between the two, which the text outlines.

This back-to-back comparison of news stories on the same topic also sheds light on international news narrative practices, since each of the media in the example comes from a different country (US, UK, and Qatar, respectively). Each example displays idiosyncrasies and medium-specific characteristics, which were already mentioned earlier, yet all three have surprisingly similar patterns of visualizing and organizing their stories. The iconic representations of Eric Holder and his downfall might once again revive the notion of visuals as a universal language.

CLARITY AND CONTEXT IN THE NEWS SAMPLE

The closer look at the online news sample confirms the findings of the general overview: The analyzed websites strive for clarity and a sound semblance of neutrality, even if they occasionally fall short of true objectivity. Their visualizations are carefully selected and always pertinent to the subject matter of the specific piece. The lead visual is in clear, direct relationship with the accompanying text, and the second visual nucleus, if present at all, is likely to be relevant as well. They tend to carry little emotional load and certainly not one that would invite judgment or emotional response. The color schemes are neutral or vaguely warm, while the camera distances are medium or close-up, making the photographic subjects relatable. The surrounding visual satellites tend to be dissociated from the main story (though exceptions exist as discussed previously), and this is a manifestation of hypermodality becoming more complex: Although textual hyperlinks are still the most widespread nodes to the World Wide Web, predominantly visual linkages like image and video thumbnails are also gathering critical mass. Narrative consonance and clear organization of the multimodal elements via the principle of spatial contiguity are the norm, and a couple of examples display the even more sophisticated dual scripting practice.

Some interesting divergent trends pop up in the analyses above as well. One is the contextual embedding that CNN utilizes in its Latino article. It demonstrates how properly themed satellites can serve as an outer support structure for the main multimodal unit and support it even in a split-attention arrangement. This is only one insight into the deep synergetic multimodal relationship between images, text, and layout. Another is the unabashed usage of emotionally charged visuals, such as those of Elaine Riddick, or the candid depictions of Eric Holder speechless or struggling to get a word across. While unexpected in the serious news–reporting context, these images manage to fit the context and even connect tightly and meaningfully with the rest of their respective articles. What lends these emotional visuals the credibility worthy of serious news is their textual embedding in the story. Without the serious reporting and commentary of the professional news media, these images could easily appear in a tabloid or a gossip website. However, reading the backstory and understanding the events behind the emotion provides a powerful anchor. While visual research often works under the premise of images' instantaneous and complete perception and appraisal, there is ground for a competing theory here. More specifically, the possibility that the accompanying text has the power to actively shape and change appraisal becomes all the more real when a serious institution such as the BBC publishes not one but two emotional visuals of a woman crying and mutely pleading for justice as an illustration to a local US political piece. The valence of the images finds its explanation in the verbal account of the tragic maiming of Elaine Riddick. The visuals make the most potent argument explicit, namely that it is a disgrace to allow so many women to suffer and then refuse to compensate them under the pretense of lacking funds. In a very real sense, they give emotional credit where it is due. This is a persuasive technique that promises to spark a telling discussion of evolving trends, changing norms, and exchange of conventions. It is also a prime example of why it is useful and necessary to study visuals in direct relation to their context and to extend semantic analyses to all possible communication modes that take active part in semiosis.

POLITICAL CAMPAIGNS

Campaign websites have long become a staple of US politics. The higher the stakes, the more important—and elaborate—the candidates' Web presence becomes. At only about fifteen years of age, the campaign website has already risen in popularity and importance at least to the level of the traditional television spot campaign component. Furthermore, since Barack Obama's historic victory in 2008, campaign websites have become the best voter base mobilization tool—whether they involve organizational activity at the grassroots level or small- to medium-scale fundraising. The current dissertation focuses on the websites of the two big-party presidential contenders, namely Barack Obama (D), who is seeking reelection, and Mitt Romney (R), who has chased after the Republican presidential nomination before on several occasions and has now officially become the Republican candidate for the White House. Therefore, analyzing their two respective websites makes for a pertinent comparison and will also check for the existence of specific visual strategies (e.g., Müller, 1997) and multimodal strategies on the two political rivals' campaign websites.

Political campaigning, in sharp contrast to news, is persuasive by definition. We expect it to employ as many communication tricks and gimmicks as possible to capture attention, to convince, and to convert. It differs from news because it pursues a purposeful ideological agenda. But on the other hand, political campaigning is similar to news production in terms of the levels of professionalism and the know-how that characterize the production process. Hence, we have an interesting comparison to make here with the help of ICON. Additionally, the two campaigns (Barack Obama vs. Mitt Romney) are like the Super Bowl of political persuasion: They pit two experienced and powerful politicians in a contest for one of the most powerful political offices in the world. Given these stakes, both camps employ the greatest campaign minds in their ideological field, and we can expect the results to be a litmus test of the best practices in online political campaigning today.

Both campaigns make generous use of visuals. There is not a single campaign webpage without a visual, and 51.06% of all visuals focus on a person (not exclusively the campaign sponsor!) followed by 44.68% depicting objects. The objects come mostly from the Romney campaign, which relies on graphic symbols for its main policy positions. All visuals have a discernible secondary motif, unlike in the news subsample. The most common secondary motif is text embedded into the image, which accounts for 53.19% of all cases. Other persons, usually groups of supporters, are the second most common visual backdrop (29.79%). This testifies to both campaigns' urge to send clear and simple visual messages that carry little or no risk of misinterpretation. Showing the campaign sponsor surrounded by waving and smiling rally-goers is one such image with an unmistakable message. Objects also form a notable secondary motif group (17.02%) and most often constitute handheld microphones or state symbols (presidential logo, national flag, the White House, etc.).

The campaign subsample also offers a greater variety of visual genres. Photographs are still the most prominent category (55.32%), followed by drawings (21.28%), most of which come from the Romney campaign, as already stated above. Different information visualizations account for 15% of the visuals, and 8.51% cover miscellaneous visualization (such as logos and symbols which do not fit any other proper code above). This variety of visuals may well stem from the persuasive nature of political campaigns. Modern PR professionals are well aware of visuals' power as well as of their differential perception, so covering a wide gamut of genres casts an equally wide net over potential audiences.

When it comes to the visuals' specific realizations, only 17.02% utilize a warm color scheme, while neutral (42.55%) and cold (40.43%) color schemes are almost equally present. While cool tones are sometimes used in order to create a feeling of unease and coldness, they also bring a sense of assertiveness, control, and determination. These are crucial qualities of the US president as leader of the nation and commander in chief. Avoiding a warm and fuzzy color ambience makes sense here. In addition, the political and economic background of the 2012 campaign mostly precludes the effective use of feel-good tactics. The economic crisis, the continuing war on terror, and other pressing issues require that the US president show immutable determination and readiness to lead. The cool and sleek color schemes of both campaigns are a visual statement of these personality traits. The camera distance variations lend additional support to this claim. The prevalence of long (21.28%) and medium shots (29.79%) presents the campaign sponsors as leaders, either in a solo spot or surrounded by supporters. A large share of the visuals (44.68%) consists of iconic representations rather than proper visualizations of reality, so camera distance is not an applicable category. The few close-ups (4.26%) reaffirm the drive to emphasize the leadership qualities of the two candidates. Both Obama and Romney are visually removed from the average viewer because they are meant to lead. The possible negative effects of this social distance are toned down by the prevalence of level camera angles (42.55%); the viewer is on equal grounds with the candidates. In this sense, though meaning to lead and showing enough determination and potential for it, neither Obama nor Romney choose to position themselves clearly above their audience and voter base. The same goes for the endorsers who appear as their substitutes in some campaign visuals. Heroic low angles appear in 13.79% of the cases, while high angles can be seen in only 3.45% of all cases.

Like political news, campaigns also use predominantly textual (56.25%) or evenly distributed visual-verbal (25%) layouts, which leave less room for alternative interpretations. In combination with the mostly neutral visualizations, this is a conscious strategy that favors simple, straightforward narratives. The emphasis is on facts and truths about each campaign and about the situation, in which the election will take place. Given the complexity of the matter, neither campaign takes the risk of sending out visual messages which are open to (mis)interpretation. This is also evident in the analyses of visual-to-visual relationships. Visual nuclei harmonize in 50% of all cases and clash openly in only 12.50% of all cases. The campaign webpages offer a single visual satellite for a compact and straightforward multimodal narrative in 37.50% of the cases, in the style of many news pages discussed above. The lack of visual satellites also supports the notion of visual clarity. On the rare occasions when satellites are present, they associate closely. Text-based attention guiding through hyperlinks and headings dominates (80%). Unlike political news, the campaigns' signaling efforts are mostly internal (56.25%), guiding voters through the webpages of policy material. External links (25%) and mixed signaling (18.75%) also stay within the respective candidate's campaign rather than leap to third-party events or persons.

Political campaigns' multimodal narratives feature a very high degree of consonance (81.25%) and no trace of dissonance. Disjunctive visual-verbal intersemiosis appears only 18.75% of the time. This is in line with the determination and discipline that the two campaign websites demonstrate. Of all the campaign webpages, 75% utilize the organizational principle of spatial contiguity, and 43.75% go a step further to apply dual scripting. The latter cases mostly come from the Obama campaign. The 56.25% of pages that shun dual scripting come mostly from the Romney campaign. This has to do with his team's choice to break down his policy positions into several individual pages, which makes high levels of integration unnecessary since content is naturally segmented and dispersed. Overall, both campaigns achieve remarkable visual-verbal cohesion and, somewhat unexpectedly, move away from the stereotypical emotional campaigning style that used to dominate American politics (e.g. Brader, 2005). The specific examples presented below discuss the categories in detail and offer explanations for these novel and somewhat unexpected trends in presidential campaigning.

A COMPARISON OF ECONOMIC POLICIES

The examples in this section make the most sense when compared back to back. This provides an opportunity for some telling conclusions at first sight already, like the surprisingly similar general design of the two websites. Different shades of blue form the basic color scheme and make the bright red "Donate" button prominent in the top right-hand corner. However, when we dive into the first example—economic policies—the similarities end there. Mitt Romney's website follows a linear text-flow organization, while Barack Obama's economic message comes in a series of boxes, each featuring text, visuals, or data graphics. The Republican's webpage breaks down the topic "Jobs and the Economy" into multimodal teasers: textual hyperlinks accompanied by symbols. Examples include "Taxes" and an icon showing a calculator or "Spending" accompanied by scissors. The Democratic candidate also breaks down the complex issue into segments; however, all the information appears already on the same webpage, neatly "packed" in the box design. Each of these designs has important implications for the policies' narrative structures.

96 *Findings from News and Campaignse*

The campaigns present their respective sponsors as active public speakers in both cases. Romney appears in a visual header at the very top, while Obama appears twice: once in a photograph in the right column, and once more in a video still, diagonally to the left. All three presidential candidate depictions feature the respective campaign sponsor speaking at a podium and turning his head to the left; furthermore, Obama makes a characteristic gesture with his hands in both instances. Romney is accompanied by the text, "Believe in America: Mitt Romney's Plan for Jobs and Economic Growth," which is a fairly generic intersemiotic combination—in the same vein as a speech balloon. Conversely, Obama is backed by an SUV in the assembly process in the photograph and by a group of people in the video still. Both lend him power—a mighty vehicle and a sizable crowd often speak louder than any text, even in all caps and bold.

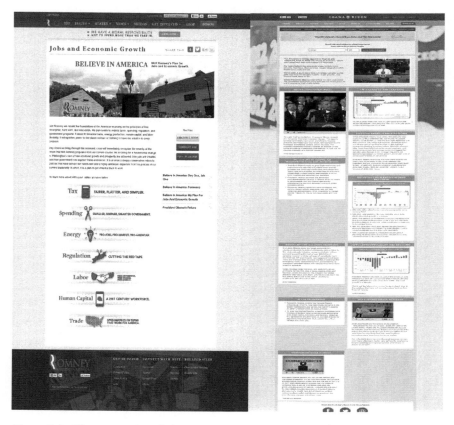

Figure 5.6 The economic policies as seen on Mitt Romney's (left) and Barack Obama's campaign websites

(*segments; sources:* Romney <www.mittromney.com/jobs>; Obama <www.barackobama.com/record/economy>).

The visual genres that populate the two pages are varied. The Romney campaign relies on a lone photograph (long shot, neutral color scheme, low camera angle) and a number of iconic drawings, while the Obama camp uses a photograph, several video stills (they all feature mostly warm color schemes, medium and long shots, and level camera angles) and information graphics. Overall, Romney's campaign dedicates more space to visuals than text, while Obama's campaign uses both modes evenly. The Republican webpage relies on intertwining of icons and text, which presents an intriguing case of cross-modal ingrowth. For all its creative implementation, however, Romney's webpage features visual nucleus dissociation: His rally photograph and the icons do not form a consistent narrative, and the icons themselves are not grouped meaningfully. A calculator, scissors, light bulb, another pair of scissors cutting red tape, a handshake, a smart phone showing a hard hat, and a geographic outline of the USA with arrows in it, all in one sequence, leave much to the imagination. Their consistent red-white-and-blue color realization is the only unifying cue in the ensemble. The Obama counterexample creates a more consistent visual narrative by establishing the incumbent president as a decisive leader who has ushered in economic growth demonstrated by the charts and figures, with a particular emphasis on the automotive industry and on the support of the people. Small businesses and consumers also find their share of visual attention here. Neither campaign webpage makes use of visual satellites. The signaling is mostly textual (apart from Romney's iconic inserts). The direction is internal in Obama's case, as it guides the reader through the page at hand, while Romney relies on external signaling to the different aspects of his economic policy, each of which gets an individual page.

In their own specific ways, both webpages create consonant multimodal narratives. Mitt Romney's dissociated visual nuclei find cohesion with the help of text, which clarifies the otherwise cryptic series of blue-red icons. After a thorough multimodal analysis, the page's spatial congruity design fleshes out—a finding that the visual analysis alone would miss. The Obama campaign, on the other hand, goes a step further into multimodal cohesion and relies on dual scripting. The multimodal layout blends the content seamlessly and guides the reader through the series of boxes via an intuitive zigzag reading path, which the differently sized boxes form. The differences outlined here are likely to result from the different campaign strategies of the two candidates. Müller (1997) provides an exhaustive description of visual styles and strategies in presidential campaigning, and one of the distinctions she draws is between incumbents running for reelection and contenders who seek to oust them. A similar principle applies here as well, only on a multimodal scale. Barack Obama has a long list of accomplishments at the end of his first term. Hence, he can rely on statistics and information graphics to speak for him, and he can summon consumers and small businesses to vouch for his achievements in the economic sector. He can also display himself speaking with confidence in front of a half-assembled car because of the work his administration did to bail out the automotive industry. All of Obama's achievements naturally converge into a flowing design, each box of which completes the puzzle picture of him as a successful president who manages the national economy well. Mitt Romney, on the other hand, is a former governor and a longtime Republican presidential nominee, first-time Republican presidential candidate. He does not have a record convincing enough to lean on; therefore, he has the task of explaining his economic platform in pure rhetoric and in much more detail. This is why one webpage is not enough, and the hyperlinks to the separate portions of the economic package he is offering have to be attractive to keep the readers clicking through. Hence, the icons and symbols come into play. Although they do not immediately make sense, they still help grab the readers' attention. The risk of visual dissociation is offset by the attention-guiding benefits of this approach, and this is what Mitt Romney's lengthy economic plan requires.

SPECIFIC ISSUES: HEALTHCARE

The second back-to-back comparison reveals even more about the two campaign strategies based on the multimodal narratives they create. The debate regarding healthcare provides an excellent opportunity to compare argumentation and information presentation styles. It is a point of very heated debate between the two camps: President Obama counts his healthcare reform among the biggest achievements of his first term, while Mitt Romney threatens to repeal the Affordable Care Act (also known as "Obamacare") as soon as he steps into office. The issue persisted long after the campaign and the election were over, and it eventually led to the government shutdown in October 2013.

The campaign sponsors are visually absent this time. In fact, the Romney webpage shuns visualization completely, apart from the icon of a Caduceus (two snakes wrapped around a staff), which traditionally symbolizes medicine or medical care. The Obama camp goes in the opposite direction: There are a total of five video stills, three of which feature persons (a cancer patient, a young adult, and two small children) and two that feature text as an opening frame. In both examples, the secondary visual motif is text in image. All visuals stick to a neutral color scheme. The Obama camp shows the persons described above in close-up or medium shots in an effort to emphasize the human element and the care President Obama has provided to the depicted groups. The camera angles are level, even in the case of the two baby girls, which underscores the importance the campaign places in the common man. Despite their varying use of visualization, both pages rely on text in similarly high measure: It occupies much more space than the visuals, and it features prominently in every image, too. This is a conscious decision on the part of both campaigns, and it reflects the complexity of the issue, which only allows discussion and persuasion in the clearest possible terms.

Findings from News and Campaigns 99

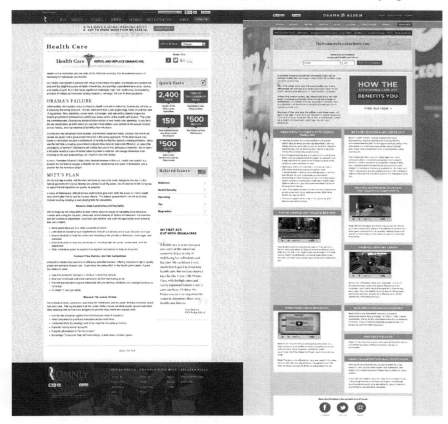

Figure 5.7 Mitt Romney's (left) and Barack Obama's healthcare policy webpages (*segments; sources:* Romney <www.mittromney.com/issues/health-care>; Obama <www.barackobama.com/record/health-care?source=primary-nav>).

The images on the Obama campaign webpage form a uniform visual narrative, which introduces the Affordable Care Act and then features representatives of some groups of patients and citizens it benefits. The Romney campaign, on the other hand, relies on a single visual, so no visual narrative as such is at hand. Both pages use extensive textual signaling. The Obama campaign relies on it to highlight major points and to guide the reader through the already known zigzag information flow described in the previous section. The Romney campaign, unlike in the previous example, also resorts to internal signaling here. Differently colored passages as well as headings and subheadings help organize and make sense of the text's rhetorical structure. The two main headings—"Obama's Failure" and "Mitt's Plan"—also reflect the recurrent structure of the Romney policy pages. They all feature a prominent hook for shortening the distance between Romney and his voter base:

His opponent is mentioned by surname only, which immediately creates distance, while he appears with his (shortened) first name. The juxtaposition of the two is reasserted through the contextual opposites "failure" vs. "plan" (for improvement) attached to the two names. Still, compared to Obama's dual scripting, heavily multimodal pattern, this seems a lot more frugal and "old-school," like an online pamphlet rather than an interactive website.

Both webpages feature consonant multimodal narratives. Even though text dominates, the images still play an important role in the overall message transfer. The semantic organization principle is spatial contiguity in the case of Romney and dual scripting for Obama once again. This, too, points towards consistency in the campaign websites and confirms the professionalism of the strategists and communicators behind them. The second set of examples also lets clearer campaign strategies flesh out. The Obama camp bets on a clear approach that presents the incumbent president's achievements in a relentlessly logical order, supported by photographs, videos, and information graphics. Romney's campaign, on the other hand, focuses on verbal argumentation and uses visuals for attention grabbing rather than information relay.

STRATEGY TAKES EXPRESSIVE CONTROL

Like the news website sample, the Romney and Obama campaign websites display certain similarities. Design is one such avenue; both rely on sleek cool colors and significant amounts of text. Impassioned campaigning takes a step back in favor of an air of expertise and argumentation rather than emotional persuasion. The persuasive effort focuses on a range of clearly defined topics, namely a list of seven or eight issues of national importance, which mostly overlap between the two camps. Despite the different amounts of visualization the two websites use (Obama definitely prevails here), they share distinct similarities in terms of multimodal narrative creation. Factual depictions are more common than "orchestrated reality," and people are in the visual focus. The campaign sponsors are present visually, but they tend to share the spotlight with other relevant persons. Barack Obama's campaign includes a number of regular people, mostly individually; it puts a human face on the numbers and achievements from the first presidential term. Romney's imagery emphasizes the mass view to show how well supported his candidacy is. Both campaigns make use of computer-generated visuals and drawings, although to different ends. The Obama camp often uses information graphics and other data visualization to present the incumbent president's track record on the important issues, while the Romney team utilizes signs and symbols to help orient the readers through his verbose policy proposals. In other words, the graphics are important meaning carriers for Obama, while they merely play a navigational role for Romney.

The multimodal comparison of the two campaigns also affirms the existence and implementation of distinct campaign strategies. As an incumbent, Barack Obama has much more clout when his campaign makes positive statements about him because it can always back them up with evidence, both visual and verbal, of his achievements while in office. Obama surely has a lot to show and to spin in the most positive light possible. He is also at considerably more freedom when it comes to layout and semantic design: There is much less explaining to do, since every move of his administration gets instant national coverage, and political analysts break down and regurgitate it profusely. Therefore, the Democratic campaign focuses more on reminding the audience of the administration's achievements and illustrating them appropriately, like in the example of healthcare reform. "Obamacare" is reviewed succinctly, and different patient groups who benefit from it particularly appear to testify how good it is for the American nation. The examples are supported by well-visualized statistics, which add some dry numbers and data for good measure. This freedom also seeps into the multimodal design of the Obama campaign's webpages. The Lego-like structures that are characteristic of the Democratic candidate's website present portions of information in a continuous narrative and employ the highest semantic organization principle of dual scripting—an elaborate content design choice that the campaign picks up and utilizes with remarkable ease. The president's activities and accomplishments from his first term provide a rich multimodal databank, which fills up the structures of the principle nicely and makes for an effective incumbent strategy of a new generation.

Mitt Romney's campaign, on the other hand, is a good example of a contender's effort. Having much less to show than an incumbent, the Republican candidate focuses on elaborating his policy positions and intentions with a view of the possible future when he assumes office. Compared to Obama's constant emphasis on achievements and presidential acts, Romney's overwhelming verbal focus seems much less convincing. With little under his belt, he has to do a lot more explaining and rationalizing, which the fundamental structure of his website reflects, too. While the Obama campaign dedicates one webpage to each important topic, the Republican's website has webpage trees which go deeper into the various aspects of every main issue. Had Romney followed the "one webpage per issue" policy of his opponent, his website would have been flush with impossibly long text passages. Due to the definite lack of appeal in this text-heavy communication design, the campaign focuses on making the signaling towards those "issue branches" as attractive and outstanding as possible. This becomes the crux of the Romney visualization effort. After a lead visual, most likely to show the former governor in crowd interaction, and a short introductory text, a series of textual hyperlinks guide the reader to the specific policy pages. Each of these hyperlinks is accompanied by a thematic symbol: a pair of scissors cutting red tape to illustrate fairer access to jobs, a pocket calculator to accompany the discussion of taxes, and so on. Compared to Obama's photographic illustrations and data visualizations, these drawings are on a much lower level of realism and appeal. However, they are there with the purpose to keep the audience reading and clicking through to the next page, and it is likely they did their job. The long texts are a lot less likely to grab and hold the attention than the discrete blocks of focused content the Democratic opponent is using; therefore, atypical internal signaling is needed, and the Romney camp has found it.

Another traditionally important campaign task is to make the candidates relatable. The Obama campaign goes about the task visually: The incumbent president often appears in warm colors and at level angles and short distances. Other persons regularly appear by his side. Mitt Romney, on the other hand, usually appears in a leadership position: He either gives stump speeches or bends down in order to talk to soldiers or common people. His higher status is emphasized visually, and he demonstrates he is fit to lead in this way. As with other important communicative tasks, the attempt to make him relatable comes in the text. In his specific policy pages, the opposition is between "Obama's Failure" and "Mitt's Plan"—the two prominent headlines found in every example. The repetition of Romney's nickname is the closest he gets to making himself like a common person. Being a Republican and a very wealthy man, however, not much more can be expected, because overplaying that card might make him seem insincere. It is notable, however, how even in this aspect of the campaign Obama holds the higher ground in terms of visual and multimodal message implementation. Overall, the two campaigns offer a very intriguing comparison, and the major insights could not have come without a multimodal approach. Despite the similarities that appear at face value, the two presidential candidates consistently utilize different campaign strategies, which have clear semantic and semiotic implications.

TRADITIONAL POLITICAL COMMUNICATION WITH AN ONLINE TWIST

The results from the two traditional political communication samples already hint at new and sometimes counterintuitive trends in both news reporting and campaigning online. A direct comparison between the two traditional genres reveals some expected similarities, like sound multimodal orchestration, clear message relays, and professional layout. The truly telling insights, however, come when we look at the differences between as well as within those two genres and when we juxtapose the online with the offline experience. Only then can we fully grasp the nature and extent to which the specific properties of the Internet influence the communication process, and ICON's worth in this process of genre remapping becomes apparent.

One of the first unique characteristics ICON uncovered in the traditional genre sample is the shift in the modality functions visual and verbal material performs in each subsample. The emotional and impassioned work, traditionally delegated to campaign visuals, moves over to text, especially in the case of Mitt Romney, whose policy webpages consistently speak of "failure" and restoring America's greatness—formulation with great emotional charge. Barack Obama, despite placing much more importance on visuals, also refrains from making strong visual statements and rather lets imagery bolster the facts of his four years in office. This unimpassioned approach is what could be expected of the news sample, but instead it comes forward with a different agenda. Cases of distinct visual-verbal dissonance and emotion-laden information design break away with the traditional journalistic value of objectivity. Here, the visuals carry the "blame" of breaking with the norm, while texts remain comparatively impartial. This is a shift in modal function worth exploring further, as it carries the seeds of Internet-specific communicative subgenres.

Another important finding here has to do with case-specific differences between communicative agendas and strategies. In the campaign sample, there is evidence for a clash of contender vs. incumbent campaigning styles, and the original theory by Müller (1997) finds support from the new media environment as well. The one defining characteristic of both styles, nevertheless, is the faithfulness to factual claims. This is another direct corollary of the Internet's rising importance in politics: As claims are increasingly easy to verify, campaign messages hone in on real issues and cite real examples rather than prevarications and exaggerations. The differences in the news subsample, on the other hand, are more subtle, but they still hint at each news medium's specific agenda. The use of emotional narratives and visualizations that establish positive or negative social relationships between the viewer and the photographic subject is not a trademark of traditional news media. Online, however, it comes with the added value of sparking a reaction, which can lead to instant communicative response thanks to the Web's interactivity. Comments, forums, and citizen journalism all benefit from the boost that expressive news reporting brings, and the extent to which different news media practice it can be a good gauge for their social engagement and responsibility.

Overall, the differences within the traditional political communication sample point towards the evolution of specific subgenres of political campaigning and news reporting, which find distinct multimodal expressions. These new developments would not have been apparent without the comprehensive approach of multimodal document design. It helps uncover not only webpage- or website-specific trends, but it also maps out global tendencies and shifts in traditional communication practices, which can be directly attributed to the World Wide Web's qualities and capabilities. The basics of each subgenre are still there, but they find new realizations and extensions online, which make continued multimodal research in the field necessary and worthwhile.

6 NGOs and Social Movements
Political Communication With Social Origins

As soon as the Internet's potential for a more inclusive kind of political communication became apparent, a tsunami of optimism washed over countless democracy supporters and campaigners worldwide. The empirical investigations in that direction came without delay and continuously strive to verify the new medium's potential for wider engagement, dialogue, and inclusion. For instance, Best and Krueger (2005) analyze political communication online from the perspective of resource theory. That is to say, they consider the costs rather than the benefits of political engagement, both online and offline. In their analyses, the primary determinants of political participation offline and online are civic skills and internet skills, respectively. Other authors (e.g. DiMaggio, Hargittai, Celeste, & Shafer, 2004; Hargittai & Shafer, 2006; Norris, 2001; Scholzman, Verba, & Brady, 2010) came to similar conclusions as well. Furthermore, "[t]hose who possess the most important determinant of online participation also tend to possess the most important determinant of offline participation" (Best & Krueger 2005, p. 196). In other words, the role the Internet plays for political participation among the general public comes into question: If the same people who are likely to participate offline are also likely to participate online, the Internet might not be the panacea of inclusion and dialogue in politics after all.

Apart from its telling findings, the study by Best and Krueger (2005) is an excellent example of transdisciplinary research, combining political science, sociology, and economic theory to test a communication medium's potential for stimulating political participation. While it does not focus on media content, it tells a lot about the potential audiences this medium reaches and speaks to. It also raises the central question of access: Who has the resources to make use of political communication online? What determines its efficacy? Can politics move online without bringing the same rules and relations that characterize it offline? All these questions point towards the audience side of the communication cycle and also apply with full strength to the phenomenon of prosumption, which is central to the rationale of this dissertation. They also relate to questions of design complexity and production values, which are analyzed and interpreted here.

This chapter's focus on NGO and social movement Web content is not entirely novel. Some political communication studies have already looked beyond traditional campaigning online. Adamic and Glance (2005), for instance, examine the blossoming area of political blogging—another, arguably more covert, form of campaign communication. This is a truly fascinating field that is growing in importance, particularly in light of the Obama 2008 campaign, where massive grassroots mobilization occurred because of the coordination opportunities presented by the World Wide Web. Gerbaudo (2012) covers the power of social media in a book tellingly titled *Tweets and the Streets*. Loader and Mercea (2012) dedicate a whole volume to the effect social media have on the practice and quality of democracy. The less formal environment of social media and semi-professional online communication generation also merit the introduction of emotion into the analytical mix. A host of recent scholarship is mapping the constantly evolving ways of online emotional expression (e.g. Paltoglou, Theunis, Kappas, & Thelwall, 2013; Skowron, Theunis, Rank, & Kappas, 2013; Thelwall et al., 2013). While we do not take this direction in this chapter, it is helpful to approach the material with heightened awareness of emotion expression as a more overt part of information relay.

Political communication research is well aware of the exponential growth in communicative opportunities that the Internet offers to political actors, and it effectively extended this very term from politicians and campaigners to the wider public as well. Different studies touch upon various aspects, characteristics, and stages of the political communication cycle that the Internet has enabled, and this affirms the field's drive to keep up with current developments and to provide answers. This section analyzes examples of political communication coming from non-traditional sources, that is from the habitual receivers of political content. By adding this important new prosumer audience, it is possible to paint a thorough picture of how political communication continues developing online as the conditions and limitations under which it grows change almost by the day. This book aims to continue working towards this goal of a heightened combined understanding by placing the principle of transdisciplinarity at its core.

NGOs

Almost every NGO has political goals and, in contrast to its proper name, relevance for government and politics in general. Like other forms of political communication, NGOs too have found a new working space online. They, however, are not commonly researched to the same extent and with the same methodologies that are applied to other artifacts of political communication, like campaign materials or news media. Since the trend for communication to move online has not passed NGOs by, and many of them actively utilize the World Wide Web for message relay and membership base organization, it makes sense to apply ICON to their online presence, too.

NGOs, much like politicians, face the task of presenting a platform or a cause and rallying social and financial support for it. Therefore, the comparison between campaign and NGO websites is expected to be particularly intriguing in terms of strategies and approaches to intersemiosis.

The first prominent NGO analyzed here is Freedom House. Founded in New York City in 1941, it has established itself as a steeple for research into media freedom and democracy globally, and its annual reports inform both scholarship and government. According to the organization's website, from its inception "Freedom House was notable for its bipartisan character. Its founders were a diverse group of prominent and influential Americans: journalists, business and labor leaders, academics, and former government officials" (FreedomHouse.org, 2012). The leadership of the NGO also reflects its goal towards inclusion and objectivity:

> The organization's Board of Trustees, which includes Democrats, Republicans and Independents, is composed of a mix of business and labor leaders, former senior government officials, scholars and journalists who agree that the promotion of democracy and human rights abroad is vital to America's interests abroad and to international peace. (FreedomHouse.org, 2012)

This information, as well as Freedom House's mission to spread democracy regardless of political alignments, promises discourse beyond party politics. The content focus of the sampled pages remains in North America, and all stories but one focus on the US in particular. It will be telling to map out the image-text relations in a political environment that goes beyond competition and political-party slant and, therefore, find hints towards a causal relationship between changes in function, which influence semantic structures.

Another influential organization's website that deserves scrutiny is Reporters Without Borders (originally *Reporters sans frontiers* or RSF in French). This NGO was founded in 1985 in Paris, France, and, alongside Freedom House, is the leading source of information on media freedom and journalistic practices around the world. In addition to reporting on the levels of press freedom around the world, RSF also takes an active position in defending journalistic rights and freedoms. Its US office is headed by a professional journalist, and at the core of its press freedom ratings are expert interviews with prominent media professionals from each country under scrutiny. This, together with its active citizen position, makes RSF an interesting counterpoint to the more neutral, descriptive approach of Freedom House. The multimodal semiotic patterns of the two organizations in comparison are likely to reflect these differing starting positions. This case study presents another opportunity to look into the nature of multimodal meaning making that nongovernmental political organizations utilize online. It also provides the first non-US example in this dissertation's sample, while it still focuses on US topics and the way RSF treats them.

The web presence of NGOs—and their PR work altogether, one might add—is not too far from the model of political campaigns. Just like politicians running for office, NGOs aim to persuade and to win over the support of as many users as possible by focusing on specific issues and presenting their cause as the right one. NGOs are also likely to be at the top of the online communication game since they have arguably more limited access to resources than campaigns or news organizations, and because the Internet offers the cheapest and widest-reaching communication platform nowadays. Therefore, financial resources aside, it is reasonable to assume similar levels of communicative sophistication between a politician's and an NGO's online presence. NGOs, however, are just as easily comparable to political news websites since they, too, present news stories that are relevant to their causes. Though as with political campaigns, NGOs' stakeholders and interests are more easily deducible and, therefore, their communication efforts are more prone to overt spinning. As a result of that, NGOs websites are more likely to display emotionally laden or otherwise suggestive visualization as opposed to neutral compositions, as well as more highly cohesive multimodal narratives in order to drive their persuasive points home.

The most common visual motif in NGO online visualizations is objects (61.54%), only then followed by people (30.77%). Of the subsample, 7.69% do not feature any visuals at all. This is a strange finding, given the main purpose of NGOs is to persuade, and since human depictions tend to have the most profound influence on attention and perception. Most such object visualizations involve the organization's logo accompanied by its name, like in the case of Freedom House, where other visualization is very scant. Other similar examples include computer-produced drawings (see examples below). To make the picture even drier, 46.15% of these visuals do not have a discernible secondary motif. In other words, the lone object is the sole image focus of the webpage almost half the time. Text-in-image is the other most common secondary motif with 38.46%, usually accompanying the NGO's logo or the odd drawing or photograph. In terms of genre, photographs account for 30.77% of the subsample, and drawings add another 23.08%. The most populous category is "miscellaneous," though, with 46.15%, and it consists exclusively of the Freedom House logo, which is often the sole visual in that NGO's webpages. This scant visualization goes against the initial expectations of full-on persuasion and visual gimmickry.

The same goes for the prevalence of neutral or cold colors (38.46% each) against 15.38% warm color schemes. While in the abundantly visual political campaign subsample the cool colors carry a message of determination and leadership, here they give the NGOs' web presence a touch of blandness and gravity. Whenever photographs are present, however, they do aim to influence. They are most often in close-up format (23.08%) and, thus, can create a more emotional bond with the viewer. One photograph is a medium shot (7.69%). The camera angles are level or low (15.38% each), creating a generally positive impression of the depicted person(s), framing them as either equal to the viewers or otherwise worthy of their attention or admiration. Still, these are rare instances since 100% of the NGO subsample is characterized as predominantly textual. Not a single webpage therein gives notable space to visuals. This may indicate a determination to deal with issues rather than with persuasion, and text is simply better suited to this task due to its unambiguous semantic organization. Nevertheless, NGOs leave a lot to be desired in the visualization department.

The visual neglect is even more evident when the relationships between the few visuals are examined. Visual nuclei are twice as likely to be dissociated as consociated (20% vs. 10%), while in the remaining 70% there is either a single main visual or none at all. Visual nuclear-satellite relations are harmonious in 11.11% of the cases when present but absent in 88.89% of all cases. Since visual satellites are often lone or absent altogether, their interrelationships are 100% "n/a." NGOs, just like any other communication entity in our sample, make use of the signaling principle and do so textually in 90.91% of the instances. The remaining 9.09% of instances describe a couple of cases of visual-verbal hyperlinking, which was much more common in the other subsamples discussed above. The orientation of the signaling is 100% external. This puts NGOs in the likely position of commentators and pundits of external information and might be one explanation of the austere multimodal designs they employ: While they handpick the visually rich general information from the outside, their in-house web content focuses on analyses and commentary, which are best realized in textual form. This hypothesis is pursued below.

In terms of multimodal narratives, NGOs achieve consonance 50% of the time and disjuncture 10% of the time, without any traces of dissonance. Given the scarcity of visuals, however, this is not too hard to achieve since the few and relatively simple images that the NGOs employ can easily find a place in the overarching narrative. Of all the pages, 50% employ spatial contiguity to this effect, and 30% rely on simple, uninterrupted text flow. There is no evidence of dual scripting in this subsample, which once again points towards the likely attempt at layout simplicity for the benefit of high-quality content. It does, however, raise important questions as to how relevant these two NGOs can hope to be in the increasingly complex and attention-grabbing multimodal environment, which the fast-paced technological developments on the World Wide Web have cultured.

FREEDOM HOUSE: NON-VISUAL TEXTS

Freedom House is, beyond any doubt, the least visual and the least visually appealing website in the sample. The first example we consider in this section illustrates this clearly. The only visual can be found in the organization's logo and represents a burning torch—a standing association to hope and freedom (e.g. the Statue of Liberty, the Enlightenment as a celebrated age in human development, etc.). The logo, therefore, qualifies as a visual with object as a main motif, accompanied by text-in-image. It is a miscellaneous visualization (logos are not part of the list), and it relies on a cold, navy-blue color scheme. This imbues the otherwise pedestrian webpage with a sense of professionalism and weight—the lone logo on a white line at the top left, completely isolated from the rest of the page's grey background and black text. Although it shuns elaborate design or visualization, Freedom House's website manages to concoct an air of authority and expertise. Behind this air, however, there is very little happening in terms of layout and intersemiosis. There are no additional visual nuclei and no satellites at all to check con- or dissociation in. The webpage is markedly textual, and so is the attention guidance, which mostly leads the reader to external links. Due to the lack of real visuals, we cannot speak of visual-text narratives proper, and the semantic organizational principle is simple text flow, which does not support any identifiable kind of intersemiosis.

Figure 6.1 "Damaging cuts to foreign operations . . ."—a typical webpage from the Freedom House website
(*source*: <www.freedomhouse.org/article/damaging-cuts-foreign-operations-budget-proposed-house-appropriations-committee>).
ICON codes: 113 – objects | 123 – text-in-image | 211 – photograph | 223 – NGO | 313 – cold | 329 – n/a | 339 – n/a | 342 – textual | 419 – n/a | 429 – n/a | 439 – n/a | 4412 – textual signaling | 452 – mostly external | 519 – n/a | 529 – n/a | 532 – no dual scripting.

The emphasis on dull, neutral, or cold colors combined with a clear focus on text seems to be the trademark of Freedom House's online presence. The example discussed above is representative of the NGO's overall multimodal style, as the pattern repeats. The only variable is the length of the article's text. Regardless of length, the text itself also usually follows a pattern of neatly separated, short paragraphs reminiscent of the news website style. The only deviation from this pattern is an article that mourns the passing of Congressman Donald Payne and features his mug shot. Apart from this short visual escapade, the article follows the exact same structure of the example above.

Overall, Freedom House seems to employ a light version of the news style: short, informative paragraphs, good amounts of external links, and a focus on specific, relatively simple issues. The verbosity of the campaign websites, for instance, is nowhere to be found here. A point of difference between Freedom House and most news websites, however, is the lack of internal attention guides, which are essential to effective news information relay. In the case of the NGO, such internal guides are not very necessary in the first place because article length is typically not an issue, and orientation in the few short paragraphs can be left to the mechanics of text flow itself. The external orientation of the hyperlinks, however, brings us back to a new term that was coined earlier in this book, namely hyper-nodality. While they are not engaging in complex intersemiosis, the Freedom House webpages always feature a fair amount of hyperlinks (an average of four links per page), which stand out even more in the austere layout and the short text. It is likely, therefore, that Freedom House's online communications team chose not to invest resources into developing complex multimodal web designs and rather to make the news section of the website a hub for digging out relevant stories, providing short insights into them, and assembling a few highly relevant links for further reading. This "freedom digest" is certainly an interesting take on modern-day online communication, and it also places Freedom House high on the hyper-nodality scale with little resource or expertise investment. This is a very good way for an NGO to establish a meaningful presence without overspending, since such organizations typically are strapped for liquid assets and best invest them elsewhere. Overall, while seeming dull and uninspired at first, Freedom House's website scores points in the realm of online political communication.

It is also important to remember that Freedom House's forte lies in country reports, which do feature considerably more visuals than the news section. This is another aspect of interest to such comparative analyses: When dealing with communicators whose financial means are limited, it is useful to consider all other communication outlets and forms they utilize and to get information or at least estimate the allocation of funds towards each one. Since the country reports are what make Freedom House a world leader in political and media rights research, it is also normal for other aspects of its communication to be further from the cutting edge.

RSF: REAL ISSUES AND COMPUTER-GENERATED VISUALS

Compared to its American "brother," the French-based Reporters Without Borders (henceforth RSF) offers a different multimodal style mix altogether. Some of the difference can be attributed to the two organizations' different natures and missions: Freedom House has the overarching goal of measuring and supporting democracy worldwide, while RSF has the more narrow focus on journalistic freedom and access to information. Mass media figure prominently in both organizations' practical work since they are the main channels though which citizens receive their political information and knowledge; these, in turn, are essential to the advancement of civil society and healthy democratic practices. Therefore, it is reasonable to expect Freedom House and RSF to cover a similar range of issues in their news sections. The difference, however, comes when we look at the people working for each of these NGOs. RSF's staff and contributors are mostly volunteers who are still practicing journalists in their respective countries. They are often the most outspoken and active members of their national journalist guilds. Unlike Freedom House, RSF does not support large headquarters or foreign offices; it merely relies on trusted volunteer contributors who provide their country insights, which are then systematized into the media freedom rankings that the NGO presents at regular intervals.

The differences in professionalization and expertise outlined above should have clear effects on the multimodal styles the two NGOs adopt. The prevalence of practicing journalists in RSF should result in a more news-like webpage design, since this is the most comfortable presentation style for most of the organization's contributors. Unlike Freedom House, RSF does not publish corporate-style country reports, and its website is the main source of information for interested users. This more news-oriented approach is evident in the first example below (Figure 6.2), which covers the executive order that Barack Obama signed on April 23, 2012, to sanction individuals and entities who enable the Iranian and Syrian governments to track down and hassle dissidents on the Web. The lead (and only) visual is a close-up shot of US President Obama with a big smile on his face. No secondary motifs can be identified. The photograph relies on a warm color scheme and level camera angle, which relate well to the president's bright smile. The webpage is overwhelmingly textual, and there are no inter-visual relationships for lack of more than one visual. Signaling is ubiquitous and takes a textual form. Hyperlinks are clearly separated from regular text via a bright magenta color, as opposed to the more traditional and widespread sky blue found in virtually all other examples so far. Like in the Freedom House's sample, the signaling is oriented mainly towards external websites as sources of relevant additional information.

Perhaps due to the major emphasis on text, the multimodal narrative is classified as disjunctive: the wide smile on President Obama's face does

112 *Findings from NGOs and Social Movements*

Figure 6.2 "US sanctions on Iranian and Syrian entities and individuals . . ."—RSF news story

(*segment; source:* <http://en.rsf.org/united-states-us-sanctions-on-iran-syria-for-26-04-2012,42380.html>).

ICON codes: 111 – persons | 129 – n/a | 211 – photograph | 223 – NGO | 311 – warm | 321 – close-up | 332 – level | 342 – textual | 419 – n/a | 429 – n/a | 439 – n/a | 4412 – textual signaling | 452 – mostly external | 513 – disjunctive | 522 – split attention | 532 – no dual scripting.

not correspond with the content of the article. The multiple text references to him ascertain there is no visual-verbal dissonance; however, contentwise the two modes do not send a uniform message. A happy face does not relate to censorship and international sanctions. For this reason, the spatial semantic relations here are coded as "split-attention." The photograph of Barack Obama is a separate meaning-carrying element in the page's construction, and it is hard to place it in direct relation to any one part of the text. The third paragraph may be a good candidate for a close multimodal knot: The text provides a direct quote from the US president. Still, the distance between the two meaning-bearing elements and the unsynchronized visual and verbal expressions make a strong case for a split-attention design. By that token, there is no dual scripting here, either. This page is a good example of RSF's pseudo-news multimodal design: The page's layout is very evocative of classic news website designs like CNN's or the BBC's. The dominant red-white-black color scheme reinforces this impression, as do the series of visual-verbal links in the column to the right of the main text. On the other hand, the yellow "Donate" button, prominently placed on the top right, recalls the two campaign websites' content distribution. Still, the main inspiration behind the RSF webpage here definitely stems from online news. The differences, however, come at the level of semantic organization. In the case of RSF, the visual content is much scarcer, and it does not coexist in close physical or meaningful proximity with the rest of the page.

The other example page coming from RSF deals with protesting a bill that invades users' online privacy. It is presented in Figure 6.3 and takes on a very

Figure 6.3 "Internet advocacy coalition announces . . ."—RSF news story (*segment*; *source*: <http://en.rsf.org/etats-unis-internet-advocacy-coalition-16-04-2012,42283.html>).

ICON codes: 113 – objects I 129 – n/a I 212 – drawing I 223 – NGO I 312 – neutral I 329 – n/a I 339 – n/a I 342 – textual I 419 – n/a I 429 – n/a I 439 – n/a I 4412 – textual signaling I 452 – mostly external I 511 – consonant I 521 – spatial contiguity I 532 – no dual scripting.

114   *Findings from NGOs and Social Movements*

similar format, only this time the small lead photograph is substituted for a computer-generated image.

The structure of the webpage is identical to the one described above, with the exception of the lead visual: Instead of a photograph, it is a drawing of a computer mouse hooked up to the Earth's globe. This connection is interrupted halfway by the well-known red "No Entry" traffic sign. Apart from it, the whole composition is in shades of grey. This makes the overall color scheme of the visual neutral. Unlike in the example above, however, the multimodal narrative is consonant. The "No Entry" sign appears halfway through the connection between the mouse (a metonymy for a computer) and the globe (a symbolic representation of the World Wide Web), just like the controversial monitoring and surveillance system is to always stand between users and their web content, collecting information from both ends of the dyad. The description of this invasive surveillance system appears in the opening paragraph, up close to the visual. Together with the appropriate use of internal textual signaling further down in the text, this makes up a classic spatial contiguity page design. There is no evidence of dual scripting, however. Despite the subtle differences between the two pages, they follow the same general format and are truly representative of the RSF sample overall.

COMMENTARIES ON OUTSOURCED CONTENT

While the two NGO websites employ different organizational and content-generational principles, they do share one important function: providing commentary. Their news sections do not follow the traditional approach of factual reporting with pertinent visualization and focusing on hard facts. Rather, each of the organizations takes up comparatively simple events (e.g. specific bills, isolated political events, activities of public figures who are somehow related or important to the organization, etc.) and provides its own commentary thereof. There is usually ample external signaling to take the readers to the information source, which then takes care of providing the facts. What the two NGOs publish is a glimpse of the facts with their own spin and interpretation. In this sense, the NGO subsample is reminiscent of what we usually associate with political campaigns, namely selective content publication and commentary geared towards a specific agenda. Although they share this general approach and a dedication to political and media freedoms, the two organizations go about their tasks in rather different communicative ways.

Freedom House makes it a point to rely on almost exclusively monomodal layouts. The austere layout, where the NGO's logo is usually the sole visual element, firmly lays the emphasis on the text. In this, it is vaguely reminiscent of Mitt Romney's exhaustive policy clarification pages. However, because Freedom House rarely goes to great lengths in its news, there is no need for extensive internal and external signaling to keep the reader interested. The text is usually separated into short, neat paragraphs, which also enhances readability. The persuasive power is fully invested into verbal constructs, such as the use of globally recognizable phrases, loaded with clear positive or negative valence (e.g. "difficult budget," "universal values," "human rights," "strong democratic institutions"). There is only one example of a multimodal design in the sample, and it only reaffirms that Freedom House has opted out of using visuals for anything more than mere illustration. Keeping in mind the size, reach, and importance of this NGO, it is reasonable to assume that it can afford any level of web design sophistication, and the multimodal frugality it displays in its news section is intentional. It is meant to redirect reader attention to Freedom House's forte, namely the country and regional reports it publishes annually, which present the hard facts about political and media freedom in the world, also multimodally.

The articles in the news section, therefore, are carefully handpicked to reflect specific developments, separated by world region, which are relevant for the general country reports. For instance, the various acts and bills that the House of Representatives discusses or passes have direct implications on the degree of government control and intervention into domestic and foreign activities on the political and media scene. As such, they affect the rankings and conclusions of the country reports. The news section of the Freedom House website is, therefore, a kind of appendix to the detailed reports and follows current developments, presenting the NGO's stance on them and, thus, hinting at how these developments affect the analyses and conclusions in the most recent country reports. Since this involves argumentation and clear formulation, visuals are generally shunned in favor of a simple, clear text-flow design.

On the other hand, RSF invests more into its multimodal web design. While it also selects news stories with direct relevance to its operations and provides in-depth commentary on specific issues, this NGO does not publish the elaborate country reports of its counterpart. It rather has a general overview of press freedom in the world along with a number of regional reports, which do not come out according to a schedule but more in a crisis-response fashion. The most recent "mission reports," as the organization calls them, deal either with countries or regions where press freedom is currently being trampled (e.g. South Sudan, Colombia, Russia), or with global issues (e.g. online surveillance). Similar topics resurface in RSF's news section as well, building the same kind of bond between formal reports and news and commentary, as in the case of Freedom House.

The implementation of the similar concept is, however, different. As a smaller organization with arguably smaller reach, RSF invests more into creating a vibrant online presence. It features a page layout that many of the sites in the news sample employ, down to the color scheme. This is likely a move towards additional credibility and influence—mimicking serious news outlets' visual style builds an almost direct association to their professional

116 *Findings from NGOs and Social Movements*

weight. The move towards a richer online presence also reflects the desire of the RSF to stay on top of current trends. While Freedom House relies on its traditional clout, RSF aims to establish itself more aggressively by following recent trends in web design and online communication. It manages to do so without sacrificing message clarity or substance as well. The visuals it employs are mostly well-related to the accompanying text, even if exceptions do occur. Although RSF follows the general news layout with a lead image and longer textual elaboration, the images are never leading semantic elements but, rather, illustrations with little meaningful contribution. This, too, reflects a strategy of economizing on online communication efforts in favor of professional reports, which are available for download and immediate consumption. Although it employs a much livelier layout and a more professional-looking design, RSF follows a similar highlighting strategy, which guides the user multimodally to the organization's main efforts.

The NGOs provide one of the most consistent subsamples in terms of semantic function. Their news sections serve the explicit purpose of highlighting content that is meaningful for the information in the country reports they publish. This subsample also illustrates how different multimodal structures can still serve one and the same function.

CITIZEN WEBSITES

The previous case studies cater to the professional side of political communication, which is also traditionally much better researched than any other political media genre. The extensive discussions on framing, political parallelism, and external influence that traditional media often display and, some might say, suffer from make it even more pertinent to look at non-profit, independent, and non-professional media products and to compare how they structure their messages and get their meanings across multimodally. This is an opportunity to check for the influence of communication sources and aims in the final media product and to test whether the novel annotation scheme ICON is useful for differentiating between media outlets based on these general authorship criteria. As examples, the dissertation focuses on the Occupy Wall Street movement and its online presence's evolution from the "We Are the 99 Percent" blog-like webpage. On it, individuals would post their stories of hardship and protest in words and pictures; then the slicker, dedicated website titled "Occupy Wall St" came long. Its mission is to provide information on the movement's pan-American network and to filter through the everyday information flow for relevant material to its users.

This is the place where prosumption makes an empirical appearance in this book, and a direct comparison between professionally produced and amateur/semi-professional online content becomes possible. By following the development from a typical blog interface to a dedicated website, the changes that take place during this "professionalization" and identity formation become apparent. There is little need for an elaborate content filter since all items here directly refer to the US. Therefore, simply the most recent stories at the time of data collection appear in the sample. All of them present a rather unique example in the genre of political persuasion. This field is normally characterized by high levels of professionalism and painstaking research and information design, while here we deal with the product of prosumption. As such, the citizen website subsample is especially relevant in direct juxtaposition to the political campaign subsample, since both aim to mobilize and persuade. The vast differences in available resources are likely to make a big difference in message design, production values, and implementation.

The websites dedicated to the Occupy! movement go one step further away from the standard actors behind political communication. Unlike the other examples already covered, these citizen-built, prosumer works do not have the backing of abundant finances and the expertise of professional communicators. They also do not have the luxury of a carefully designed agenda and polished messages, which are characteristic of high-grade PR. The Occupy movement and its predecessor, "We Are the 99 Percent," do try to persuade and make an emotional connection to the viewer; however, it is not expected of them to make a carefully crafted appeal. Rather, the focus here is on telling poignant individual stories in words and pictures and letting them do the persuading. A good amount of webpages in this subsample carry out the other important social movement function of the World Wide Web: community organization. As such, they list the details about events in specific locations and call to action, but all this happens without the sophisticated persuasion techniques. In a way, the Occupy movement is preaching to the choir. Therefore, the expectations are to have a more or less equal distribution of visual attention to persons and their stories and posters and other event materials. The emotionality is likely to be higher than in the other subsamples, and the sophistication of the multimodal narratives somewhat lower due to the assumed lower professionalism of the communicators.

As both websites represent a people's movement, it is expected that people are in the visual focus—this is so in 57.14% of cases, followed by objects, which account for the remaining 42.86% of cases. The objects in question are usually the main motifs of event posters, such as trees, books, or microphones. The only secondary motif is text-in-image (83.33%) or none at all. This reflects the simple communication pattern that the subsample tends to follow: plain images closely related to a textual message, the two elements meant to reinforce one another. It also reflects the pattern that the "We Are the 99 Percent" movement followed in its prime. All prosumers who joined the movement contributed self-portrait photographs in which they hold up sheets of paper, usually handwritten, telling the story of their battle with poverty and deprivation. It is notable that this visual mold does not spill over to the more professional-looking website of the Occupy Wall Street movement. More on that follows later on in this chapter.

In terms of material property, 50% of the visuals in this subsample are photographs, and 16.67% each are either drawings or miscellaneous. The latter are usually event ads and posters, which play an important role in promoting events and organizing the Occupy supporters in specific locales. Another 16.67% of the webpages do not feature any visualization; they are problem- and argument-oriented pieces from the official website of the movement. These visualizations come in mostly warm (42.86%) or neutral (28.57%) color schemes. Cold and gray scale account for 14.29% of cases each. This is the only subsample that utilizes warm colors to such an extent. This is a move, conscious or unconscious, to better relate to the audience, to create a positive emotional connection with the viewer by instilling a sense of kindness, which naturally comes with that color palette. This works well with the prevalence of long shots—also 42.86% of the sample. Depicting large crowds or landscapes in cold colors is more likely to create feelings of alienation or even hostility, while the warm color scheme emphasizes the connection between the crowds and the viewer. It is a cue that these people's battle is right, and it can become our own, too. Close-ups and medium shots account for 14.29% of cases each, making sure that the movement also gets associated with human faces and not just angry groups of people, regardless of the warm colors. Level camera angles dominate (42.86%), along with an unusually high incidence of high angles (28.57%), which is best explained by the visual subject matter here. The focus of the movement are people in difficult financial circumstances; therefore, the high camera angle emphasizes visually how down on their luck they are and contributes to the feelings of sympathy and pity in the audience's eyes. The "We are the 99 Percent" webpage is the only predominantly visual one in the sample (counts for 16.67%), while the rest of the pages are mostly textual (50%) or even in text and visuals (33.33%). This signifies a certain level of professionalism and a drive to make compelling arguments not only with emotional visuals but also with verbal lucidity.

The relationships between visual nuclei and between nuclei and satellites, when present, are uniformly consonant (20%), but most of the time there is a single visual, and no inter-visual relationships are possible (80%). Satellite-satellite relationships, in particular, do not appear at all. This is a visual frugality that speaks not only of the producers' possibly limited know-how but also of their purpose to make a simple message and offer a departure from the complex communication designs professional PR creates. Therefore, in this case the ideological aspect of the communication at hand dictates form and function to a large extent. Signaling takes the form of textual hyperlinks exclusively, also emphasizing a simple, no-flashiness approach. The orientation of the signaling is evenly distributed between external (50%) and mixed (50%).

The expectedly least professional subsample returns the highest levels of visual-verbal narrative consonance—83.33%, and not a single case of dissonant or disjunctive image-text relations. This is not too much of a surprise, nevertheless, given both the webpages' relative simplicity compared to the other subsamples as well as the lack of extensive PR experience and technical prowess. These constraints have the positive effect of facilitating straightforward narratives which hang together well without loose ends. This is also evident in the prevalent organizational principle of spatial contiguity (66.67%) as opposed to only 16.67% for split-attention designs. Dual scripting is evident in 33.33% of the cases, which again points towards the drive for maximum effectiveness while keeping things simple. This approach is evident in the first example, which focuses on page 1 of the "We Are the 99 Percent" blog-styled website from where the Occupy movement garnered momentum.

The webpage structure, unlike any of the previous examples, is based around visuals and not text this time. A series of user-generated photographs create the main column of meaning, and there is a smaller textual navigation column on the left-hand side. The photographs follow the same logic: a visual depiction of one or more persons accompanied by text that places the image in perspective. These photographs rely on neutral or warm color schemes, which help establish rapport with the viewer. The level or low camera angles do the same, evoking feelings of equality or of compassion, respectively. The distance is usually a close-up in the case of individual depictions or a long shot to emphasize the mass support of the movement. It is called the 99 Percent, after all, and it needs to appear online in its numbers.

The snapshot under scrutiny appears in Figure 6.4. The visual nuclei consociate: They all tell the story of deprivation, unhappiness, and dissatisfaction with the economic and social status quo in the United States. There are no visual satellites, which lends additional power to the nuclei. The signaling remains textual, as ever, and external. The most common attention guide takes aims to redirect readers to the official Occupy Wall Street website. The visual-text narrative is consonant, and it provides a great example of dual scripting: each visual adds another facet to the 99 Percent storyline, and the accompanying texts form natural bonds with their respective images. The top three images, which are shown in the figure above, also form an elaborate visual narrative on their own: The first one being an extreme close-up of a sheet of paper with only three fingertips visible to hint at the human presence in the photo, the second one featuring a young woman holding another piece of paper with another story, and the third one showing a mass protest accompanied by a third story. The visuals simulate a camera panning out, gradually taking in more and more content into its focus. This is also a (likely unintended) visual metaphor for the movement's own growth and reach at the time. This is how the supposedly least professionally backed political communication channel excels at building a strong, focused multimodal narrative with a clear message and effective realization.

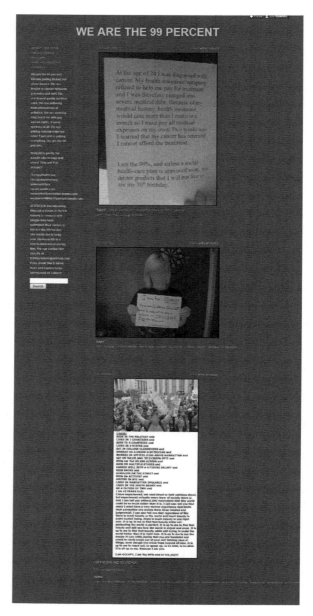

Figure 6.4 "We Are the 99 Percent"
(*segment; source:* <http://wearethe99percent.tumblr.com/>).

Typical ICON codes: 111 – persons | 123 – text-in-image | 211 – photograph | 224 – citizen | 311 – warm & 312 – neutral | 321 – close-up & 323 – long shot | 332 – level & 333 – high | 341 – visual | 411 – visual nuclei consociation | 429 – n/a | 439 – n/a | 4412 – textual signaling | 452 – mostly external | 511 – consonant | 521 – spatial contiguity | 531 – dual scripting. NB: Recognizable persons' faces have been blurred intentionally for privacy reasons.

Findings from NGOs and Social Movements 121

Another even more palpable manifestation of the development of Occupy Wall Street is the transition from the blog-styled online presence exemplified above to a much more professional-looking website explicitly dedicated to the movement. The first example (Figure 6.5) displays much more elaborate production values. It calls to action in support of the Cruz family, who are being evicted from their home after PNC Bank did not acknowledge an online payment on time and sent the Cruzes' house into foreclosure. The piece calls for a wide protest against the bank and goes on to document meticulously the ordeal of the family in the past few months.

The webpage features one visual nucleus, which leads into the story and shows a group of young protesters sitting on the porch of a house. The secondary motif is text-in-image: Two chunks of text in the top and bottom quarters of the visual summarize the Cruzes' ordeal and make the call to stand up against PNC Bank on June 21. The color scheme of the image is mostly cold despite the presence of numerous people. This helps make the gravity of the situation even more palpable and emphasizes the determination of the depicted protesters to see this through. The distance is long in order to capture as many people as possible; the composition, however, shows the row of protesters at different distances from the camera, since they all sit in a row. The people towards the end of the row gradually go out of focus, which enhances the feeling of a multitude of supporters for the cause. The camera angle is level to establish immediate rapport with the viewer. The ratio of images to text is mostly even, with the inclusion of the one visual satellite that appears further down into the article. It features of a photograph, supposedly of the same house where the protesters are pictured above, with a banner in front of it which reads, "Foreclosure Free Zone." The visual nucleus and satellite stand in consociation: The nucleus establishes the facts and the need for action, and the satellite presents the final goal, namely to make the Cruzes' property a foreclosure-free zone. Despite the visual richness of the page, most of the attention guides take on textual form, both within the main text and on the left-hand column. The signaling takes the reader to other pages, with the exception of a subheading in the main text, which introduces the backstory of the conflict between the family and the local bank.

The multimodal narrative is consonant: The visuals tell the story of the civil protest that has been taking place so far and also call to further action, which is also doubled in the text. Furthermore, the text clarifies the motivation behind what the visuals call for by relating the complete story of the conflict between the Cruzes and PNC Bank. The spatial semantic organization principle is that of spatial contiguity, although no dual scripting is evident. This example features a rather concise and effective instance of multimodal narration, one that relies on carefully designed and placed visuals that relate to the textual component organically and serve both an illustrative and a persuasive role. This, along with the prominent role that text plays in the visual semiosis here, echoes the dominant approach we saw in the campaign subsample and reasserts the main similarity between these two forms of political communication: the drive to mobilize the viewers into action.

122 *Findings from NGOs and Social Movements*

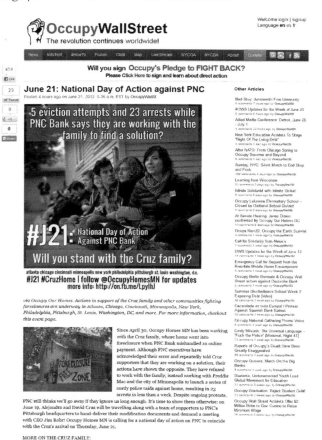

Figure 6.5 "June 21: National day of action against PNC"—Occupy Wall Street news story

(*segment; source:* <http://occupywallst.org/article/june-21-national-day-action-cruz-family/>).

ICON codes: 111 – persons | 123 – text-in-image | 211 – photograph | 224 – citizen | 313 – cold | 323 – long shot | 332 – level | 343 – even | 419 – n/a | 421 – visual nucleus-satellite consociation | 439 – n/a | 4412 – textual signaling | 452 – mostly external | 511 – consonant | 521 – spatial contiguity | 532 – no dual scripting.

Another such call appears in the following example (see Figure 6.6.). It calls New Yorkers to an event commemorating *Juneteenth*, the anniversary of abolishing slavery in the United States. It takes place in Bed Stuy, the site of the first free African-American community after the Emancipation, and it aims to put different local communities together in an attempt to fight the remnants of slavery and racial segregation, which the event organizers are still able to detect. The lead visual is a poster that relates the story of Bed

Findings from NGOs and Social Movements 123

Figure 6.6 "Bed-Stuy: Juneteenth Free University"—news story from Occupy Wall Street
(*segment; source:* <http://occupywallst.org/article/bed-stuy-juneteenth-free-university/>).
ICON codes: 113 – objects | 123 – text-in-image | 212 – drawing | 224 – citizen | 314 – grayscale | 329 – n/a | 339 – n/a | 343 – even | 419 – n/a | 429 – n/a | 439 – n/a | 4412 – textual signaling | 453 – mostly mixed | 511 – consonant | 521 – spatial contiguity | 532 – no dual scripting.

Stuy as an African-American community in the NYC area and presents the mission of the event to be an educational and entertainment opportunity directed mainly at local residents. The visual focus is on a large tree growing out of an open book. This composition is ripe with symbolism: The book alludes to knowledge, wisdom, and understanding, and the tree it supports is likely a synecdoche for the strong and united community, which naturally grows out of these virtues.

While the text in the image is the main secondary motif, the stylized human silhouettes holding balloons and kites—clearly county fair goers—are an important visual detail that adds to the community message of the poster. The genre of the visual nucleus is a drawing in black and white. It is a fitting realization since the article refers to the abolition of slavery, which happened 150 years ago; therefore, the old-fashioned visual style matches the starting point of the narrative. The "community tree" and the happy fair goers are supported by the textual component of the image, and they all congeal into an invitation to a community-building event celebrating the Emancipation and continuing its mission of integration and mutual learning. This elaborate poster is the only visual on the page, so no visual relationships are discernible here. It is quite prominent, so it drives the image-text ratio to about even. The signaling is textual, as usual, but in this case many of the attention guides are meant for internal rather than external navigation. There are numerous phrases in bold, variable font sizes and types, which all aim to help the readers go through the page in an orderly fashion and with the right content emphases. There is also the usual selection of external links in the right-hand column.

The multimodal narrative here is consonant. The visual and its embedded text provide the back story of the Juneteenth event 150 years ago, and the main text below describes the motivation behind the 2012 event, to which the readers are cordially invited both as attendees and contributors. The page's organization is based on spatial contiguity: The historical overview happens at the top and is close to the old-fashioned visual illustration, and the reference to the present day follows logically after. There is no evidence for dual scripting, since the content is not anchored visually and semantically. Nevertheless, this is one more example of effective consonant multimodal narration. While one might argue that this is easily achieved in the Occupy Wall Street website's "less is more" design environment, the harmonious intersemiosis and simplicity of the communicative efforts here nevertheless deserve praise, and they likely account for at least some of the social movement's success and relevance in its heyday.

THE PROFESSIONAL NARRATION OF AMATEUR WEBSITES

The citizen website subsample brings a good deal of positive surprises. Granted, its narratives are by far the simplest, least multimedia-packed, and not too rich or extensive content-wise. Nevertheless, everything that does appear on the citizen webpages is, almost without exception, built on harmoniously coexisting multimodal relationships and features coherent intersemiosis. When other sources with supposedly more professional origins and wider access to costly tools and expertise opt out of multimodal designs altogether (e.g. Freedom House), this choice gains even more power and speaks louder than ever in favor of citizens' rapidly growing technological expertise.

The gratuitous use of images is the first major characteristic of the Occupy sample. There is only one article that lacks visualization, and most others have one or typically two images to accompany the textual content. What is more impressive, in the cases of multiple-image illustrations, a distinct visual narrative fleshes out of their sequential viewing. The Cruz article above is a prime example of that, first documenting the protest and then visualizing the goal of turning over the foreclosure on the family's home. Since the Occupy movement was never centrally organized, and the website merely serves as a hub for coordinating local action at best, it is safe to treat the individual news articles as products of prosumption, and this is an excellent sign of how far this phenomenon has gone in its short lifespan so far. Another example of effective visual narration is the "We Are the 99 Percent" webpage, which takes the form of a long photo series and where the stories are embedded into the visuals themselves. The panning-out effect of the leading photographs at the time of sampling works brilliantly to pinpoint the stories of individuals while visualizing the growing mass support as more and more stories add up and decry the unfair status quo. This "visual growth" is an impressive multimodal design feat, which no professional communicator in the sample attempted. Therefore, it speaks even more loudly in favor of non-standard, creative online political communication, at least in this particular case.

While the visual coherence is impressive, it is even more remarkable how well it ties with the textual components of the pages, too. While the "We Are the 99 Percent" visuals usually do not depict particular actions, their compositional aspects (camera angle and distance, color scheme, etc.) directly relate to the stories each picture presents via the embedded texts. Poor people cheated out of healthcare, employment, or even the roof over their heads appear in subdued lighting, at close range and from level or high camera angles—all conscious visual design choices to enhance the emotional dialogue with the viewer. As such, this webpage in particular represents the single most emotion-laden example in the whole sample analyzed here. Despite expectations to find more emotional charge and sway in campaign materials, for example, the prosumer source delivers it instead. It is also notable that this affective communication occurs without involving sophisticated techniques or strategies; rather, basic photographic skills and well-placed textual content blend together seamlessly into a powerful statement which speaks to heart and reason equally well. Occupy Wall St's website retains this quality of close multimodal spatial contiguity, but the visual emotional charge is toned down. However, the official website retains the visual simplicity which nevertheless builds powerful narratives. Even in the case of single visuals, like the Juneteenth poster considered above, the visualization technique is simple yet symbol laden and persuasive. The book and the tree at the core of the fair of black silhouettes in celebration carry a strong symbolic message, which finds its textual realization close by, thus forming a cohesive multimodal unit.

126 Findings from NGOs and Social Movements

The citizen website sample presents a rather unique entry into this analysis with its "less is more" approach towards intersemiosis. It demonstrates how a presumed lack of expertise or extensive technical and PR knowledge need not prevent public communicators from developing powerful multimodal messages which hit the nail on the head even without the latest tricks in web design. The sampled webpages also carry a subtle emotional charge, which is characteristic of communication "from the people to the people." It relies on shared conventions in interpersonal online communication, acquired by experience in social networking and sharing content for both friends and the general public. This is where the production values of the "We Are the 99 Percent" webpage come from, and through there they also seep through into the more professional-looking Occupy Wall St website. While the summary is not meant to be an "ode to prosumption," it is important to admit the phenomenon's strong influence and admirable function in situations of citizen and community organization.

THE SOCIAL POLITICAL COMPLEX

Diving into the less traditional sample of political communication content proves to be as equally revealing an endeavor as the previous chapter's focus. Amid the variety of emotions and expectations tied to the political Web, our first look at some concrete manifestations of citizen empowerment and nonpartisan social engagement yields a variety of exciting findings. They relate to both structure and function, as in the previous chapter, and point towards different trends in the phenomenon of "non-political" political communication online.

The biggest surprise in the analyses above has to do with the juxtaposition of perceived and actual levels of professionalization. NGOs, despite their expected higher levels of sophistication, display much more modest capabilities than social movements when it comes to multimodal message presentation. Social movements, on the other hand, bring in a positive surprise with a variety of visualizations and complex, lucid visual-verbal designs. Unlike the traditional political sample, which displayed case-by-case variations, here the representatives of the two genres put forth solid multimodal presences which do not display much inner variation. This is one side of the professionalization debate: While campaigns and news corporations have experienced communicators who can cover a larger playing field of multimodal presentations, citizens at different levels of social organization stick to more or less predefined communicative strategies and avoid variation, for fear of message dilution or miscommunication.

Another, positive, side of the professionalization gap has to do with the communicative functions that the social political webpages in the sample carry out. Here we find high levels of message clarity and discipline, supported by clear communication goals. The NGOs take on the role of information hubs and broadcasters rather than content generators. Their mostly minimalist information designs support this function well: Solid verbal argumentation with little visual support, followed by an external hyperlink to a relevant source of further information, is all it takes to fulfill the basic function of information relay. This approach also hints at the NGOs' target audiences, which mostly consist of already converted followers. Rather than persuasion, they need information and argumentation that they can then transform into action if need be. Social movements, on the other hand, take the persuasive road consistently and clearly. Their more complex multimodal designs are executed effectively with simple yet aptly designed visual-verbal narratives that often include emotional displays as well. The target audience here requires a direct call to action rather than just information presentation. In that, social movements are like political campaigns, and it is no wonder some of the examples in our sample share many multimodal characteristics.

The findings from the social political communication sample provide further evidence for the Internet's power to reshape traditional communicative habits. The wider variety of media affordances allows for new structures to evolve to the service of particular functions, be they persuasive, informative, or argumentative. As shown by the strict adherence to clear communicative strategies, less professional political communicators have the potential to carry out similarly effective and sophisticated message relay online, and this can largely be credited to the natural inclusiveness of the World Wide Web as a communication channel with low technological prerequisites and a steep learning curve. Overall, this chapter's findings provide reasons for reviving Internet optimism when it comes to the Web's game-changing potential, and further investigations should bolster this argument.

7 Moving Forward

Evolving Genres and Future Research Directions in Political Communication Online

Despite its relatively small size, the sample of online political communication documents at the heart of this book's empirical component deserves further breakdown by genre. The discussions in the previous sections demonstrate the different approaches each online outlet takes towards realizing instances of multimodal (or, at times, mono-modal) political communication. By going through the five ICON layers, each genre—and sometimes, each specific outlet—forms a distinct multimodal pattern. Before going in that direction, however, a discussion of some elemental and structural differences among the different sampled media is in order.

The positioning and the function of the visual(s) is one important token by which the sampled online communication genres can be differentiated. It is interesting to note that, overall, visuals are not as prominent as the "visual turn" (e.g. Griffin & Kagan, 1996) prophesizes, despite the ease of visual integration and publication on the Web nowadays. That does not mean visuals are scarce—quite the contrary—but rather that they get passive narrative roles more often than not. They illustrate, reinforce verbal points, and occasionally help guide readers' attention, but they are rarely the central meaning-bearers on the page. The only exception to this trend comes from the citizen website subsample, where images often form continuous narratives that are not subordinate to a textual story. This subsample is also the only one that uses photographs' emotional charge more extensively. Via a purposeful combination of production features, a subtle valence creeps into each of the protest visualizations and lends them additional resonance. This is a feat most commonly found in professional persuasive genres, such as political campaigns; in the current sample, however, these are much more subtle than usual and most often bet on neutral compositional values, thus placing the focus on the direct intended meaning rather than any emotional appeals.

Although not center stage most of the time, visuals have a clearly designated place in their respective narratives, where they participate in the meaning-making process harmoniously. Most multimodal texts are of uniformly consonant natures. The rare examples of disjunction come from the campaign sample where Mitt Romney's symbolic attention guides are bound to raise a few eyebrows. With only a few exceptions, therefore, visual-verbal relations are complementary, which shows a high standard of meaning creation that all genres in the sample seem to share. The NGOs present something of an exception in this regard, not because they do not integrate their different communication modes meaningfully but because oftentimes they simply shun images altogether. This example is particularly strong in the case of Freedom House, whose news section tends to rely on simple text flow rather than on any more elaborate multimodal composition approach. Reporters Without Borders, on the other hand, often does use visuals, but only to mirror passages in the text or to visually refer to actors who play a verbal role therein. So, these are cases of visual-verbal consonance because text and image overlap, but they do not make equal narrative contributions, and this differentiation should be taken into account.

When considering relationships between visuals, these are most commonly absent due to the visual scarcity outlined previously. One main visual is what many pages in the sample rely on. Still, there are positive examples. Political campaigns, particularly Barack Obama's, tend to feature more than one visual nucleus, and half the time these nuclei converge to form common narratives. This strengthens the narratives and imbues them with additional layers of meaning. The common incidence of photographs and data visualizations in this subsample also reinforces the factual weight of the statements in there. News websites, on the other hand, have the highest level of visual nucleus-satellite consociation, which echoes their characteristic of clustering similarly themed news together and providing exhaustive information on a given issue at the users' fingertips. Most often the consonant visual satellites also play the role of hyperlinks or video "play" buttons, that is, they trigger additional content intake and, hence, serve as information hubs within the space of the webpage.

The topic of hyperlinks and attention signaling is also important here since every single webpage in the sample relies on some form of signaling. Apart from the news example above, all signaling is textual or prevalently so and takes the reader to other webpages. This is an example of hypermodality at work, even though it is beyond the scope of this book to investigate the hypermodal narratives that this action spawns. The one exception from this trend comes from campaigns, where more than half of all signaling efforts are directed inwards, that is, they guide the reader through the page at hand rather than towards a different one. This has to do with a couple of general and case-specific characteristics. Overall, campaigns are a high-concentration communicative genre due to their ultimate purpose of persuasion. This requires nothing short of a stranglehold on reader attention, and internal signaling helps achieve that. Additionally, the internal signaling score is driven up by the Romney campaign in particular because of its high-density textual statements. Extended readings are a veritable pest when it comes to effective communication, but they are necessary in this case because Mitt Romney has no other way to present his policies but to theorize about their benefits textually. Therefore, a large amount of attention guiding is necessary to keep the reader moving through the important theses on each policy webpage—something like passing through literary checkpoints. This is an approach which most of the genres shun because they do not have to rely on such long texts and they tend to separate their pieces into neat little paragraphs rather than complex rhetorical statements.

Complexity—visual, verbal, or multimodal—is another point of comparison, and it relates directly to the spatial-semantic organization of content on the page. News websites are expectedly multilayered, but Barack Obama's website from the campaign sample is an unlikely addition to this group. Complex designs are unavoidable when it comes to providing high quality and quantity of information, but when one aims at persuasion, simplicity is the high road. Nevertheless, the campaign opts for a complex design, which it holds together via the extensive use of dual scripting—more than any other sampled website, in fact. This example truly illustrates the importance of semantic organizational principles and how they can compensate for mismatches between purpose and message form. Spatial contiguity is the norm for most websites, as it keeps most-similar content chunks together and eases. On the other end of the layout spectrum, news media afford themselves the highest levels of split attention designs, also unexpected for the genre with likely the most densely packed contents. Citizen websites, on the other hand, demonstrate the least amount of complexity while still sticking to the spatial contiguity principle more than half the time. The complex visual narratives and their clear embedding into the accompanying texts hint at dual scripting in a third of all citizen webpages, which is remarkably high for the least professional producers in the sample.

TYPOLOGIES OF MULTIMODAL POLITICAL COMMUNICATION ONLINE

The previous discussion provides a summary of the important multimodal traits of the different genres in the webpage sample and demonstrates the applicability and usefulness of ICON as a multimodal annotation tool. Since the purpose of this book is to explore both structures and functions of political communication online, here we systematize the findings of the ICON content analysis and provide a first typology of layouts and their accompanying functions. It is important to keep in mind these represent idealized types, and they are derived from a limited sample. Their purpose is not to identify general trends but to illustrate how ICON annotations can best be summarized. In that sense, they are valuable theoretical constructs that, along with ICON itself, welcome further application, testing, and development as more and more content gets filtered through them. The typology is not explicitly separated according to genre, because on several occasions during the discussion of results it became apparent that online political communication genres have not solidified yet, and often similarities across genres are greater than those within. Nevertheless, the genre-likely types are clearly marked, and the exceptions that apply are also discussed briefly. The names of the ideal types usually revolve around the visuals because of their empirically proven perceptual primacy. Of course, the discussions of each type consider all relevant semantic page elements.

Before going into the examples, there are a few points to keep in mind. The structural types do not consider every aspect of the ICON annotation scheme. This is so because some structural and meaning-bearing elements, such as visual motifs and production characteristics or nature and direction of attention guides, have already been discussed at length in the previous results chapters. The same goes for the prevalence of text over visuals in terms of crude space dedicated to each communication mode. Even though they are not considered at length during the structural discussions, they do appear prominently in the ensuing characterization of typical functions, which each page design takes on. Therefore, all meaningful page elements contribute to the overall type creation.

LEAD VISUAL NUCLEUS, WITH OR WITHOUT SATELLITES

This is by far the most common multimodal design in the sample. The headline and the visual either form a cohesive unit or are directly superimposed on each other. There is often a direct connection between the two, that is, the headline clarifies at least in part what can be seen in the lead visual. If this connection is not made explicit that early, the opening paragraph usually takes care of that. In these two cases, we are dealing with a spatial contiguity design—which is the most common one in the sample. More rarely, the content is organized in a split-attention fashion, and the lead visual finds its textual reference only later on. The satellites, if any, are not too far away from the main visual even though they are more likely to be dissociated from it than otherwise. They also tend to group together, which does not necessarily guarantee their semantic association. There are examples for both possibilities in our sample.

The most common function this structure carries out is to inform. The lead visual relates closely with a distinct paragraph or several paragraphs of the main text, and the two form a cohesive multimodal unit, which sheds light on an aspect of the story as is the spatial contiguity tradition. The lead visual serves mostly illustrative purposes but often can go beyond that and make more meaningful contributions to the narrative. This structure is typical of news websites due to its clarity and pliability. It is also used occasionally by the Romney campaign as well as by RSF, though in the latter case the visual nucleus is a rather superficial illustration most of the time. This is the simplest kind of multimodal design, and it stems from the print newspaper convention of having one photograph for attention grabbing and general topic orientation. This is why it is very common in the online sample as well.

MULTIPLE VISUAL NUCLEI, WITH OR WITHOUT SATELLITES

This design might seem similar to the first one, but the difference turns out to be crucial. All cases of multiple visual nuclei (usually between two and three) also feature dual scripting. This is a good illustration of the power visuals wield in a multimodal page design. While one lead visual allows one to emphasize any aspect of the story and place the relevant blocks of text closer to the image, the stacking of several main visuals together demands a more sophisticated method of organization, in which the visuals play the role of semantic anchors. Again, the presence or absence of satellites does not play a major role in this complex meaning-making process. The visual nuclei may or may not create a distinct narrative on their own. Given the characteristic dual scripting, the natural content flow is guaranteed either way.

This Web structure is typical for persuasive communication genres or for specific webpages where opinion formation is at least as important as information relay. It finds its clearest manifestation in the Obama campaign's policy pages where multiple visual nuclei are interspersed among boxes of text, forming a cohesive persuasive narrative of the incumbent president's successes and aptitude when it comes to any matter of national security and prosperity. The same goes for the subtle but powerful narrative that the "We Are the 99 Percent" movement creates on its blog-like webpage. There, the series of photographs with embedded texts not only inform us of individuals' plights but also aim to make us realize we are not different from them and should spring into action against the broken status quo. Finally, the BBC also provides one such example even though persuasion is not among its overt goals. The article about Elaine Riddick and the forced sterilization campaign in North Carolina not only presents the information on the matter, but also creates a subtle but clear value judgment. It does so through the empathy-inducing photographs of Riddick, an outspoken victim of the illegal acts, which are placed in the direct vicinity of the verbal account of her suffering and her reaction to the news that the state Senate will not offer any monetary compensation in the end. This is also a rare display of emotional visualization, which finds a good home in the dual-scripting design because it is the only content organization scheme with enough clarity and power to restrain unwanted irrational appraisals.

NO VISUAL; TEXT-FLOW, WITH OR WITHOUT INTERNAL SIGNALING

In spite of the ever-lessening production constraints online, the monomodal text-flow design appears quite often in the sample. These articles rely exclusively on text flow for their organization; thus, we cannot speak of spatial contiguity or any other multimodal semantic organization principle. In a way, this design is a return to the print pamphlet style of political communication that was in vogue for a long time until the World Wide Web came about, and some early politician websites even tried to transfer it to the new medium, much to scholars' and citizens' dismay.

The text-only design is the trademark of Freedom House and the Romney campaign's specific policy pages, and it is used to comment and reason on specific issues. The NGO takes the simple text design to an extreme and applies no form of internal signaling whatsoever, merely stringing sentences and paragraphs together. The only deviation from simple text is the occasional hyperlink to the relevant country report at the end of the article or to the information source—usually a news website or another NGO. As discussed above, this has to do with Freedom House's resource allocation and mission rather than with a deliberate anti-visual agenda. For the purposes of analysis, commentary, and steering attention towards relevant news items found on other websites, the NGO is doing well. The Romney campaign, on the other hand, employs various internal signaling measures: from headlines, to bold or italicized text passages, to different font colors, all in an effort to mark the important points and keep the reader moving from checkpoint to checkpoint. The play with colors and the stylized icons on top of each policy page (e.g. calculator when discussing taxation) are the closest the Romney camp comes to displaying content intersemiotically. As discussed above, it is next to impossible for Mitt Romney to provide multimodal evidence of competence and achievement; therefore, the way forward is to argue and reason, and this is what the text-flow design does best.

DISTRIBUTION OF THE SAMPLE ACROSS THE THREE WEBPAGE TYPES

After having discussed the three types which emerged from the ICON content analyses, finding out how the sample distributes across them helps put the current research into perspective.

The most prevalent design, covering exactly half of the whole sample, is the lead visual nucleus, whose main purpose is to inform. This is partially due to the news-media bias of the sample, but this is far from the only cause. Within the sampling period, every single genre of political communication utilizes this design at least twice, and every single sampled medium at least once. The multiple visual nuclei design comes second with a 27% occurrence, and it reasserts the importance of persuasion for political communication of any genre. Text flow, characteristic for communication artifacts that focus on reasoning, covers the remaining 23% instances.

This distribution has its roots both in the nature of the sample (which is news heavy) but also in what could be a paradigm shift of political communication to persuade informatively rather than emotionally, at least when it comes to online settings. The ever-growing number of alternative news sources makes it easy to cross-check the habitual campaign exaggerations,

134 *Evolving Genres and Future Research*

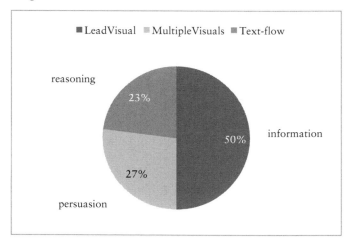

Figure 7.1 The distribution of the sample across the three typical structures and their respective functions.

conflations, and prevarications of all magnitudes. Users (i.e. audiences) are now prepared and able to check every claim and every news item in a matter of minutes. This and the 24-hour news cycle are game changers for the field of political communication online, and the response is to put information in the spotlight. Some support for this claim comes from the summary report on misleading argumentation in the 2012 election, compiled by FactCheck.org (Robertson, 2012), a major agent for truth in campaigning on the national and local level. The "Whoppers of 2012," or biggest lies the Obama and Romney campaigns propagated, come from television ads, televised debates, and campaign speeches exclusively. Not a single contentious statement originated in online form. This is not to say the misleading information from other media did not seep into each of the online campaigns—for example, TV content often finds its way into the video sections of the election websites. Rather, the "information turn" points towards a new production ethic when it comes to exclusively online content for campaigns, and also for NGOs and social movements that face similar vetting criteria, though they enjoy much less public attention at this point.

The ubiquity of multiple-visual designs in the more persuasive portion of the sample is hardly surprising. It is much more crucial to note how it ties with the discussion of information values above. Digging deeper into the Obama pages, which are by far the most visual and intricately designed in terms of meaning generation, one finds the core value of informative and much less emotional persuasion than is characteristic for US campaigning (e.g. Brader, 2005; 2006). The same cannot be said of the photo streams from the We Are the 99 Percent movement, which employ multiple visuals with the explicit goal of stirring emotions through candid and touching narratives. The different approaches evident in these otherwise similar multimodal patterns confirm the flexibility that visual and layout variations inject into communication designs.

Text flow also makes a prominent appearance in an otherwise persuasion-heavy genre: Mitt Romney's specific policy positions come without any visual aids, be it illustrations, attention guides, or significant narrative contributions. In this austere design, which is not very characteristic of the World Wide Web's palette of layout options, the information distortion patterns from other media formats resurface. For instance, the Romney policy page on health care contains the claim that the Obama administration is financing the Affordable Health Care Act by "gutting" another program, Medicare, and redirecting almost a trillion US dollars from it into the new project (Robertson lists this as one of the big whoppers of the 2012 election). Although making this claim a campaign steeple when it comes to health care debates definitely was a concerted strategic decision, it is telling that the deviation from truthful persuasion consistently employs multimodal designs, which are uncharacteristic of the genre of online political communication at hand. This hints at a possible profound connection between structures and functions, between information design and content.

These structure-functional typologies transcend the original notions of genre, according to which the webpage sample got subdivided. This in itself is another contribution of the ICON analysis: By painting a comprehensive semantic picture, it paves the way for novel multimodal content orchestrations to become stable genres in their own right. The pilot test already hints at the viability of inductive genre development as well as differentiation within established and confirmed genres according to specific communicative goals and functions. Given sufficient empirical backing, we may soon see the birth of the Obama-style vs. Romney-style of online campaigning, based on the different kinds of mono- or multimodal persuasion a candidate employs. Working with ICON also captures the fluidity and flexibility of the World Wide Web as a communications platform, and this is another good starting point for the definition of the medium's new genre structures and functions.

CONCLUSIONS

The findings in this book point towards a growing body of diverse multimodal designs. The structural diversity, in turn, necessitates growing levels of sophistication and expertise when it comes to marrying design with strategy and function. Being exploratory and preliminary, this book casts a wide net across different instances of political communication in an attempt to both present some preliminary multimodal characteristics they employ and to test a newly developed annotation tool. In doing so, it asks four specific research questions. The empirical portion of this book provides the bulk of their answers. This section systematizes the findings in the context of the research

136 *Evolving Genres and Future Research*

questions, considers the limitations of the study design, and outlines some crucial avenues for further multimodal research in political communication.

SUMMARY OF FINDINGS

The first question was *How do the different communication modes (visual and verbal) interact in the multimodal documents examined?* The answer to this question is mostly contained in Layer 5 of ICON. As discussed previously, in 73% of all cases the two communication modes formed a harmonious, uniform relationship in terms of meaning generation. The incidence of dissonant image-text relations was the lowest (3.85%), and in a few cases there was no discernible interaction between visual and textual elements (11.54%). This outlines a trend towards multimodal cooperation and harmonious orchestration that crosses genre boundaries in online political communication. Since we are addressing a *how* question here, it is also helpful to consider the hierarchical relations between the different communication modes. In Layer 3, the visual-verbal ratio was computed and indicated text's supremacy, with over 71% of the webpages dedicating considerably more space to verbal content. This finding may point towards some path dependency: Although visuals are on the rise and canvas constraints online play a diminishing role in information design, image material rarely receives a lead role and is more often used as illustration and reiteration of verbal points. This is also evident in the findings in Layer 4, where most commonly there is a single visual nucleus, and it is dissociated from the visual satellites, if any. In other words, visual narratives are still scarce. Nevertheless, when they are present, they tend to be consistent and, thus, support the observation of a trend towards consonant information design, within and across communication modes. Hence, a clear semantically uniform structure is at the core of most sampled webpages, and the functions visuals and texts carry out in it are complementary, with visuals taking a secondary role in the meaning-construction process more often than not.

The second question was *How do the different communication modes relate to meaning-construction patterns of the content?* The answer is spread around all five ICON layers, since each mode makes a contribution to meaning production. The visual characteristics that the first few analytical layers cover paint a picture of a move towards realistic and truthful reporting, with a people focus and textual or action accompaniment. The realization of the visuals is in mostly neutral colors and even angles and distances. Complex visual narratives are mostly rare, taking a step back into illustrative roles while the text creates the story. Barack Obama's policy pages are a notable exception, where visuals and layout are instrumental to creating the narrative, but this is more an exception that proves the rule than anything else at this point in the analyses. There is a clear direction towards harmonious semantic relationships, both among visual nuclei (when multiple ones are present) and between images and text. This is also reflected in the predominantly contiguous placement of similarly themed elements from different modes—what is referred to here as "spatial contiguity." Therefore, the answer to the second question ties in with the findings from the first one, and it confirms the structural patterns found in the sample. The hierarchical relationships between the two communication modes also become apparent when considering the typologies outlined previously.

The third question was *How do political websites contextualize their content visually and verbally?* The answer lies in ICON's Layer 5 classifications of information design patterns. The clearest way to explore contextualization in this case is to look at the ways content is organized in the sampled webpages. Of all the webpages, 65% of them employ the organizational principle of spatial contiguity, which means most multimodal pages placed visual and verbal content in meaningful contexts, that is, context enhanced rather than diluted the message and did not create potential confusion. Split-attention designs, which keep contextually linked multimodal elements apart in the page layout, appeared rarely (19.23% of the whole sample), which signals that the prevalence of spatial contiguity is very likely to be the intentional application of a principle for semantic clarity. This is also a reflection of the most important functions of the political communication items sampled here, namely to inform, to persuade, or both. The content organization illustrates the merging of structure and function to a degree, where the structure actively supports the embedded function, and the function necessitates certain structures—what was termed "semiotic affordance" before and was tied to genre characteristics in previous discussions (e.g. Kress, 2010). Affordances aside, this characteristic of many multimodal documents in the sample also speaks of a uniform information-design decision, of a careful orchestration of modes towards a distinct communicative goal in a good portion of the sample. Therefore, one of the major challenges of the prosumer era, namely the varying degrees of expertise and skill on both sides of the content, seems to be receding, as examples from multiple genres and multiple levels of expertise mostly conform to the standard of multimodal consonance.

The fourth and final research question asked was *Are there clearly identifiable medium- and genre-specific patterns of multimodal interaction?* Answering it involves looking across all five ICON layers and also keeping in mind the relationship between genre and semiotic affordance. The degree and the uniformity of difference between the four subgenres of online political communication is a good indicator of how unique these genres really are and whether it is worthwhile to consider them separately at all. In fact, the typologies speak of three distinct genres instead of four, and the separation is based on the structure-function complex to a large degree. The main genre, which is defined by the function to "inform," tends to feature a single visual nucleus, with or without satellites, consonant image-text relationships structured in spatial contiguity (and sometimes even in dual scripting), and reality-centered, even-tempered visualizations (i.e. mostly photographs with little emotion-inducing characteristics). This multimodal genre is mostly in the realm of online news, but political campaigns and NGOs also make use of it often enough to blur any clear boundaries.

The "persuasion" multimodal genre, which is mostly found in Barack Obama's campaign website and to a much lesser extent in Mitt Romney's, is a definite upgrade on the complexity of multimodal design. This one is also very visual, often involving multiple consociated visual nuclei that actively form a narrative to go along with the textual component of the webpage. Here photographs also dominate, but a notable amount of images are also computer-generated (icons, data visualizations, banners, etc.). The genre achieves persuasion through multimodal mutual support, that is, images and texts either directly repeat each other's messages, or their messages are closely linked and reinforce each other to make a stronger common point than each mode would formulate alone. In a departure from the habitually emotional campaign style of the past (e.g. Brader, 2005), these multimodal persuasive structures rely on information and on disciplined message repetition and elaboration rather than on affective formulation. Although it is most typical of the Obama campaign, the persuasion design also appears in some news media, like the BBC example considered at length above. Therefore, this design is not genre-specific, either.

The third and last distinct genre is dubbed "reasoning" and involves text exclusively. It is the design genre closest to being uniformly associated with a communication genre, as almost all NGO webpages and most of the Romney campaign webpages rely on it. Its defining characteristic is the absence of visuals in favor of purely verbal reasoning, mostly austere (in the case of Freedom House) but sometimes aided by color-coded headlines or other attention guides (in the case of Mitt Romney). It is an unexpected design decision to carry out persuasion via a single communication mode, and it occurs strictly in situations where new information needs to be presented and a logical case needs to be constructed. This holds true for Freedom House's announcements of rejected bills and how they hurt press freedom or international peace as well as for the Romney campaign's attacks on Barack Obama's policies and how they ought to be changed. Nevertheless, there is no perfect genre agreement here, either, and this completes the overall picture of *functional* rather than thematic genres in the sample. We, therefore, may not speak of solid online political communication genres according to definition, scope, or subject, but rather group media according to their multimodal structures and functions. This is another area where the ICON approach proves useful and necessary.

LIMITATIONS AND CHALLENGES STILL AHEAD

Being an initial, exploratory study, the empirical portion of this book is definitely not without its shortcomings. Keeping an active awareness of those shortcomings is essential in developing ICON further and finding wider applications for it in the future. This section serves as an overview of the challenges still ahead of multimodal research in political communication online and, thus, provides a summary of the third thematic component of this book's manifold goals.

The first and most obvious limitation is the small sample size. Although the study covers a reasonable variety of online political communication genres, it does not feature a large number of examples from each. Therefore, some of the findings outlined above might be due to the small amount of cases considered here. A related limitation pertains to the distribution within the sample: news websites form by far the most populous subsample, followed by political campaigns and then by an equal distribution of NGO and citizen movement websites. This skewed distribution should be taken into account particularly when talking about the overall coding results. When it comes to discussing variation within subsamples, the exploratory qualitative nature of the investigation allows for more telling conclusions. Nevertheless, all summaries and inferences are regarded as preliminary and subject to follow-up testing and approval. This is also the nature of the empirical investigation from the outset, but it bears repeating here as well.

Another limitation concerns the sampling period. As with any one-shot random study, there is a possibility that the events of the day shaped the content generation and presentation processes. Although most of the sampled websites, if not all, clearly aim at establishing a recognizable layout identity and display sufficient levels of design expertise and forethought to keep design discipline, the nature of the content can often dictate its presentation. For instance, breaking news can necessitate coverage, but no visual material is yet available, so news and commentary appear in text form only; or an NGO is short on staff capable of maintaining their Web presence, so the designs of the latest five articles are not typical of its established online identity. The scenarios are numerous and of varying plausibility, but the fact is that in order to draw reliable conclusions, multiple waves of data collection and analysis are a must, and at least one of those waves has to be purposefully placed in a time of crisis or a major event, which would provide excellent conditions for direct comparison of reporting and presentation styles among different websites. This would, naturally, exclude presidential campaign websites from the sample since the time of their activity is limited. Nevertheless, all other politically engaged website genres can keep their place in the sample and contribute material from different points in time, which can then be analyzed comparatively at deeper and more conclusive levels. Enlarging the sample will also take care of another problem, namely the ability to do only a basic statistical analysis. While different techniques exist for standardizing scores and running non-parametric tests on such small-N, skewed samples, the best way to reliably compare across different cases and to draw conclusions about significant similarities and differences is to collect a large enough pool of data.

A shortcoming that became apparent during the analyses of the two largest subsamples (news and campaign webpages) was the inability of the current research to fully analyze video material. On a number of occasions moving images were embedded into the multimodal document design. They were signified by the opening film frame and a standard "play" button on top of it, hinting at the multimedia character of the visual. In such cases the video still was treated as a visual nucleus and analyzed as a regular photograph. There are good reasons for this decision, both objective and argumentative, but a thorough multimodal analysis would have to consider video content in full. The inclusion of spoken narrative and other audio features will be of particular relevance and interest when it comes to characterizing each webpage's overall multimodal meaning creation strategies and structures.

The fact that all the theory building and the empirical analyses were carried out by a single researcher is also an obvious limitation. Although all analyses were done with great care and with carefully documented intra-rater reliability, this remains a study setup that is prone to bias. This is another reason that all analyses are exploratory and all conclusions are preliminary. Still, ICON promises to be a valuable resource for exploring image-text relations in page-based documents, both on- and off-line. A final limitation concerns the lack of a dedicated software application that would serve ICON's needs best. This is not a limitation of the research since the data were collected and analyzed successfully; it is more an observation that a better-suited software application could have saved much effort. The UAM Image Tool is a good application, but it is mostly an extension of the UAM Corpus Annotation Tool, which was originally designed for vast text passages. Therefore, it has a text-based working logic, and this makes applying some of the ICON layers to webpages difficult and cumbersome. The cases with a higher number of visuals were particularly daunting to code. Hence, the next step of ICON annotation would greatly benefit from a dedicated software application. This and all the other limitations mentioned above paint an accurate picture of a new method at the start of its development. They are meant both as constructive criticism and as words of caution when interpreting the preliminary findings.

OUTLOOK

The preliminary analyses illustrate ICON's applicability to studying image-text relations in online documents, with special attention to the visual component, unlike the model's SFL-centered multimodal predecessors. As some of the limitations suggest, the first follow-up application of ICON should involve a larger pool of data. The present exploratory study uncovered a set of preliminary characteristics common to several genres of online political communication as well as trends and approaches unique to each of them. The most natural extension of this research project is its repetition

Evolving Genres and Future Research   141

with a larger number of cases. This is also the best way to support and direct the theory-building effort of this book, and it will also clarify the typologies discussed above. One viable design would be to construct an artificial week over the course of two months, which brings randomization into the equation and paints a more accurate picture of each medium's multimodal strategy, and collect the five most recent stories from each weekday at a given hour. The hour itself might also change for each day. Since all websites in the current sample concern current events, they are dynamic enough to provide such a mass of content. Although the US presidential campaign is over, there are numerous other smaller-scale campaigns to follow. Alternatively, prominent politicians' personal websites can be included instead—also in support of the notion of the "permanent campaign" (e.g. Blumenthal, 1980). Such a follow-up study will help ICON congeal further and will provide more detailed and reliable typologies of image-text communication relations online.

Comparative designs are not the sole research avenue where ICON can make a contribution. It can also find application in the deep qualitative study of specific topics and media phenomena such as an online news medium coverage style of a particular topic of relevance. From covering conflict and war to internal political crises and scandals, ICON can act as an aid to or upgrade of traditional media framing research, which rarely is truly multimodal. Such an in-depth study would also entail the involvement of several researchers with linguistic and framing expertise. Given ICON's own multidisciplinary motivation and origins, this is a welcome addition. Such a study design would also allow tracing the evolution of an online medium's coverage of a certain topic, since accessible archives of old news going back at least five years are common nowadays. In this way, topical coverage of mass shootings, abortion rights, the war on terror, or any other subject can be traced and analyzed for presentation patterns, which then can provide insight into both the medium's ideological position on the issue and its likely influence on public opinion. Such an extended study can then also be made comparative by adding different media to the sample and uncovering their meaning structures.

Much was made of the presence and kinds of multimodal content designs, described and tested by Holsanova and colleagues (2008), among others. Roughly 85% of all webpages fit the characteristics of one of the most prominent print newspaper page designs. While informative, this does not negate the possibility that better-fitting, purely online multimodal designs do not exist. One promising direction for further research in this area is to replicate the original eye-tracking studies, which helped the currently used designs find precise definition, and this time use webpages as stimuli. This will be a definitive test for the viability of the existing models, and it is also likely to provide an answer regarding the roughly 15% of webpages which had a "miscellaneous" content structure. Such an analysis would also be well complemented by a series of expert interviews with webmasters who have worked on different websites that fall under our definition of political communication here. This double-sided approach will shed new light on this constantly evolving and relevant phenomenon of the 21st century globally connected society.

ON ICON's PLACE IN POLITICAL COMMUNICATION RESEARCH

Political communication as a research field is in a state of perpetual growth and development since it opened up to the Internet. The fluid dynamism of the World Wide Web is a blessing as well as a challenge for political media scholars. ICON is a natural reaction to that. It acknowledges the complexity of the analytical task by incorporating facets of different disciplines into its approach to multimodal document analysis. It does so in an environment where transdisciplinary work is still at a nascent stage, and many traditionalists still frown upon crossing scientific and methodological borders. Apart from its contribution to creating insights into political semiosis online, ICON's impact also stems from its hybrid nature. It provides a clear demonstration of the benefits of transdisciplinarity and creates a useful precedent for other similar approaches to evolve around specific research questions and goals.

Among the major novelties ICON brings to the table of communication research is the heightened awareness of genre as communicative as well as social action. This is one of the many synergetic benefits of the marriage between communication studies and linguistics this volume has presented. The notion of genre as a set of semiotic affordances is of tremendous help in the process of charting new scientific territories, and the Internet is arguably the widest field communication research has had to map to date. Embedding individual multimodal narratives in such a wider context, as ICON has shown here, increases the potential for telling insights and breaks the mold of traditional media analysis. Since genre structures and functions congeal based on insights from a much larger volume of data, genre mapping in political communication online is one very fruitful direction which can be pursued via ICON or similar multimodal annotation schemes.

ICON also contributes to greater understanding of modern-day political communication by pushing the limits of what we consider political. It incorporates social action online into its pilot test, and it maps out its communicative characteristics and scopes with the same precision it scrutinizes traditional channels for political communication. Moreover, it finds similarities across the multimodal expressions of traditional and social political communication. This breathes new life into the notion of language (and, by extension, communication in general) as social action based on shared norms and notions. It also poses the exciting task to political communication researchers to find out whether today's political prosumers are not taking up traditional political campaigning strategies and adapting them for their own social-political goals. This would also present an interesting case of media convergence taking a long leap, that is communicative strategies developed for TV and print political persuasion seeping through the online communication of social movements.

Such a "widened" view of media convergence has direct implications for how prosumption can be integrated into the analytical equation. The awareness of genre, context, and modal co-deployment that the ICON analyses demonstrate is an excellent starting point for characterizing the user-driven component of political communication online. Thanks to previous mono-modal research in the field, we have a good understanding of how "professional" political communicators create and display content. Chapter 5 also shed multimodal light on the subject. This allows us to create a timeline for the development of prosumer-generated content from its inception, assuming it started out with mimicry and is still evolving into a genre of its own. Some of the findings presented in Chapter 6 certainly point in the direction of borrowed strategies (e.g. NGOs' textual argumentation in line with the Romney campaign; social movements' persuasive designs reminiscent of the Democratic effort as well as the BBC's occasional emotional news reporting). Such trends merit the contextual embedding of communication studies and the further tracing and elaboration of genre development in political communication online.

Although it relies on principles, methods, and insights from different disciplines, ICON is still a construct designed for use in communication science. As such, it brings innovation not only to theory but also to methodology. The cross-pollination with systemic-functional linguistics is a particularly strong component here, and it will shine through even more in a large-N follow-up. As communication science—and visual communication in particular—has long struggled with a certain lack of unique methodologies, ICON makes a contribution to the expansion of the discipline's toolbox of reusable approaches. Just as the Internet is flexible, so is the annotation tool infinitely pliable. Layers can be amended, removed, or inserted to address more aspects of political communication online. With its adaptable nature, ICON represents a new generation of research tools, which is in pace with the constantly changing data source online that communication scientists have to handle. Its application and its founding principle are a solid contribution to the field in their own right: they aim to open up the way for more such flexible, effective, and quite possibly better analytical tools to develop.

Last but not least, this book is not alone in its aim to shed light on the Internet's role in political life. As part of the Routledge Series in Political Communication, it joins a rich tradition of encompassing volumes, each of which focuses on a specific aspect of politics' move online. Scullion, Gerodimos, Jackson, and Lilleker (2013) and Nixon, Rawal, and Mercea (2013) take a societal view, looking for the effects of online politics across different societies in a series of comparisons. Lees-Marshment, Rudd, and Stromback (2009) make the comparison global and scrutinize political parties' online activities in the context of different political systems. Gouliamos, Theocharous, and Newman (2013) as well as Kluver, Jankowski, Foot, and Schneider (2007) examine political marketing online from the vantage point of culture. Lilleker and Jackson (2011) compare elections in the US, the UK, France, and Germany and focus on the use of Web 2.0 tools for party and candidate branding. Loader and Mercea (2012) take the Web 2.0 focus further and focus entirely on social media applications and their growing impact on political participation and outcomes. This volume joins the group by offering a Web- and content-centered approach that is ready for application on a global scale. Its flexible nature makes it ready to accommodate the expertise and knowledge of previous scholarship, and it can be embedded in the cultural, social, or systemic context of any of the above examples. As such, ICON is a natural next step in the study of political communication online, and it is one of many that the field will take in the direction of understanding and realizing the Internet's potential in this process.

Works Cited

Adamic, L., & Glance, N. (2005). The political blogosphere and the 2004 US election: Divided they blog. *Proceedings of the 3rd International Workshop on Link Discovery,* New York. 36–43.
Aday, S. (2010). Chasing the bad news: An analysis of 2005 Iraq and Afghanistan war coverage on NBC and Fox News Channel. *Journal of Communication, 60*(1), 144–164. doi: 10.1111/j.1460–2466.2009.01472.x
Alexander, B., & Levine, A. (2008). Web 2.0 storytelling: Emergence of a new genre. *EDUCAUSE Review, 43*(6), 40–48.
Ansolabehere, S., & Iyengar, S. (1997). *Going negative. How political advertisements shrink & polarize the electorate.* New York, NY: The Free Press.
Appelgren, E. (2004). Convergence and divergence in media: Different perspectives. *8th ICCC International Conference on Electronic Publishing,* Brasilia—DF, Brazil. 237–248.
Aronoff, M., & Reese-Miller, J. (2003). *The handbook of linguistics.* Malden, MA: Blackwell.
Baird-Olson, K. (2003). Colonization, cultural imperialism, and the social construction of American Indian mixed blood identity. In L. Winters & H. DeBose (Eds.), *New faces in a changing America: Multiracial identity in the 21st century* (pp. 194–221). Thousand Oaks, CA: Sage.
Baldry, A., & Thibault, P. J. (2006). *Multimodal transcription and text analysis.* London and New York: Equinox.
Barthes, R. (1964). Rhetoric of the image [Rhetorique de l'image]. *Communications, 4,* 40–51.
Bateman, J. (2007). Towards a *grande paradigmatique* of film: Christian Metz revisited. *Semiotica, 167*(1/4), 13–64.
Bateman, J. (2008). *Multimodality and genre: A foundation for the systematic analysis of multimodal documents.* New York, NY: Palgrave-Macmillan.
Bateman, J., Delin, J., & Henschel, R. (2002). A brief introduction to the GEM annotation schema for complex document layout. *Proceedings of the 2nd Workshop on NLP and XML (NLPXML-2002)—Post-Conference Workshop on the 19th International Conference on Computational Linguistics (COLING-2002).* Taipei, Taiwan. 13–20.
Bateman, J., Delin, J., & Henschel, R. (2004). Multimodality and empiricism: Preparing for a corpus-based approach to the study of multimodal meaning-making. In E. Venola, C. Charles, & M. Kaltenbacher (Eds.), *Perspectives on multimodality* (pp. 65–87). Amsterdam, the Netherlands: John Benjamins.
Bell, P. (2001). Content analysis of visual images. In T. van Leeuwen, & C. Jewitt (Eds.), *Handbook of visual analysis* (pp. 10–34). London: Sage.

Works Cited

Bennett, W. L., & Livingston, S. (2003). Editors' introduction: A semi-independent press; Government control and journalistic autonomy in the political construction of news. *Political Communication, 20*(4), 359.

Benson, R. (2006). News media as a "journalistic field": What Bourdieu adds to new institutionalism, and vice versa. *Political Communication, 23*(2), 187.

Berger, G. (2009). How the internet impacts on international news. *International Communication Gazette, 71*(5), 355–371. doi: 10.1177/1748048509104977

Best, S. J., & Krueger, B. S. (2005). Analyzing the representativeness of internet political participation. *Political Behavior, 27*(2), 183–216.

Bianco, J. S. (2009). Social networking and cloud computing: Precarious affordances for the "prosumer". *Women's Studies Quarterly, 37*(1/2, Technologies), 303–312.

Biber, D., Conrad, S., & Reppen, R. (1998). *Corpus linguistics. Investigating language structure and use.* Cambridge, UK: Cambridge University Press.

Blackwood, R. (1983). The content of news photos: Roles portrayed by men and women. *Journalism Quarterly, 60,* 710–714.

Blumenthal, S. (1980). *The permanent campaign.* Boston, MA: Beacon Press.

Boczkowski, P. J., & de Santos, M. (2007). When more media equals less news: Patterns of content homogenization in Argentina's leading print and online newspapers. *Political Communication, 24*(2), 167.

Boyatzis, R. (1998). *Transforming qualitative information: Thematic analysis and code development.* Thousand Oaks, CA: Sage.

Boyd-Barrett, O. (1998). Media imperialism reformulated. In D. Thussu (Ed.), *Electronic empires: Global media and local resistance* (pp. 157–176). London, UK: Arnold.

Braden, R., & Hortin, J. (1982). Identifying the theoretical foundations of visual literacy. In R. Braden & A. Walker (Eds.), *Television and visual literacy* (pp. 169–179). Bloomington, IN: International Visual Literacy Association.

Brader, T. (2005). Striking a responsive chord: How political ads motivate and persuade voters by appealing to emotions. *American Journal of Political Science, 49*(2), 388–405.

Brader, T. (2006). *Campaigning for hearts and minds: How emotional appeals in political ads work.* Chicago, IL: University of Chicago Press.

Bruns, A. (2007). Produsage: Towards a broader framework for user-led content creation. *Creativity & Cognition, 6,* 1–7.

Bruns, A. (2008). *Blogs, Wikipedia, Second Life: From production to produsage.* New York, NY: Peter Lang.

Callaghan, K., & Schnell, F. (2001). Assessing the democratic debate: How the news media frame elite policy discourse. *Political Communication, 18*(2), 183.

Castells, M. (2000). *The rise of the network society.* San Francisco, CA: Wiley & Sons.

Castells, M. (Ed.). (2005). *The network society: A cross-cultural perspective.* Northampton, MA: Edward Elgar Pub.

Chmiel, A., Sienkiewicz, J., Thelwall, M., Paltoglou, G., Buckley, K., Kappas, A., & Holyst, J. A. (2011). Collective emotions online and their influence on community life. *Plos One, 6*(7), e22207. doi: 10.1371/journal.pone.0022207

Coleman, S. (2001). Online campaigning. *Parliamentary Affairs, 54*(4), 679–688. doi: 10.1093/parlij/54.4.679

Comor, E. (2011). Contextualizing and critiquing the fantastic prosumer: Power, alienation and hegemony. *Critical Sociology, 37*(3), 309–327. doi: 10.1177/0896920510378767

Cook, T., & Campbell, D. (1979). *Quasi-experimentation: Design and analysis for field settings.* Boston, MA: Houghton Mifflin.

Cooke, L. (2005). A visual convergence of print, television, and the internet: Charting 40 years of design change in news presentation. *New Media & Society, 7*(1), 22–46. doi: 10.1177/1461444805049141

Cooperstock, J. R. (2007). Human-computer interaction. *Wiley encyclopedia of computer science and engineering*. New York, NY: John Wiley & Sons, Inc. doi: 10.1002/9780470050118.ecse524

Corbin, J., & Strauss, A. (2007). *Basics of qualitative research: Techniques and procedures for developing grounded theory.* London, UK: Sage.

Costa, C., Antonucci, F., Pallottino, F., Aguzzi, J., Sun, D., & Menesatti, P. (2011). Shape analysis of agricultural products: A review of recent research advances and potential application to computer vision. *Food and Bioprocess Technology, 4,* 673–692. doi: 10.1007/s11947–011–0556–0

Curtiss, D. (1987). *Introduction to visual literacy.* Englewood Cliffs, NJ: Prentice Hall.

Daft, R., & Lengel, R. (1984). Information richness: A new approach to managerial behavior and organizational design. In L. Cummings & B. Staw (Eds.), *Research in organizational behavior 6* (pp. 191–233). Homewood, IL: JAI Press.

Dahl, R. (1990). *Democracy and its critics.* New Haven, CT: Yale University Press.

de Vries, J. (2008). Newspaper design as cultural change. *Visual Communication, 7*(1), 5–25. doi: 10.1177/1470357207084862

de Saussure, F. (1959 [1916]). *Course in general linguistics* (2nd ed.). London, UK: Peter Owen.

Denton, R., & Woodward, G. (1990). *Political communication in America.* New York, NY: Praeger.

Derks, D., Fischer, A. H., & Bos, A. E. R. (2008). The role of emotion in computer-mediated communication: A review. *Computers in Human Behavior, 24*(3), 766–785. doi: 10.1016/j.chb.2007.04.004

DiMaggio, P., Hargittai, E., Celeste, C., & Shafer, S. (2004). Digital inequality: From unequal access to differentiated use. In K. Neckman (Ed.), *Social inequality* (pp. 355–400). New York, NY: Russell Sage Foundation.

Djonov, E. (2007). Website hierarchy and the interaction between content organization, webpage and navigation design: A systemic functional hypermedia discourse analysis perspective. *Information Design Journal, 15*(2), 144–162.

Dondis, D. (1973). *A primer of visual literacy.* Cambridge, MA: MIT Press.

Druckman, J. N., Kifer, M. J., & Parkin, M. (Winter 2007). The technological development of congressional candidate web sites. *Social Science Computer Review, 25*(4), 425–442. doi: 10.1177/0894439307305623

Dubrovsky, V., Kiesler, S., & Sethna, B. (1991). The equalization phenomenon: Status effects in computer-mediated and face-to-face decision-making groups. *Human Computer Interaction, 6,* 119–146.

Endres, D., & Warnick, B. (2004). Text-based interactivity in candidate campaign web sites: A case study from the 2002 elections. *Western Journal of Communication, 68*(3), 322–342.

Entman, R. M. (1993). Framing: Toward clarification of a fractured paradigm. *Journal of Communication, 43*(4), 51–58. doi: 10.1111/j.1460–2466.1993.tb01304.x

Entman, R. M. (2006). Punctuating the homogeneity of institutionalized news: Abusing prisoners at Abu Ghraib versus killing civilians at Fallujah. *Political Communication, 23*(2), 215.

Fahmy, S. (2004). Picturing Afghan women: A content analysis of AP wire photographs during the Taliban regime and after the fall of the Taliban regime. *Gazette, 66*(2), 91–112.

Fahmy, S., & Kim, D. (2008). Picturing the Iraq War: Constructing the image of war in the British and US press. *International Communication Gazette, 70,* 443–462.

Farnsworth, S. J., & Owen, D. (2004). Internet use and the 2000 presidential election. *Electoral Studies, 23*(3), 415–429. doi: 10.1016/S0261–3794(03)00029–5

Foot, K. A., & Schneider, S. M. (2002). Online action in Campaign 2000: An exploratory analysis of the U.S. political web sphere. *Journal of Broadcasting & Electronic Media, 46*(2), 222.

Galtung, J., & Ruge, H. (1965). The structure of foreign news: The presentation of the congo, cuba, and cyprus crises in four Norwegian newspapers. *Journal of Peace Research, 2*, 64–91.

Garcia, A. C., Standlee, A. I., Bechkoff, J., & Yan Cui. (2009). Ethnographic approaches to the internet and computer-mediated communication. *Journal of Contemporary Ethnography, 38*(1), 52–84. doi: 10.1177/0891241607310839

Gerbaudo, P. (2012). *Tweets and the streets. Social media and contemporary activism*. London: Pluto Press.

Gibson, R. K., Lusoli, W., & Ward, S. (2005). Online participation in the UK: Testing a 'contextualised' model of internet effects. *British Journal of Politics & International Relations, 7*(4), 561–583. doi: 10.1111/j.1467–856X.2005.00209.x

Gibson, R., & Römmele, A. (2001). Changing campaign communications: A party-centered theory of professionalized campaigning. *The Harvard International Journal of Press/Politics, 6*(4), 31–43. doi: 10.1177/108118001129172323

Goffman, E. (1974). *Framing analysis*. New York, NY: Free Press.

Gouliamos, K., Theocharous, A., & Newman, B. (Eds.) (2013). *Political marketing: Strategic 'campaign culture'*. New York, NY: Routledge.

Green, D., & Gerber, A. (2008). *Get out the vote: How to increase voter turnout* (2nd ed.). New Haven, CT: Brookings Institution Press.

Griffin, M., & Kagan, S. (1996). Picturing culture in political spots: 1992 campaigns in Israel and the United States. *Journal of Political Communication, 13*, 43–61.

Grittmann, E., & Ammann, I. (2009). Die Methode der quantitativen Bildtypanalyse. Zur Routinisierung der Bildberichterstattung am Beispiel von 9/11 in der journalistischen Erinnerungskultur. In T. Petersen & C. Schwender (Eds.), *Visuelle Stereotypen* (pp. 141–159). Cologne, Germany: Herbert von Halem Verlag.

Grittmann, E., & Ammann, I. (2011). Quantitative Bildtypenanalyse. In T. Petersen & C. Schwender (Eds.), *Die Entschlüsselung der Bilder* (pp. 163–178). Cologne, Germany: Herbert von Halem.

Grittmann, E., & Lobinger, K. (2011). Quantitative Bildinhaltanalyse. In T. Petersen & C. Schwender (Eds.), *Die Entschlüsselung der Bilder* (pp. 145–162). Cologne, Germany: Herbert von Halem.

Grudin, J. (1990). The computer reaches out: The historical continuity of user interface design. *Proceedings of the CHI'90 Conference on Human Factors in Computer Systems*. New York. 261–266.

Gueorguieva, V. (Fall 2008). Voters, MySpace, and YouTube. *Social Science Computer Review, 26*(3), 288–300. doi: 10.1177/0894439307305636

Halliday, M. (1973). *Explorations in the functions of language*. London, UK: Edward Arnold.

Halliday, M. (1985). *An introduction to functional grammar*. London, UK: Edward Arnold.

Halliday, M. (2004). *An introduction to functional grammar* (3rd ed.). London, UK: Edward Arnold.

Halliday, M., & Hasan, R. (1985). *Language, context and text: Aspects of language in a social-semiotic perspective*. Oxford, UK: Oxford University Press.

Hallin, D., & Mancini, P. (2004). *Comparing media systems: Three models of media and politics*. Cambridge, MA: Cambridge University Press.

Harding, F. (2003). Africa and the moving image: Television, film and video. *Journal of African Cultural Studies, 16*(1), 69–84. doi: 10.1080/1369681032000169276

Hargittai, E., & Shafer, S. (2006). Differences in actual and perceived online skills: The role of gender. *Social Science Quarterly, 87*, 432–448.

Hinduja, S., & Patchin, J. W. (2008). Personal information of adolescents on the internet: A quantitative content analysis of MySpace. *Journal of Adolescence, 31*(1), 125–146. doi: 10.1016/j.adolescence.2007.05.004

Hodge, R., & Kress, G. (1988). *Social semiotics*. Cambridge, UK: Polity Press.

Holmqvist, K., Holsanova, J., Barthelson, J., & Lundqvist, D. (2003). Reading or scanning? A study of newspaper and net paper reading. In J. Hyönä, R. Radach, & H. Deubel (Eds.), *The mind's eye: Cognitive and applied aspects of eye movement research* (pp. 657–670). Amsterdam, Netherlands: Elsevier Science.
Holsanova, J. (2008). *Discourse, vision, and cognition.* Amsterdam, Netherlands: John Benjamins.
Holsanova, J. (2012). New methods for studying visual communication and multimodal integration. *Visual Communication, 11*(3), 251–257. doi: 10.1177/1470412912446558
Holsanova, J., Holmberg, N., & Holmqvist, K. (2008). Reading information graphics: The role of spatial contiguity and dual attentional guidance. *Applied Cognitive Psychology, 22,* 1–12.
Holsanova, J., Rahm, H., & Holmqvist, K. (2006). Entry points and reading paths on newspaper spreads: Comparing a semiotic analysis with eye-tracking measurements. *Visual Communication, 5*(1), 65–93. doi: 10.1177/1470357206061005
Holtz-Bacha, C. (2004). Political campaign communication: Conditional convergence of modern media elections. In F. Esser, & B. Pfetsch (Eds.), *Comparing political communication: Theories, cases, and challenges* (pp. 213–230). Cambridge, UK: Cambridge University Press.
Howard, P. (2005). Deep democracy, thin citizenship: The impact of digital media in political campaign strategy. *Annals of the American Academy of Political and Social Science, 597,* 153–170.
Howard, P. (2011). *The digital origins of dictatorship and democracy: Information technology and political Islam.* New York, NY: Oxford University Press.
Iyer, A., & Oldmeadow, J. (2006). Picture this: Emotional and political responses to photographs of the Kenneth Bigley kidnapping. *European Journal of Social Psychology, 36*(5), 635–647. doi: 10.1002/ejsp.316
Jacobs, A. (2006). Using self-similarity matrices for structure mining on news video. In G. Antoniou, G. Potamias, C. Spyropoulos, & D. Plexousakis (Eds.), *Advances in artificial intelligence* (pp. 87–94). Berlin & Heidelberg: Springer. doi: 10.1007/11752912_11
Jensen, K. (2010). *Media convergence: The three degrees of network, mass, and interpersonal communication.* New York, NY: Routledge.
Jones, S. (1995). Understanding community in the information age. In S. Jones (Ed.), *Cybersociety: Computer-mediated communication and community* (pp. 10–35). Thousand Oaks, CA: Sage.
Kaid, L. L., Gerstle, J., & Sanders, J. (Eds.). (1991). *Mediated politics in two cultures: Presidential campaigning in the USA and France.* New York, NY: Praeger.
Kaid, L. L., & Postelnicu, M. (2005). Political advertising in the 2004 election. *American Behavioral Scientist, 49*(2), 265–278. doi: 10.1177/0002764205279421
Kappas, A., & Krämer, N. (2011). *Face-to-face communication over the internet: Emotions in a web of culture, language and technology.* Cambridge, UK: Cambridge University Press.
Kappas, A., & Müller, M. G. (2006). Bild und Emotion—ein neues Forschungsfeld. *Publizistik, 51*(1), 52–66.
Kidder, L., & Judd, C. (1986). *Research methods in social relations* (5th ed.). New York, NY: CBS University Publishing.
Kluver, R., Jankowski, N., Foot, K., & Schneider, S. (Eds.) (2007). *The Internet and national elections: A comparative study of Web campaigning.* New York, NY: Routledge.
Kotler, P. (1986). The prosumer movement: A new challenge for marketers. *Advances in Consumer Research, 13*(1), 510–513.
Kraidy, M. (2005). *Hybridity, or the cultural logic of globalization.* Philadelphia, PA: Temple University Press.

Kress, G. (2003). *Literacy in the new media age*. London, UK: Routledge.
Kress, G. (2010). *Multimodality: A social semiotic approach to contemporary communication*. Oxon, UK: Routledge
Kress, G., & van Leeuwen, T. (1990). *Reading images*. Geelong, Australia: Deakin University Press.
Kress, G., & van Leeuwen, T. (1996). *Reading images: The grammar of visual design*. London, UK: Routledge.
Kress, G., & van Leeuwen, T. (2002). Colour as a semiotic mode: Notes for a grammar of colour. *Visual Communication, 1*(3), 343–368. doi: 10.1177/1470357220200100306
Kress, G., & van Leeuwen, T. (2006). *Reading images: The grammar of visual design* (2nd ed.). London, UK: Routledge.
Kriesi, H. (2004). Strategic political communication: Mobilizing public opinion in 'audience democracies'. In F. Esser & B. Pfetsch (Eds.), *Comparing political communication: Theories, cases, and challenges* (pp. 184–212). Cambridge, UK: Cambridge University Press.
Lang, P., Bradley, M., & Cuthbert, B. (1997). International affective picture system (IAPS): Technical manual and affective ratings. Retrieved from www.hsp.epm.br/dpsicobio/Nova_versao_pagina_psicobio/adap/instructions.pdf
Lang, S. (2004). Local political communication: Media and local publics in the age of globalization. In F. Esser & B. Pfetsch (Eds.), *Comparing political communication: Theories, cases, and challenges* (pp. 151–183). Cambridge, MA: Cambridge University Press.
Lawrence, R. G. (2006). Seeing the whole board: New institutional analysis of news content. *Political Communication, 23*(2), 225.
Lees-Marshment, J., Rudd, C., & Strömback, J. (Eds.) (2009). *Global political marketing*. New York, NY: Routledge.
Lemke, J. L. (1998). Multiplying meaning: Visual and verbal semiotics in scientific text. In J. Martin & R. Veel (Eds.), *Reading science: Critical and functional perspectives on discourses of science* (pp. 87–113). London, UK: Routledge.
Lemke, J. L. (2000). Opening up closure: Semiotics across scales. In J. Chandler & G. van de Vijver (Eds.), *Closure: Emergent organizations and their dynamics* (pp. 100–111). New York, NY: New York Academy of Science Press.
Lemke, J. L. (2002). Travels in hypermodality. *Visual Communication, 1*(3), 299–325. doi: 10.1177/1470357220200100303
Liebes, T. (2000). Inside a news item: A dispute over framing. *Political Communication, 17*(3), 295.
Lilleker, D., & Jackson, N. (2011). *Political campaigning, elections and the Internet: Comparing the US, UK, France and Germany*. New York, NY: Routledge.
Lincoln, Y., & Guba, E. (1985). *Naturalistic inquiry*. London, UK: Sage.
Loader, B., & Mercea, D. (Eds.) (2012). *Social media and democracy: Innovations in participatory politics*. New York, NY: Routledge.
Luntz, F. (2006). *Words that work: It's not what you say, it's what people hear*. New York, NY: Hyperion.
Mann, W., & Thompson, S. (1988). Rhetorical structure theory: Towards a functional theory in text organization. *Text, 8*(3), 243–281.
Martin, J. (1992). *English text: System and structure*. Amsterdam, Netherlands: John Benjamins.
Martinec, R., & Salway, A. (2005). A system for image-text relations in new (and old) media. *Visual Communication, 4*(3), 337–371. doi: 10.1177/1470357205055928
Mayer, R. (2005). Principles for managing essential processing in multimedia learning: Coherence, signaling, redundancy, spatial contiguity and temporal contiguity principles. In R. Mayer (Ed.), *Cambridge handbook of multimedia learning* (pp. 183–200). New York, NY: Cambridge University Press.

McFarlane, D. C., & Latorella, K. A. (2002). The scope and importance of human interruption in human-computer interaction design. *Human-Computer Interaction, 17*(1), 1–61.
McLuhan, M. (1960). Effects of the improvements of communication media. *The Journal of Economic History, 20*(4), 566–575.
McNair, B. (2003). *An introduction to political communication* (3rd ed.). London, UK: Routledge.
McQuail, D. (1987). *Mass communication theory* (2nd ed.). London, UK: Sage.
Mellese, M. A., & Müller, M. G. (2012). Mapping text-visual frames of sub-Saharan Africa in the news: A comparison of online news reports from Al Jazeera and British broadcasting corporation websites. *Communication, Culture & Critique, 5*(2), 191–229. doi: 10.1111/j.1753-9137.2012.01123.x
Messaris, P. (1994). *Visual literacy: Image, mind, and reality.* Boulder, CO: Westview Press.
Messaris, P. (1998). Visual aspects of media literacy. *Journal of Communication, 48,* 70–80.
Messaris, P., & Abraham, L. (2003). The role of images in framing news stories. In S. Reese, O. Gandy, & A. Grant (Eds.), *Framing public life: Perspectives on media and our understanding of the social world* (pp. 215–226). Mahwah, NJ: Erlbaum.
Miller, C. (1984). Genre as social action. *Quarterly Journal of Speech, 70,* 151–167.
Mitchell, W. J. T. (1984). What is an image? *New Literary History, 15*(3, Image/Imago/Imagination), 503–537.
Mitchell, W. J. T. (2005). There are no visual media. *Journal of Visual Culture, 4*(2), 257–266. doi: 10.1177/1470412905054673
Moriarty, S., & Popovich, M. (1991). News magazine visuals and the 1988 presidential election. *Journalism Quarterly, 68*(3), 371–380.
Morris, M., & Ogan, C. (1996). The internet as mass medium. *Journal of Computer-Mediated Communication, 1*(4), 0–0. doi: 10.1111/j.1083-6101.1996.tb00174.x
Morris, N. (2002). The myth of unadulterated culture meets the threat of imported media. *Media, Culture & Society, 24*(2), 278–289. doi: 10.1177/016344370202400208
Müller, M. G. (1997). *Politische Bildstrategien im amerikanischen Präsidentschaftswahlkampf 1828–1996.* Berlin, Germany: Akademie Verlag.
Müller, M. G. (2003). *Grundlagen der visuellen Kommunikation.* Konstanz: UVK.
Müller, M. G. (2007). What is visual communication? Past and future of an emerging field of communication research. *Studies in Communication Sciences, 7*(2), 7–34.
Müller, M. G. (2008a). Iconography. In W. Donsbach (Ed.), *The international encyclopedia of communication* (pp. 2159–2161). Oxford, UK: Wiley-Blackwell.
Müller, M. G. (2008b). Visual competence: A new paradigm for studying visuals in the social sciences? *Visual Studies, 23,* 101–112.
Müller, M. G. (2011a). Iconography and iconology as a visual method and approach. In E. Margolis & L. Pauwels (Eds.), *The SAGE handbook of visual research methods* (pp. 283–297). London, UK: Sage.
Müller, M. G. (2011b). Ikonographie und Ikonologie, visuelle Kontextanalyse, visuelles Framing. In T. Petersen, & C. Schwender (Eds.), *Die Entschlüsselung der Bilder: Methoden zur Erforschung visueller Kommunikation* (pp. 29–56). Cologne, Germany: Herbert von Halem Verlag.
Müller, M. G., & Kappas, A. (2011). Visual emotions—emotional visuals. emotions, pathos formulae, and their relevance for communication research. In E. Konijn, K. Döveling, & C. von Scheve (Eds.), *Handbook of emotions in mass media* (pp. 310–331). London, UK: Sage.
Müller, M. G., Kappas, A., & Olk, B. (2012). Perceiving press photography: A new integrative model, combining iconology with psychophysiological and eye-tracking methods. *Visual Communication, 11*(3), 307–328. doi: 10.1177/1470357212446410

Müller, M. G., Özcan, E. A., & Seizov, O. (2009). Dangerous depictions: A visual case study of contemporary cartoon controversies. *Popular Communication, 7*(7), 28–39.

Nachmias, C., & Nachmias, D. (1992). *Research methods in the social sciences* (4th ed.). London, UK: Edward Arnold.

Nakamura, Y., & Kenada, T. (1997). *Semantic analysis for video contents extraction—spotting by association in news video*. Unpublished manuscript.

Newell, A., & Card, S. K. (1985). The prospects for psychological science in human-computer interaction. *Human-Computer Interaction, 1*(3), 209.

Nixon, M. S., Liu, X. U., Direkoğlu, C., & Hurley, D. J. (2011). On using physical analogies for feature and shape extraction in computer vision. *Computer Journal, 54*(1), 11–25.

Nixon, P., Rawal, R., & Mercea, D. (Eds.) (2013). *Politics and the Internet in comparative context: Views from the cloud*. New York: Routledge.

Norris, P. (2001). Political communication. In N. Smelser & P. Baltes (Eds.), *International encyclopedia of the social & behavioral sciences* (pp. 11631–11640). Oxford, UK: Elsevier.

Norris, S. (2004). Multimodal discourse analysis: A conceptual framework. In P. LeVine & R. Scollon (Eds.), *Discourse and technology: Multimodal discourse analysis* (pp. 101–115). Washington, DC: Georgetown University Press.

Nöth, W. (2011). Visual semiotics. In E. Margolis, & L. Pauwels (Eds.), *The SAGE handbook of visual research methods* (pp. 298–316). London, UK: Sage.

O'Halloran, K. (2004). *Multimodal discourse analysis*. New York, NY: Continuum.

O'Halloran, K. (2008). Systemic Functional-Multimodal Discourse Analysis (SF-MDA): Constructing ideational meaning using language and visual imagery. *Visual Communication, 7*, 443–475.

O'Halloran, K. (2011). Multimodal discourse analysis. In K. Hyland, & B. Paltridge (Eds.), *Companion to discourse* (pp. 120–136). New York, NY: Continuum.

O'Reilly, T. (2007). What is Web 2.0: Design patterns and business models for the next generation of software. *Communications & Strategies, 1*, 17–38.

O'Toole, M. (1994). *The language of displayed art*. London, UK: Leicester University Press.

O'Toole, M. (1999). *Engaging with art*. Perth, Australia: Murdoch University.

Palen, L., Vieweg, S., Liu, S. B., & Hughes, A. L. (2009). Crisis in a networked world: Features of computer-mediated communication in the April 16, 2007, Virginia Tech event. *Social Science Computer Review, 27*, 467–480. doi: 10.1177/0894439309332302

Paltoglou, G., Theunis, M., Kappas, A., & Thelwall, M. (2013). Predicting emotional responses to long informal text. *IEEE Transactions on Affective Computing, 4*, 107–115.

Parks, M. R., & Floyd, K. (1996). Making friends in cyberspace. *Journal of Computer-Mediated Communication, 1*(4). doi: 10.1111/j.1083-6101.1996.tb00176.x

Patterson, T. (2002). *The vanishing voter: Public involvement in an age of uncertainty*. New York, NY: Knopf.

Peirce, C. (1931–58). *Collected papers*. Cambridge, MA: Harvard University Press.

Qi, W., Gu, L., Jiang, H., Chen, X., & Zhang, H. (2000). *Integrating visual, audio and text analysis for news video*. Unpublished manuscript.

Ragin, C., & Becker, S. (Eds.). (1992). *What is a case? Exploring the foundations of social inquiry*. New York, NY: Cambridge University Press. Ramirez et al 2002

Ramirez, A., Walther, J. B., Burgoon, J. K., & Sunnafrank, M. (2002). Information-seeking strategies, uncertainty, and computer-mediated communication. *Human Communication Research, 28*(2), 213–228. doi: 10.1111/j.1468-2958.2002.tb00804.x

Rheingold, H. (1994). *The virtual community: Finding connection in a computerized world*. London, UK: Secker & Warburg.

Richardson, K., Parry, K., & Corner, J. (2012). *Political culture and media genre beyond the news*. London, UK: Palgrave-Macmillan.
Ritzer, G., & Jurgenson, N. (2010). Production, consumption, prosumption. *Journal of Consumer Culture, 10*(1), 13–36. doi: 10.1177/1469540509354673
Robertson, L. (2012). Whoppers of 2012, final edition. Retrieved from http://factcheck.org/2012/10/whoppers-of-2012-final-edition/
Rössler, P. (2012). Comparative content analysis. In F. Esser & T. Hanitzsch (Eds.), *Handbook of comparative communication research* (pp. 459–468). London, UK: Routledge.
Royce, T. (1998). Synergy on the page: Exploring intersemiotic complementarity in page-based multimodal text. *JASFL Occasional Papers, 1,* 25–49.
Royce, T. (2002). Multimodality in the TESOL classroom: Exploring visual-verbal synergy. *TESOL Quarterly, 36*(2), 191–205.
Royce, T. (2007). Intersemiotic complementarity: A framework for multimodal discourse analysis. In T. Royce & W. Bowcher (Eds.), *New directions in the analysis of multimodal discourse* (pp. 63–109). London, UK: Lauwrence Erlbaum Associates.
Ryfe, D. M. (2006). The nature of news rules. *Political Communication, 23*(2), 203.
Scholzman, K., Verba, S., & Brady, H. (2010). Weapon of the strong? Participatory inequality and the internet. *Perspectives on Politics, 8,* 487–509.
Schramm, W. (1997). *The beginnings of communication studies in America*. Thousand Oaks, CA: Sage.
Schreier, M. (2012). *Qualitative content analysis in practice*. London, UK: Sage.
Scullion, R., Gerodimos, R., Jackson, D., & Lilleker, D. (Eds.). (2013). *The media, political participation, and empowerment*. New York, NY: Routledge.
Simpson, J. (2002). Computer-mediated communication. *ELT Journal: English Language Teachers Journal, 56*(4), 414.
Skowron, M., Theunis, M., Rank, S., & Kappas, A. (2013). Affect and social processes in online communication—Experiments with an affective dialog system. *IEEE Transactions on Affective Computing, 4,* 267–279. doi: 10.1109/T-AFFC.2013.16
Swales, J. (1990). *Genre analysis: English in academic and research settings*. Cambridge, UK: Cambridge University Press.
Sweller, J., van Merrienboer, J. G., & Paas, F. G. W. C. (1998). Cognitive architecture and instructional design. *Educational Psychology Review, 10*(3), 251–296.
Tellaeche, A., Pajares, G., Burgos-Artizzu, X. P., & Ribeiro, A. (2011). A computer vision approach for weeds identification through support vector machines. *Applied Soft Computing, 11*(1), 908–915. doi: 10.1016/j.asoc.2010.01.011
Thelwall, M., Buckley, K., Paltoglou, G., Skowron, M., Garcia, D., Gobron, S., Ahn, J., Kappas, A., Küster, D., & Holyst, J. A. (2013). Damping sentiment analysis in online communication: Discussions, monologs and dialogs. *Computational Linguistics and Intelligent Text Processing / Lecture Notes in Computer Science, 7817,* 1–12.
Thibault, P. J. (2001). Multimodality and the school science textbook. In C. Torsello-Taylor, G. Brunetti, & N. Penello (Eds.), *Corpora testuali per ricerca, tradizione e apprendimento linguistico* (pp. 293–335). Padua, Italy: Unipress.
Thorne, S. (2008). Computer-mediated communication. In N. Van Deusen-Scholl (Ed.), *Encyclopedia of language and education* (pp. 1–12). New York, NY: Springer Science.
Tian, Y., & Stewart, C. M. (2005). Framing the SARS crisis: A computer-assisted text analysis of CNN and BBC online news reports of SARS. *Asian Journal of Communication, 15*(3), 289–301. doi: 10.1080/01292980500261605
Toffler, A. (1980). *The third wave*. London, UK: Collins.
van de Vijver, F., & Leung, K. (2011). Equivalence and bias: A review of concepts, models, and data analytic procedures. In D. Matsumoto & F. van de Vijver (Eds.),

Cross-cultural research methods in psychology (pp. 17–45). New York, NY: Cambridge University Press.
van Leeuwen, T. (2001). Semiotics and iconography. In T. van Leeuwen & C. Jewitt (Eds.), *Handbook of visual analysis* (pp. 92–118). London, UK: Sage.
van Leeuwen, T. (2008). New forms of writing, new visual competencies. *Visual Studies, 23,* 139–151
Waller, R. (1987). Using typography to structure arguments: A critical analysis of some examples. In D. Jonassen (Ed.), *The technology of text* (pp. 105–125). Englewood Cliffs, NJ: Educational Technology Publications.
Walther, J., Liang, Y., DeAndrea, D., Tong, S., Carr, C., Spottswood, E., Amichai-Hamburger, Y. (2011). The effect of feedback on identity shift in computer-mediated communication. *Media Psychology, 14*(1), 1–26.
Ward, J. (2005). An opportunity for engagement in cyberspace: Political youth web sites during the 2004 European parliament election campaign. *Information Polity: The International Journal of Government & Democracy in the Information Age, 10*(3), 233–246.
Wirth, W., & Kolb, S. (2004). Designs and methods for comparative political communication research. In F. Esser, & B. Pfetsch (Eds.), *Comparing political communication: Theories, cases, and challenges* (pp. 87–114). Cambridge, MA: Cambridge University Press.
Wirth, W., & Kolb, S. (2012). Securing equivalency: Problems and solutions. In F. Esser & T. Hanitzsch (Eds.,), *Handbook of comparative communication research* (pp. 469–485). London, UK: Routledge.
Wolfsfeld, G., & Sheafer, T. (2006). Competing actors and the construction of political news: The contest over waves in Israel. *Political Communication, 23*(3), 333.
Wright, P. C., Fields, R. E., & Harrison, M. D. (2000). Analyzing human-computer interaction as distributed cognition: The resources model. *Human-Computer Interaction, 15*(1), 1–41.
Wright, T. (2011). Press photography and visual rhetoric. In E. Margolis & L. Pauwels (Eds.), *The SAGE handbook of visual research methods* (pp. 317–337). London, UK: Sage
Xenos, M. (2008). New mediated deliberation: Blog and press coverage of the alito nomination. *Journal of Computer-Mediated Communication, 13*(2), 485–503. doi: 10.1111/j.1083–6101.2008.00406.x
Xenos, M. A., & Foot, K. A. (2005). Politics as usual, or politics unusual? Position taking and dialogue on campaign websites in the 2002 U.S. elections. *Journal of Communication, 55*(1), 169–185. doi: 10.1111/j.1460–2466.2005.tb02665.x
Yin, R. (2009). *Case study research: Design and methods* (4th ed.). London, UK: Sage.
Young, R. (1995). *Colonial desire: Hybridity in theory, culture, and race*. London, UK: Routledge.
Zakon, R. (2010). Hobbes' internet timeline. Retrieved from www.zakon.org/robert/internet/timeline/

WEB SOURCES

Al Jazeera English (June 21, 2012). *Catholic nuns protest against US budget cuts.* Retrieved from www.aljazeera.com/video/americas/2012/06/2012620142917511451.html
Al Jazeera English (June 21, 2012). *US police beating victim Rodney King dies.* Retrieved from www.aljazeera.com/news/americas/2012/06/201261716454859368.html
Al Jazeera English (June 21, 2012). *US to halt deportations of young immigrants.* Retrieved from www.aljazeera.com/news/americas/2012/06/2012615145446521318.html
BBC Online (June 21, 2012). *Congress contempt charge for US Attorney General Holder.* Retrieved from www.bbc.co.uk/news/world-us-canada-18528798

Works Cited

BBC Online (June 21, 2012). *North Carolina rejects funds for sterilisation victims.* Retrieved from www.bbc.co.uk/news/world-us-canada-18529735

CNN Edition (June 21, 2012). *Holder contempt vote could come next week.* Retrieved from http://edition.cnn.com/2012/06/21/politics/holder-contempt/index.html

CNN Edition (June 21, 2012). *Latino boom makes Orlando proving ground for Obama.* Retrieved from http://us.cnn.com/2012/06/21/politics/florida-hispanic-vote/index.html

CNN Edition (June 21, 2012). *Obama campaign says it will be outraised in June.* Retrieved from http://politicalticker.blogs.cnn.com/2012/06/20/massive-money-being-raised-by-republican-side-worries-top-obama-campaign-officials-2/

Freedom House (June 21, 2012). *Damaging cuts to foreign operations budget proposed by House Appropriations Committee.* Retrieved from www.freedomhouse.org/article/damaging-cuts-foreign-operations-budget-proposed-house-appropriations-committee

MSNBC Online (June 21, 2012). *First thoughts—Romney's immigration challenge.* Retrieved from http://firstread.msnbc.msn.com/_news/2012/06/21/12337055-first-thoughts-romneys-immigration-challenge?lite

Obama for America (June 21, 2012). *The president's record on equal rights.* Retrieved from www.barackobama.com/record/equal-rights?source = primary-nav

Obama for America (June 21, 2012). *The president's record on health care.* Retrieved from www.barackobama.com/record/health-care?source = primary-nav

Obama for America (June 21, 2012). *The president's record on jobs and the economy.* Retrieved from www.barackobama.com/record/economy

Occupy Wall St (June 21, 2012). *Bed-Stuy: Juneteenth free university.* Retrieved from http://occupywallst.org/article/bed-stuy-juneteenth-free-university/

Occupy Wall St (June 21, 2012). *June 21: National day of action against PNC.* Retrieved from http://occupywallst.org/article/june-21-national-day-action-cruz-family/

Reporters without Borders (April 16, 2012). *Internet advocacy coalition announces Twitter campaign to fight privacy-invasive bill (CISPA).* Retrieved from http://en.rsf.org/etats-unis-internet-advocacy-coalition-16–04–2012,42283.html

Reporters without Borders (April 26, 2012). *US sanctions on Iranian and Syrian entities and individuals for monitoring and tracking dissidents online.* Retrieved from http://en.rsf.org/united-states-us-sanctions-on-iran-syria-for-26–04–2012,42380.html

Romney for President (June 21, 2012). *Health care.* Retrieved from www.mittromney.com/issues/health-care

Romney for President (June 21, 2012). *Jobs and economic growth.* Retrieved from www.mittromney.com/jobs

We Are the 99 Percent (June 15, 2012). *We are the 99 Percent.* Retrieved from http://wearethe99percent.tumblr.com/

Index

Al Jazeera English 65; in-depth analysis of a webpage from 65–6, 88–9, 89–91
annotation 36, 37–8, 57–8
attention guides *see* signaling principle

Baldry, A. & Thibault, P. 11, 24, 31
Barthes, R. 21
Bateman, J. 10–12, 23, 24, 25–8, 32, 54
BBC: in-depth analysis of a webpage from 86–7, 89–91
Brader, T. 13, 95, 134

camera angle 43–4, 60–1, 80, 91, 94, 97, 98, 107, 111, 118, 121, 125
camera distance 42–3, 60–1, 80, 91, 94, 97, 98, 107, 111, 118, 121, 125
CMC *see* computer-mediated communication
CNN: in-depth analysis of a webpage from 82–4, 89–91
co-deployment 4, 7, 11, 24, 32, 143; *see also* multimodality
coding categories 53–5
color 42–3, 60–1, 91, 94, 97, 107, 111, 118, 121, 125
color schemes *see* color
comparability 51–2
comparative design 51
computer-mediated communication 15–17; emotional expressions in 105; shared conventions of 126
computer-mediated interaction *see* computer-mediated communication
content-analytical categories 53–4
content segmentation 36–7

context 3, 9–10, 19, 25, 34, 73–4, 137
contextual embedding 92
contextualization *see* context
convergence 4, 14, 50, 74, 143
corpus 26, 28, 58; image corpora 37
corpus-based linguistics *see* corpus
culture 4

data collection 36–7
Djonov, E. 12, 44–5, 47
dual scripting 49–50, 68–9, 72, 97, 101, 130, 132; *see also* eye-tracking; Holsanova, J.

equivalence 52
eye-tracking 22, 46, 71

framing 74–5, 141
Freedom House, brief history of 106; in-depth webpage analysis of 108–10

GeM 11, 23, 25–8, 36; *see also* Bateman, J.
genre 26, 27–8, 51, 142; visual genre 97; *see also* semiotic affordance
Genre and Multimodality *see* GeM
Grittmann, E. 21; *see also* visual content analysis

Halliday, M. 19, 27, 29, 31, 34; *see also* systemic functional linguistics
HCI *see* human-computer interaction
Holsanova, J. 44, 48, 69, 141
human-computer interaction 16–17
hyperlink *see* hypertext
hypermodality 11, 44, 47, 64
hypertext 11–12, 81, 92, 98, 129; *see also* hypermodality

Index

ICON: communication layer 44–7; disciplinary approaches 21–4; five layers of annotation 36–7; iconographical layer 38–40; material layer 41; multimodal layer 47–50; origins of 19–21; production layer 42–4; typologies of multimodal webpage design 131–5
image 9; *see also* visuality
Imagery and Communication in Online Narratives *see* ICON
imagery see visuality
inductive content analysis 22, 28, 135
interdisciplinarity 6–8, 19–21, 24, 33–4
Internet: brief history of 14–15; as communication network 15–17; as data source 50–1
intersemiosis *see* narratives: multimodal
intersemiotic complementarity 28–30; *see also* Royce, T.

Kaid, L. L. 13
Kraidy, M. 3–4, 54
Kress, G. 9, 27, 31, 42, 75, 137

Leeuwen, T. van 9, 11, 21, 22, 42
Lemke, J. L. 11, 32, 33, 44; *see also* hypermodality

McLuhan, M. 15
McNair, B. 12–13; *see also* political communication
McQuail, D. 15
media hybridization 3–4; *see also* convergence
metafunctions: in language 29; in multimodal documents 29–30, 31
microcontent 17
Mitchell, W. J. T. 9, 21; *see also* visuality
modal density see *co-deployment*
MSNBC: in-depth analysis of a webpage from 84–6
Müller, M. G. 9, 19, 20, 31, 39, 58
multimodal discourse analysis 31–3; *see also* O'Halloran, K.
multimodal dissonance 65–6
multimodal document 7, 11, 23, 30
multimodality 8, 10–12

narrative 21, 47–50; multimodal 23, 30, 33, 56–7, 61–5, 81–2, 100, 118–19, 121, 125–6, 127, 129–30; structures 25, 44, 95; *see also* ICON: communication layer, multimodal layer
news websites 79–80
NGOs 105–8
nucleus and satellite page elements 26, 56; *see also* visual nuclei, visual satellites

Occupy Wall St. 52, 116–17; in-depth analysis of a webpage from 121–4
O'Halloran, K. 31–3, 34
online communication 8, 14–17, 33, 105; emotional 16, 105; interpersonal 15

page-based documents 11–12
Peirce, C. 75–6
pilot coding 55
political action 39
political campaign 13–14, 92–3; permanent campaign 141; professional campaign 2; strategy 98, 101–2, 103, 107 n
political communication 1, 8, 12–14, 104, 133–4, 142
political iconography 8, 22; *see also* Müller, M. G.
political iconology 7, 22, 25, 30; *see also* political iconography
political news websites 79–80
political persuasion 2, 92, 117, 132; *see also* Brader, T.
political realities 13, 74
political websites 5–6
produsage *see* prosumption
professionalization 59, 116, 121, 126–7; lack of 2–3, 14
prosumer *see* prosumption
prosumption 1–3, 17, 105, 116–17, 125, 137

qualitative content analysis 22; *see also* Schreier, M.

Reporters Without Borders: brief history of 106; in-depth webpage analysis of 111–14
research design 6–8; exploratory 7, 14, 22–3, 78
research questions 5–6, 136–8
rhetorical structure theory 27
Royce, T. 28–30

RSF *see* Reporters Without Borders
RST *see* rhetorical structure theory

sampling 51–3, 139
Saussure, F. de 75–6
Schreier, M. 22, 24
semi-automatic multimodal content analysis 23–4
semiotic affordance 28, 41, 59, 137, 142
sense relations *see* intersemiotic complementarity
SFL *see* systemic functional linguistics
signaling principle 44, 46–7, 71, 81, 99, 108, 110; orientation 47, 63–4, 102, 118; visual and textual 47, 63, 91, 95, 124, 129–30
social media 105, 144
social semiotics 75–6
spatial contiguity design 49, 66, 72, 97, 114, 121, 130, 131, 137
split attention design 49, 66, 112, 130, 131
structure-functional webpage complexes 54–5, 71–2, 131–5, 136–8
Swales, J. 27, 28, 41
synchronous and asynchronous communication 17
systemic functional linguistics 7, 19, 24–5, 31, 33–4

text: as mixed-mode content 10–11, 19, 30, 33, 72; as verbal content 4, 7, 10, 33, 71, 108, 132–3; as visual element 56, 107
Toffler, A. 1, 2; *see also* prosumption
transdisciplinarity *see* interdisciplinarity

UAM Image Tool 37–8, 140
US presidential campaigns 51–2, 92–3; Barack Obama 67–8, 69–70, 93–5; Mitt Romney 93–5, 103; multimodal comparison of 95–100; strategic comparison of 100–2

validity 58
visual communication 9–10, 19, 30; in political communication research 73–4, 128; *see also* visuality
visual content analysis 21–2
visuality 8–10, 19
visual literacy 10
visual motif 39–40; *see also* ICON: iconographical layer
visual narratives 32, 44–6, 58–61, 99, 128–9, 136; *see also* narratives, ICON: communication layer
visual nuclei 40, 56, 58, 61–3, 81, 91, 94, 97, 108, 118, 119
visual satellites 40, 56, 61–3, 81, 91, 95, 97, 108, 118
visual turn 11, 20, 128; *see also* visual communication

Warburg, A. 22; *see also* political iconography
We Are the 99 Percent 52, 116–17; in-depth analysis of a webpage from 118–20
webpage design types: lead visual nucleus 131; multiple visual nuclei 132; text-flow 132–3
World Wide Web 14–15, 53, 72, 76; *see also* Internet

Yin, R. 6–7, 58